Praise for *Leadership, Teamwork, and Trust*

"Watts Humphrey has always emphasized the importaı  in software development, and this theme has permeate tributions in CMM, TSP, and PSP. *Leadership, Teamwoı* ues this mantra and compiles valuable lessons into priı that are consumable by executives and leaders. Measurea ımprovement ıs the differentiator of successful projects and market-leading software organizations. If you want to learn to steer such endeavors, this book will provide some valuable insights."

> —Walker Royce
> Vice President, Chief Software Economist
> IBM

"How to successfully manage knowledge workers is definitely the first of the really big business management challenges of the twenty-first century. Now Watts Humphrey and James Over are able to show how improving leadership, teamwork, and trust are at the heart of what needs to be done and to explain exactly how empowerment, productivity, and profitability are deeply intertwined. This book provides expert guidance on how to reliably bring knowledge work in on time, on budget, and to the correct specification—something that the software engineering industry has been grappling with for decades. There is a better way, and this is it!"

> —Mark Smith
> Global Director of Quality (2000 to 2010) and former Senior Executive, Global PSQ, and Certifications Director, Accenture

"Read this book if you're a team leader, manager, or executive responsible for knowledge-working teams. Benchmark your own principles and practices for team motivation, high product quality, and sustained competitive results against industry leaders. Based on their extensive software industry experience, Watts Humphrey and Jim Over present the techniques that empower self-directed knowledge-working teams to produce superior work, both predictably and at the lowest cost. Software organizations will be compelled to try the Team Software Process (TSP), as we did in Microsoft IT with great success."

> —Aiden Wayne
> Information Solutions General Manager
> Microsoft Entertainment and Devices Division

"I want you to know that TSP is one of the most valuable innovations implemented in the Beckman Coulter product development process since I joined the company in 2002. Software has become increasingly important to the success of our instrument systems. And in our business, quality is the most important factor for success. TSP gives us a path to better development time to market and superior quality. We are true believers."

> —Scott Garrett
> Chairman and Chief Executive Officer
> Beckman Coulter, Inc.

"Stock exchanges are businesses that have been shaken in recent years by new regulations and unprecedented competition driven by technology. The Mexican Stock Exchange is no exception and is currently immersed in its most important process of business and technological transformation since its creation in the nineteenth century. Understanding that the competitiveness of the exchange will come mostly from its technology platform, we have recognized the value of knowledge work and its management challenges. We adopted TSP/PSP, with coaching from the Software Engineering Institute of Carnegie Mellon, for managing the execution of our most critical software projects. Results so far are very good, and we plan to gradually extend the TSP/PSP practice across the company."

    —Enrique Ibarra
        Director, General Adjunto de Tecnologias del Grupo Bolsa Mexicana de Valores (Mexican Stock Exchange)

"Watts Humphrey has done more to advance the science of Software Quality Management than anyone I know. His work has had an immense, positive impact on how I lead software organizations. If you want software that is better quality, faster to the market, and cheaper to build, then Watts Humphrey and Jim Over have a tremendous amount of wisdom to share. Great stuff."

    —Michael J. Cullen
        Vice President, Quality
        Oracle Communications Global Business Unit

"I'm very impressed with the results of TSP in my organization. It is possible to see the difference made by applying these new knowledge-management methods. With TSP, you can adjust your processes, make them leaner, and obtain high-performance teams. This book is perfect guidance for all executives and managers who want to introduce those methods into their organizations."

    —Joao Barracose
        Senior Manager, Development Systems
        BBVA BANCOMER (Mexico)

"PSP and TSP have proved to be incredibly successful means for my engineering teams and managers to make and meet their business commitments. Getting high-quality automotive infotainment and head-unit software developed by geographically and culturally separated teams on increasingly tight schedules demands the disciplined engineering and management techniques outlined and referenced in this great new book!"

    —Peter Abowd
        President, Worldwide Automotive Business
        Altia, Inc.

Leadership,
Teamwork,
and Trust

The **SEI Series in Software Engineering** represents is a collaborative undertaking of the Carnegie Mellon Software Engineering Institute (SEI) and Addison-Wesley to develop and publish books on software engineering and related topics. The common goal of the SEI and Addison-Wesley is to provide the most current information on these topics in a form that is easily usable by practitioners and students.

Books in the series describe frameworks, tools, methods, and technologies designed to help organizations, teams, and individuals improve their technical or management capabilities. Some books describe processes and practices for developing higher-quality software, acquiring programs for complex systems, or delivering services more effectively. Other books focus on software and system architecture and product-line development. Still others, from the SEI's CERT Program, describe technologies and practices needed to manage software and network security risk. These and all books in the series address critical problems in software engineering for which practical solutions are available.

Leadership, Teamwork, and Trust

Building a Competitive Software Capability

Watts S. Humphrey
James W. Over

✦ Addison-Wesley

Upper Saddle River, NJ • Boston • Indianapolis • San Francisco
New York • Toronto • Montreal • London • Munich • Paris • Madrid
Capetown • Sydney • Tokyo • Singapore • Mexico City

 **Software Engineering Institute** | **Carnegie Mellon**

The SEI Series in Software Engineering

Many of the designations used by manufacturers and sellers to distinguish their products are claimed as trademarks. Where those designations appear in this book, and the publisher was aware of a trademark claim, the designations have been printed with initial capital letters or in all capitals.

CMM, CMMI, Capability Maturity Model, Capability Maturity Modeling, Carnegie Mellon, CERT, and CERT Coordination Center are registered in the U.S. Patent and Trademark Office by Carnegie Mellon University.

ATAM; Architecture Tradeoff Analysis Method; CMM Integration; COTS Usage-Risk Evaluation; CURE; EPIC; Evolutionary Process for Integrating COTS Based Systems; Framework for Software Product Line Practice; IDEAL; Interim Profile; OAR; OCTAVE; Operationally Critical Threat, Asset, and Vulnerability Evaluation; Options Analysis for Reengineering; Personal Software Process; PLTP; Product Line Technical Probe; PSP; SCAMPI; SCAMPI Lead Appraiser; SCAMPI Lead Assessor; SCE; SEI; SEPG; Team Software Process; and TSP are service marks of Carnegie Mellon University.

The authors and publisher have taken care in the preparation of this book, but make no expressed or implied warranty of any kind and assume no responsibility for errors or omissions. No liability is assumed for incidental or consequential damages in connection with or arising out of the use of the information or programs contained herein.

The publisher offers excellent discounts on this book when ordered in quantity for bulk purchases or special sales, which may include electronic versions and/or custom covers and content particular to your business, training goals, marketing focus, and branding interests. For more information, please contact:

U. S. Corporate and Government Sales
(800) 382-3419
corpsales@pearsontechgroup.com

For sales outside the U.S., please contact:

International Sales
international@pearsoned.com

Visit us on the Web: informit.com/aw

Library of Congress Cataloging-in-Publication Data
Humphrey, Watts S., 1927–2010.
 Leadership, teamwork, and trust : building a competitive software capability / Watts S. Humphrey, James W. Over.
    p. cm.
 Includes index.
 ISBN 978-0-321-62450-5 (pbk. : alk. paper)
1. Computer software industry—Management—Case studies. 2. Knowledge management. 3. Software engineering. 4. Computer software—Management. I. Over, James W. II. Title.
 HD9696.63.A2H86 2011
 005.068'4—dc22

                                              2010041164

ISBN-13: 978-0-321-62450-5
ISBN-10:   0-321-62450-5
Text printed in the United States on recycled paper at Courier in Stoughton, Massachusetts.
First printing, December 2010

We dedicate this book to our families and to our TSP team at the SEI. Our families, particularly our wives, Barbara Humphrey and Patricia Over, have been wonderfully supportive throughout the many years it has taken us to develop these methods and to gain the experience and understanding required to write this book. Their support has been invaluable.

Our TSP team, many members of which have worked with us for nearly twenty years, has tirelessly and creatively participated in TSP development, taught many courses, and worked with countless organizations to demonstrate the method's extraordinary effectiveness. We could not have accomplished what we have done without their support.

—Watts S. Humphrey and James W. Over

Contents

Preface

The problems of managing software have probably been annoying, but they may not have seemed fundamental to your business. You may also have noticed, however, that the amount of software work in your business has been growing and that more and more of your people's work now looks like software work. This means that, like many other senior executives and managers, you will soon find that an increasing amount of your people's work will become as hard to manage as software. If that prospect doesn't frighten you, it should.

This book is for those senior executives and managers who run modern technology-intensive businesses. It describes why software work has always been hard to manage, why more and more work will soon be as hard to manage as software, and what you can do about it. As Robert Frost once said, "The best way out is always through."

What Frost meant is that dodging problems doesn't work. You must dig into them, understand them, and then address them. The time has come to address these software management problems. That is the premise on which this book is based: Software work is manageable. To manage it, however, we must first understand *why* it has always been so hard to manage.

The fundamental reason that software has been hard to manage is that it is a new and different kind of work. The management principles of the past are not suitable for software development. Software engineering is knowledge work, which is nothing like the traditional kinds of labor for which today's traditional management methods were developed. This book describes the knowledge-based management system that this kind of work requires, the principles upon which it is based, how this new management system works, and how to introduce it into your organization.

The management challenges of the future concern knowledge work and knowledge workers. In the past, your knowledge workers were primarily doing software engineering work, but now knowledge workers are increasingly involved in all aspects of your business. Software was the first large-scale knowledge-based industry, and its management problems are well known. Now, with knowledge work and knowledge workers pervading modern business, problems that used to be restricted to software groups are becoming common in most parts of every technology-based business.

Knowledge work is not like other kinds of work, and its management problems are unique. Recent research into management methods for knowledge workers has provided new insight into why software work has been so hard to manage. In fact, it is the special characteristics of software work, and in fact of all knowledge work and knowledge workers, that have made software projects so hard to manage. This new understanding has led to a new management system specifically tailored for knowledge work and knowledge workers. When organizations use these new methods, they find that their software work is predictable and manageable and that their people have more rewarding and satisfying work lives. In addition, the quality and profitability of their products are greatly improved.

Modern work in almost all technical fields now involves software, and it also involves design and development practices that are much like those used by software people. When the management methods described in this book are used, all forms of creative work become more manageable. In addition, employee turnover drops, customers are more satisfied, and your people are more creative. This, in turn, leads to more efficient ways of working, as well as to more attractive and profitable product offerings. This book describes these changes, gives examples of organizations that are working this way today, and outlines some of the benefits they have obtained.

BOOK ORGANIZATION

This book is composed of nine chapters and five appendices. The nine chapters describe the new knowledge-working management methods, why they are required, and the principles that guide their introduction and use. The book's five appendices address many of the questions that executives and managers have raised as they explore these concepts, conduct trial studies, and introduce the methods into their organizations.

Chapter 1 describes the increasing pace of change in the modern marketplace and the threats that all organizations now face from an aggressive set of worldwide competitors. Chapter 2 addresses the bureaucratic problems of increasing corporate size and how modern knowledge-management methods can help to address them. Chapter 3 describes the nature of knowledge work and how properly led knowledge-working teams can resolve many of the intractable problems businesses face today. Chapter 4 covers the principles and methods involved in managing knowledge work, and it explains how these management practices differ from those traditionally followed.

With Chapter 5, the book switches from explaining what knowledge-work management methods are to discussing the challenges of introducing them. Chapter 5 addresses how to motivate knowledge workers to use these new management methods personally. Chapter 6 discusses how to build and maintain the disciplined and collaborative environment that knowledge-working teams need to consistently follow these practices. Chapter 7 covers the new opportunities for dynamic decision making that become available with these data-driven knowledge-management methods, and Chapter 8 describes the critical nature of quality for knowledge work. Finally, Chapter 9 describes how to make this vision of the future come true in your organization.

Following these nine chapters, the book's five appendices provide more detailed guidance on introducing and using these management methods. Hundreds of organizations have now used them, and the appendices encapsulate the guidance we have found most effective in making their efforts successful. Because all organizations are different, and because many new and unfamiliar situations will arise, your management team will need substantial guidance in following the steps outlined in this book. The appendices contain answers to the most common questions and step-by-step guidelines on how to proceed.

READING THIS BOOK

We suggest that you read the nine chapters in order. They present a logical sequence of concepts that builds a complete high-level overview of these new management methods. Building on this conceptual background, the appendices provide a deeper level of information. They can be used as a reference or guideline for introducing and using the methods. The five appendices start by covering common questions, then trial introduction and piloting, and finally the broader issues of adoption and use. We suggest using this book in one of the following ways:

- You can read this book's nine chapters to gain an overview understanding of these knowledge-management methods, why they are needed, how they could help improve your organization's performance, and how to introduce and use them.

- You can use the book, particularly its appendices, to answer questions you might have before deciding to introduce and use these methods.

- Once you have decided to introduce these methods, your people can follow the guidance in the appendices to conduct pilot studies and to then introduce the methods broadly in your organization.

WHY WE WROTE THIS BOOK

We first tried using the management methods described in this book in 1996. Since then, we have introduced them to hundreds of organizations with thousands of managers and developers. During this time, we have learned a great deal about how these methods can be used to address the many situations that arise in modern technology-intensive businesses. We have worked with organizations of every imaginable variety, and while no single book could cover all of the issues of introducing and using these methods, we were able to encapsulate the most frequently encountered issues into a single moderate-size volume. This book is that volume.

Acknowledgments

First and foremost, we must thank three organizations and their executives for letting us describe their experiences with these methods. Blanca Treviño and her people at Softtek have been instrumental in getting these new knowledge-management methods more widely recognized, particularly in Mexico, where Softtek is a leading supplier of software and software services. Cesar and Carlos Montes de Oca and Ricardo Delgadillo of Quarksoft were among the first users of these methods, and their experiences have helped to get these methods better known and to build the experience base needed for their widespread adoption.

We also thank the people at Beckman Coulter for allowing us to describe their work. Humayun Qureshi kindly allowed us to quote his early reactions to these teamworking methods, and Rick Marshall, Carl Wyrwa, John Hetzler, and Larry Whitford have also been instrumental in getting the methods properly introduced in their company. Tim Lancaster and his team also took the time to review our description of their experiences and to ensure that what we have said properly reflects what happened. We thank them all.

Unfortunately, the team we described in Chapter 3 was and still is doing highly classified work for the U.S. Department of Defense, and we were unable to get their story cleared for release. We have worked with them for several years, however, and they have pioneered many of the practices that have turned out to be most successful, particularly for large, distributed, and multidisciplined knowledge-working teams. We salute them for their groundbreaking achievements and regret that we cannot recognize them by name.

We also thank Jason Ziemer of NAVOCEANO (NAVO) for telling us about his team and letting us use his story to illustrate some key points in the appendices. The members of his team were Carissa Bedford, Lleo Garner, Brook Bell, and Bobby Roots, and they did an extraordinary job of improving the services their group provides to U.S. naval forces in battle zones throughout the world.

In addition to getting help and support from many of our users, we have also been fortunate in having a large group of reviewers who have kindly given their time to review drafts of the book's chapters and to provide helpful comments and suggestions. These reviewers are Daniel Burton, Bob Cannon, David Carrington, Noopur Davis, Agustín De La Maza, Carlos Montes de Oca, Julia Mullaney, Jan Philpot, Marsha Pomeroy-Huff, Jim Sartain, David Scherb, Gregory Such, and Alan Willett. We thank them all for their help.

We also thank the management team at the Software Engineering Institute (SEI) for their support of our work. Anita Carleton, Clyde Chittister, and Paul Nielsen have supported us over the many years it has taken to develop, refine, and transition these methods into increasingly widespread use. We cannot thank them enough for their support.

Bill Thomas, who manages technical communications at the SEI, kindly helped with the final editing and release of the manuscript for publication, and Peter Gordon and his staff at Addison-Wesley have done a masterful job of producing this volume on an aggressive schedule. Without their help and support, this book would not have been possible.

1
Creative Destruction

Change is a fact of life. The world is changing faster than ever before, and the challenges of tomorrow will almost certainly be different from and more demanding than those of today. While no one can say precisely what these challenges will be or how to prepare for them, some things are pretty obvious from our recent history. This book describes the nature of these challenges and a strategy that will help you to address them.

CORPORATE CHURN

The first new phenomenon that is obvious from our recent history is corporate churn. Industry leaders always fail, and sometimes they fail surprisingly quickly. Consider, for example, what has happened to the largest and most successful U.S. businesses. In the 24 years from 1956 to 1980, 24 firms dropped off the Fortune 500 list *every year*. However, in the 24 years from 1982 to 2006, that rate increased to 40 firms *every year* [Economist 2009]. That comes to 960 seemingly successful firms switching from being winners to being losers in 24 years.

Joseph Schumpeter studied the reasons for corporate churn and, in 1942, published a book called *Capitalism, Socialism and Democracy* [Schumpeter 1942]. In this book, he explains why organizations grow, prosper, and die. He called this concept "creative destruction." While his ideas were not well accepted at

1

the time, they are now widely recognized as perceptive and pre-scient. He describes why economies are in constant flux in the following way:

> The fundamental impulse that sets and keeps the capitalist engine in motion comes from the new consumer goods, the new methods of production or transportation, the new markets, the new forms of industrial organization that capitalist enterprise creates.

Schumpeter's work also suggests why market leaders are so often surprised by their newer and more agile competitors. It is because the rules of the game keep changing.

> As soon as quality competition and sales effort are admitted into the sacred precincts of (economic) theory, the price variable is ousted from its dominant position.

While Schumpeter's ideas sound reasonable and are now widely accepted, he does not say where these giant-killing new competitors come from. Just who are they and why are they able to topple large and established businesses?

Just as they have in the past, the challengers to industry leaders will come from unexpected quarters. These newcomers will be entrepreneurs who have found some innovative new way to make themselves unique. This has been true in a great many industries, and as indicated by the relative vigor and productivity of small businesses, it is likely to remain true in the future. The innovative advantages of small businesses are indicated by the fact that in the United States, small businesses produce many more new jobs and grow much faster in percentage terms than their larger competitors.

Consider, for example, a recent Small Business Administration study [Terleckyj 1999]. Over a three-year period, new and small companies accounted for only 25% of employment but for 39% of job growth. This means that, on average, small businesses grew nearly 60% faster per capita than their larger competitors. Clearly, being a small business has had some pretty significant advantages. In Chapter 2, we discuss how small businesses operate and examine some of the reasons for their superior performance.

Change is the name of the game for modern industry. Those organizations that do not recognize and plan for the often obvious future trends of their industries will almost certainly be replaced, and it could happen very quickly.

KNOWLEDGE WORK

Assuming that Schumpeter was correct and that the rules of the game are continuously changing, a high priority for executives should be identifying those changes that will impact their businesses. Once these changes have been identified, executives and senior managers can better judge how and when to make the adjustments needed to capitalize upon them. The key challenge, of course, is determining what these future changes are likely to be and how to take advantage of them before your competitors do.

Peter Drucker devoted much thought to the analysis of corporate management. More than 50 years ago, in his 1957 book *Landmarks of Tomorrow,* he outlined the key challenges he saw for future managers and executives [Drucker 1957]. He concluded that learning how to manage knowledge work would be the key management challenge of the next century. He described knowledge work as work that is done in the workers' heads instead of with their hands. He concluded that knowledge work would soon be the most critical and the highest-valued form of labor. Later, in his book *The Age of Discontinuity* [Drucker 1969], Drucker wrote:

To make knowledge work productive will be the greatest management task of this century, just as to make manual labor productive was the great management task of the last century.

More recently, in an article in the *Harvard Business Review* [Drucker 1997], he also said:

The productivity of knowledge workers will not be the only competitive factor in the world economy. It is, however, likely to become the decisive factor, at least for most industries in developed countries.

Drucker was the premier management thinker of the twentieth century, and it behooves us to take his views seriously. This book, in fact, does just that. It starts from the premise that knowledge work is the work of the future, and that the organizations that first recognize and capitalize on this fact will be the industrial leaders of tomorrow. Ask yourself this question: "If Drucker and Schumpeter were right, what should I do to capitalize on the opportunities of the knowledge-working age?"

This book answers that question.

THE URGENCY OF CHANGE

As is clear, both from Schumpeter's and Drucker's views and from the current rate of industrial churn, change is a fact of competitive life. Furthermore, the rate of change is accelerating. While this is not particularly surprising, what is surprising is how often changes have come as surprises, even to very successful firms. Many of these surprises, however, happened not because the new ideas were unknown in advance to the leading firms. In fact, many of these companies actually *invented* the new methods that ultimately destroyed them.

Eastman Kodak still survives, and it invented many of the technologies in modern digital photography. Eastman Kodak, however, is not a market leader in digital photography. Similarly, Texas Instruments invented many of the methods used in developing and manufacturing integrated circuits, but TI no longer leads the semiconductor industry. The reason organizations are often surprised by technologies they already know is that they refuse to accept the implications of what they know.

For example, IBM management knew very well that the personal computer was coming and that it would be big business. They also knew that programming was an increasingly important part of the computer business. However, because IBM never put these two facts together, the company literally gave the PC programming business to Microsoft. Within a few years, Microsoft jumped from being a small start-up to being a major corporation with a market value even greater than that of the once-mighty IBM.

IBM management's lack of vision probably can be attributed to the fact that its executives and senior managers had long thought of programming as an expense. Until 1968, IBM had always given its software and systems engineering services to its customers as a part of its hardware support. Even 13 years later, when IBM introduced the PC in August 1981, its executives could not visualize software as a potentially profitable business opportunity. Today, IBM's software and systems engineering services generate more revenue and are more profitable than its hardware businesses. In fact, only a few years ago, IBM actually spun off its printer and disk drive hardware businesses. Old attitudes are hard to change, and IBM management's outdated attitudes were nearly fatal for the company.

The problem in large corporations is not a lack of vision; it is a lack of courage—the courage to recognize that the world is changing. Leaders must recognize that the things that made them successful in the past are not likely to be the things that will keep them successful in the future. The question, of course, is: "What will make organizations successful in the future?" The answer is that nobody really knows, and those who say that they do will almost certainly be proven wrong. What we do know, however, is that the problems that both large and small businesses will soon face will be different from those of today, and they will principally concern management. We also know that these problems will likely be of two types.

The first type of future problem concerns questions of scale. Small businesses typically grow faster and are more dynamic than larger ones, at least in part because they are not burdened by the problems of size. The question, then, is how a business can grow and be successful without being choked by its own size. Businesses have long faced this problem, but with the Internet and the new flexibility of the "flat world," these size problems are now quite different from what they were just a few years ago [Friedman 2005]. For example, in the past, the big issue was numbers of people and spans of control. Today, while we still have the span-of-control issue, the scale problems also include managing geographically distributed groups, mixed cultures, and heterogeneous technical teams. Clearly, mastering the problems of size in this increasingly complex environment will be more challenging and more important than ever before.

The second set of future problems has been with us for some time but has largely been confined to the specialized field of software. These problems concern knowledge work and knowledge workers. As Drucker pointed out, knowledge work is work that is done in the workers' heads rather than with their hands. While we have long had knowledge workers, traditionally there have been only a few of them on most projects. The vast bulk of the work has been done by technicians and less skilled laborers or factory hands. Today, most technical work looks more like software engineering, where the workers make creative decisions and produce work products on computers. Knowledge work is the key to the future, and those who master this discipline will be the industry leaders of the twenty-first century.

The fact that knowledge work requires a new management strategy and style is obvious from the history of the software business. Software projects have always been hard to manage, and few software groups, even today, can consistently deliver quality products on committed schedules or for anywhere near their planned costs. Software development was the first technology to involve large-scale knowledge work, and while software work has always been a management problem, traditionally it has involved only a small part of most businesses.

As knowledge work becomes pervasive, new corporate management strategies will be needed. Software and other forms of knowledge work are becoming increasingly important as they involve a greater proportion of business operations and more executives and senior managers recognize that software is now the controlling element of their operations. Software controls production schedules, optimizes prices, manages costs, and calculates profits. When new business strategies are implemented, software is the gating element, and when products are late, the software work is usually furthest behind schedule. In almost all areas of modern science and industry, products are developed with methods that look very much like software development. Just about all future systems and product development work will have to be managed as knowledge work. As noted in the next chapter, many aspects of the corporate world could benefit by being managed with these methods today.

The methods described in this book are designed for knowledge work and knowledge workers. These same methods will also help you to address other key issues, including those of size. The next example shows how the new knowledge-management methods can help executives and senior managers manage their businesses.

THE SOFTTEK STORY

Blanca Treviño is CEO of Softtek, a Mexican company with headquarters in Monterrey. Softtek is the largest independent IT service provider in Latin America with almost 6,000 employees and offices in 13 countries. The company was founded in 1982 and grew steadily until 2000 when Ms. Treviño became the CEO. Since then, the corporate growth rate has exceeded 30% per year. Softtek has long operated in North and South America and Europe, but it recently opened operations in five more countries: Venezuela, Chile, Paraguay, England, and China.

From the outset, Softtek focused on quality as a key marketing discriminator. It was one of the first Latin American companies to implement the Software Engineering Institute's (SEI's) software development practices and was assessed at CMMI[1] level 3 in 2000. In 2004, Softtek's development groups achieved the SEI's coveted level 5 rating, the highest CMMI level. While this was an important achievement, it was not unique to Softtek. In fact, many of its competitors had also achieved the same high rating. To compete and be successful, the Softtek managers had to maintain their quality rating and also devise some new way to provide their customers with unique products and services.

Ms. Treviño knew that Softtek had to be unique to stay competitive and continue to grow. Trying to compete on price alone would be a losing game because, although Mexican labor costs

---

1. CMMI, Capability Maturity Model Integration, is an evaluation method and model devised and supported by the SEI to rate the process capability of technical organizations.

were below those in the United States, Canada, and Europe, companies from India and China had an even lower cost structure. She therefore established a corporate goal of being the highest-quality software provider in Latin America and among the best in the world. Her objective was to offer such high-quality products and to provide such predictable and responsive services that Softtek's customers would make it their preferred supplier.

To achieve her corporate goal, Ms. Treviño knew that Softtek had to make some significant changes to both maintain and improve the productivity and quality of its engineering work and to differentiate itself from the competition. She therefore had her technical groups introduce the method the SEI had developed for knowledge work, the Team Software Process (TSP). The success of the TSP in improving engineering performance, coupled with Softtek's "near-shore" advantages in the U.S. marketplace, has enabled the company to attract a growing volume of profitable business and to expand its IT services business rapidly.

THE SOFTTEK EXPERIENCE

Starting in 2007, Softtek has been introducing the methods described in this book. The company's early TSP pilot projects were highly manageable, its people had more rewarding and satisfying work lives, and its customers were increasingly satisfied. In those parts of the business that used these new methods, Softtek improved its project performance, enhanced its product offerings, and improved its employees' quality of work life. It also improved profitability and accelerated corporate growth.

Project Performance

The new TSP knowledge-working methods also helped Softtek's technical teams improve their record of on-time and within-cost development performance. One large global financial institution even challenged Softtek to become its highest-performing software supplier in Latin America. After introducing the methods described in this book, and for almost a full year to date, Softtek's development teams have not missed any of this customer's quality or on-time delivery goals. This performance has earned them their customer's highest rating as a services provider, and for the next year, Softtek became that customer's IT services vendor with the highest proportion of the customer's business. In fact, the customer has even asked its other software vendors to consider using the TSP methods described in this book.

Product Offering

While Softtek had previously had an excellent record of delivering products on schedule and within contracted costs, its development performance has recently improved to such an extent that it can offer more development contracts on a fixed-price basis. This convinced many clients to move from a cost-plus to a managed-services delivery model for their projects. The customers are happy to have a more predictable cost structure, and Softtek has a higher-valued set of customer contracts. While some of this improvement was due to improved project management, a major part was a direct result of Ms. Treviño's drive for superior quality.

Product quality became so predictable and Softtek's products had so few defects that the company decided to offer quality guarantees. In selected cases, Softtek even included quality warranties in development contracts and promised to refund the customer's money for every defect found in customer acceptance testing or use. Initially, Softtek set its warranty budget at one-tenth of what such a warranty would have cost the company historically, but with its TSP teams, its costs have typically run well below that. While Softtek did make a few refunds, the customers liked the guarantees, and Softtek's competitors were unable to match them without losing money. To date, the guaranteed Softtek products have had so few defects that the company has decided to offer quality guarantees on a more regular basis.

People

With the TSP methods, the developers' quality of work life has greatly improved. Now, instead of suffering through all-nighters during final test, the developers can balance their workload and recover from schedule problems without impacting their projects. They are now home for dinner nearly every night, and they can take scheduled vacations without fear of unanticipated project crises.

This work-life improvement also has had important company benefits. For the TSP teams, turnover has decreased to one-quarter the turnover rate of non-TSP teams, and the company is better able to retain its most experienced and productive talent. This maintains team stability, saves recruiting costs, and improves the company's return on its personnel investment. With its improved corporate image and reputation, particularly among students, Softtek also finds it easier to recruit and retain the best engineering talent.

WHAT NEXT?

Judging by the abominable history of the software industry, Softtek's accomplishments might seem extraordinary. But the fact is, in any other industry this level of performance would earn only a passing grade. Just delivering quality products on schedule and within planned costs is what product developers are paid to do. For software work, however, this is a significant achievement, and it is one that all businesses must soon learn to achieve with all types of knowledge work.

As you read this book, remember that the problems you face in the future will be different from and more challenging than those you face today. Chapter 2 describes the issues of managing organizations as they grow. It also discusses small businesses, bureaucracy, and the problems of managing and controlling a growing business. Chapter 3 gives an overview of knowledge work, how the knowledge-working teams of the future will work, and the issues those teams must address to be successful. Starting with Chapter 4, we describe how to change your organization to better utilize your knowledge-working people and to capitalize on the enormous potential opportunities of the knowledge-working economy.

SUMMARY AND CONCLUSIONS

This chapter describes why even very successful organizations face an urgent need to change, why these changes must be a high priority, and the issues to be addressed in making the changes. The chapter makes four principal points:

1. The corporate leaders of today are not likely to be the leaders of tomorrow because of the accelerating pace of industrial change, a phenomenon that Joseph Schumpeter called "creative destruction."

2. As Schumpeter also pointed out, the rules of successful competition are changing, and the things that made today's businesses successful are not the things that will make businesses successful in the future.

3. Businesses face two principal challenges in making the management changes that will allow them to remain competitive in the marketplace. The first challenge is managing the problems of size; this problem is discussed more fully in Chapter 2.

4. The second challenge is making knowledge work productive. As Peter Drucker said, this will be the decisive factor for future success. This topic is discussed further in Chapter 3, and the balance of this book outlines a strategy for addressing the challenges of managing knowledge work and knowledge workers.

REFERENCES

[Drucker 1957] Peter Drucker, *Landmarks of Tomorrow: A Report on the New Post-Modern World* (New York: Harper & Row, 1957).

[Drucker 1969] Peter Drucker, *The Age of Discontinuity* (New York: Harper & Row, 1969).

[Drucker 1997] Peter Drucker, "The Future Has Already Happened," *Harvard Business Review* 75, no. 5 (September–October 1997): 20–23.

[Economist 2009] "Taking Flight," *The Economist*, September 17, 2009.

[Friedman 2005] Thomas L. Friedman, *The World Is Flat: A Brief History of the Twenty-first Century* (New York: Farrar, Straus and Giroux, 2005).

[Schumpeter 1942] Joseph Schumpeter, *Capitalism, Socialism and Democracy* (New York: Harper & Row, 1975 [orig. pub. 1942]).

[Terleckyj 1999] Nestor E. Terleckyj, "Measuring Contribution of Small Business to Industry Job Growth by Data in Business Association Directories," *U.S. Small Business Administration Report for Project SBAHQ-97-M-0753*, April 30, 1999.

2

The Bureaucracy

In Chapter 1 we introduced the two key challenges facing modern businesses: managing their growing size and managing knowledge work. In this chapter, we talk about the first issue, managing and controlling a growing business. Here, the principal concern is the tension between the flexibility and innovation required by technological change and the bureaucratic procedures needed to operate a growing business.

WHY ORGANIZATIONS NEED A BUREAUCRACY

As organizations grow, they must build bureaucracies to help run the business. These bureaucracies are usually hierarchically structured and operate in accordance with defined rules and procedures. While bureaucracies are often viewed as cumbersome and destructive, they are a necessary part of any but the smallest businesses. However, they must be properly constituted and managed or they will generate delay and inefficiency. The reason is that, like human scar tissue, bureaucratic procedures offer protection, but they can also limit speed and flexibility.

The fundamental purpose of the bureaucracy is to handle the operational details of the business automatically. When properly run, it can save senior managers time and allow them to focus on the core parts of the business. For example, the bureaucracy can routinely handle such tasks as operating the cafeteria; keeping

15

the facilities clean and comfortable; handling payroll, billing, and expenses; and managing all the other daily details of the business. A bureaucratic management style in these areas rarely impacts the core areas of the business. However, bureaucratic procedures can become troublesome when they involve more critical activities. The following example illustrates how this can happen.

THE SOFTWARE CRISIS

The company's software work had always been troubled, but it was now too big and too deeply involved in the business to ignore. The software department had always been late delivering its programs, and many of the company's products were now missing their schedules because of software problems. This group was in such trouble that the VP fired the software director and asked Brandon to take over. His job was to get the software operation under control.

Brandon visited the largest three of his development groups and found that nobody had good plans or schedules. While everybody was working hard, the operations were chaotic and out of control. Brandon decided to cancel all existing schedules and to require every software group to produce detailed plans for its work. He would review and approve the plans and personally make all future commitments. After the VP approved this recovery plan, Brandon issued a directive to his managers, telling them to produce detailed plans for all of their projects and to review them with him within 60 days. After he rejected the first few plans, his people soon learned what was needed and the plans got much better. Brandon then issued a new set of commitments based on the reviewed and approved plans, and the group started delivering products on schedule.

Brandon's review system worked reasonably well as long as he was able to review every proposed commitment and to check the quality of the supporting plans personally. However, as the organization grew, the reviews took too much time, so he initiated a staff review system. The objective was to address the most common problem he had found in the plans: that activities were often missing. For example, the project's costs might not be covered in the budget; key requirements might be omitted; and testing, maintenance, or field support might be left out.

He addressed this problem by having each plan reviewed by representatives of all the key departments before that plan could be brought to him. This worked, and he no longer had to make a thorough personal review of every plan. Within about a year, however, the marketing and support groups realized that they had leverage they never had before. They started withholding approval until their special needs were addressed. Marketing would haggle over pet features, service would object to the number of deferred defect fixes, and testing would argue about the resources they would need. By the time these problems had gotten severe, Brandon had been promoted and the review system was an entrenched part of normal business. The new director did not recognize the problems or what had caused them, so it never occurred to him to abandon or change the review system.

While the original objective of Brandon's review system was laudable, it became a bureaucratic procedure, and, like many such procedures, it was soon misused. Bureaucrats often have considerable power within their narrow scopes of authority, and they can be very demanding and even unreasonable. The essential problem was that Brandon was using a bureaucratic procedure as a mechanism to force his people to do their jobs correctly.

This is an expensive and often ineffective way to make knowledge workers follow defined procedures. While it will normally work, it gives staff members who are often narrowly focused considerable power over the knowledge workers. This causes delays and limits the engineers' ability to innovate or to do almost anything quickly. Also, people soon forget why the bureaucratic process was established, and it then becomes an ineffective ritual. Perhaps the worst outcome is that such bureaucratic procedures tell the knowledge workers that management does not trust them to do their jobs correctly. While it is important to ensure that knowledge workers do their jobs correctly, a bureaucratic procedure is an expensive way to do it. The next example illustrates how a small and rapidly growing business addressed its growth problems.

THE QUARKSOFT STORY

After Cesar Montes de Oca Vazquez and Ricardo Vidrio Delgadillo had earned their engineering degrees at Tecnológico de Monterrey in Mexico and worked as software engineers for about six years, both decided to go to Carnegie Mellon University (CMU) in the United States to get master's degrees in software engineering. At CMU, they used the SEI's latest software engineering method, TSP, for doing their course project and became convinced that using a defined and measured knowledge-working process was a better way to develop software than anything they had seen in Mexico.

After graduating from CMU, they realized that they had a unique skill that could help them form a business. By establishing the first software company in Mexico to use the TSP, they believed that they could do better work than other companies and could be very successful. In 2000, they worked as software consultants, and then in May 2001, they started Quarksoft.

Even though they didn't yet have customers, they started with 11 employees whom they trained in the TSP methods. They did not get their first customer until September, but they kept the business together and grew it slowly. By 2004, they had 50 engineers and by 2006 they had 70. Then they won several large contracts, and by the end of 2009, they had 315 employees.

Because the software methods their people used required the engineers to gather and use data on their work, the company could establish a precise and effective management system. They also had their engineering teams create their own plans for meeting management's project requirements. Then, after management reviewed and approved the team's plans, the engineers were held responsible for managing to their commitments, for keeping management apprised of project status, and for calling on management whenever they needed help with risks or issues.

The development people then felt responsible for their own work and acted like part of the management team. Because they made their own plans and defined their own processes, they were motivated to follow these plans and processes. They also learned quickly to use their process data to assess their work, measure project status, and decide how to best meet their business and technical goals. To help the teams do their work, management established a coaching system to guide the project launches and team operations. The result was that the teams actually followed their defined processes and plans, so there was little need for a bureaucratic system to enforce standard corporate procedures.

This management style resulted in consistently superior team performance, and it earned the company a rapidly growing volume of business. It also earned it two major Mexican industrial awards. In 2008, Dell and American Express jointly named Quarksoft the nation's most innovative company, and in 2009, the magazine *CNN Expansion* named it one of the ten most innovative companies in Mexico.

THE QUARKSOFT MANAGEMENT SYSTEM

Judging by the poor cost and schedule performance of most companies in the software industry, software engineering is a very difficult technology to manage. However, even in this complex field, Cesar and Ricardo have built a profitable business by offering high-quality products and services to their customers. The principal reason for this superior performance is the corporate management style that Cesar and Ricardo adopted. The business benefits of this way of working can be described in four categories: precise data, team-based discipline, commitment ownership, and quality.

Precise Data

To follow the TSP method, engineering teams and all team members gather precise data on the time they spend, the sizes of the products they produce, and the defects they inject and remove. Getting engineers to completely and accurately gather data on their work is a major challenge. Even with all of their experience, Quarksoft managers describe this as a key area that requires continuing attention and emphasis. However, with detailed status reports from their TSP teams, managers can manage the business precisely and responsively. The data the engineers gather cover all of their project work, and they gather the data every day. This precise status information enables the teams to accurately report cost and schedule progress every week. Management then knows where the work stands at all times and can immediately react to project problems or quickly adjust business plans when changes are needed.

Team-Based Discipline

Most executives and senior managers would agree that teams are important, but they generally believe that their people already follow sound teamworking practices. Quarksoft, however, follows a defined process for building teams and for guiding and coaching them to follow their detailed plans and operational processes. The specifics of how the TSP process does this are covered in subsequent chapters; the objective is to build integrated and cohesive project teams that understand the business context for their work and are disciplined in the way they do that work. This ensures that all the engineers understand the reasons for their job assignments and feel responsible for following their defined processes and plans. It also empowers them to be entrepreneurs and to act like members of the management team. When they have ideas about how to improve the business or see something that needs to be changed or fixed, they can make changes themselves or raise the issue to a suitable level of management.

By encouraging team participation and self-management, Quarksoft capitalizes on its people's creativity. This enables them to make rapid and innovative improvements, and it helps to develop future managers and leaders. It also largely eliminates the need for the bureaucratic procedures that many organizations use to enforce business discipline on their development teams. However, Quarksoft management did establish a bureaucratic procedure to audit the gathering, management, and use of process data. Just as with financial data, they found that timely, complete, and accurate process data were essential for running the business and for managing and improving profitability.

Commitment Ownership

Perhaps the most important element of Quarksoft's management system is the way it handles commitments. When starting every project, the executive or manager responsible for initiating that project, together with marketing or customer representatives, meets with the engineering team to explain the company's goals for the job and why the customers want and need it. The team then spends a few days developing a plan to do the work and returns to this same management group to present its plan. In this final launch meeting, the team requests approval of the plan or negotiates any desired plan changes.

This commitment process is called the TSP launch, and it guides properly trained teams in producing complete and realistic plans. Then, with a reasonably accurate plan and a committed team, the members are motivated to do whatever it takes to meet their commitments. While all development projects run into surprises and problems, if these problems are promptly recognized and addressed, they can usually be resolved fairly quickly. As a result, Quarksoft's TSP teams rarely miss their delivery commitments.

Because a high proportion of Quarksoft's business is under fixed-price contracts, it might seem risky to allow the teams to make their own plans. However, with their extensive data on historical project performance, management has a sound basis for making and managing customer commitments. As in any other business, they recognize that the principal concerns in negotiating customer contracts should be competition and business value. While engineering cost is important, it should primarily be used to estimate a project's profitability and level of risk. Once management has decided on the optimum price and delivery date, the challenge for the team is to ensure that management provides them with adequate resources to meet the schedule and for all team members to strive to maximize corporate profit.

Quality

Quarksoft management has made quality the top engineering priority. They did this because they found that the projects that produced the highest-quality work were typically the most profitable. With quality work, rework is minimized as are development costs. For knowledge work, however, quality work is consistently done only by properly trained and highly motivated people. Quarksoft management also found that to consistently meet their schedule commitments, they had to supply properly skilled and trained resources whenever a project needed them. In addition, with the TSP all teams use a common process and gather and use identical process measures, so it is relatively easy for team members to move among projects.

Because their people's motivation, skill, and training are the principal factors governing corporate profitability, Quarksoft management invests a great deal of time and effort in motivating, recruiting, training, and developing people. To manage these areas and to ensure that a suitable cadre of skilled and competent people is available for every project, they made the VP for R&D responsible for recruiting, training, and people development. Training and personnel development plans are also an important part of every manager's responsibilities.

THE QUARKSOFT EXECUTIVE TEAM

While Cesar and Ricardo were building Quarksoft, Carlos Montes de Oca Vazquez, Cesar's brother, became TSP-trained and joined a university as a computer science professor. After a couple of years, Quarksoft had grown significantly, so Cesar and Ricardo invited Carlos to join the company as Vice President for Research and Development. They then formed the corporate management team consisting of Cesar, the Chief Executive Officer; Ricardo, the Chief Operating Officer; and Carlos, for R&D.

Since they were all TSP-trained, they decided to run the corporate office as a knowledge-working team and to review and relaunch their management plans every one and a half to two months. In these relaunches, they review their long-term goals and update the overall corporate plan for the next plan period. They also develop detailed plans and goals for the next period and assign executive team members responsibility for two or three of these goals. In their weekly status meetings, they review goal status, track performance against plan, and address any other items needing attention.

Because they have precise data on all aspects of corporate operation, the Quarksoft executive team has tried various ways to track, control, and guide the business. Some examples of what they are doing are illustrated by their recent actions in financial management, R&D improvement, and people evaluation and motivation.

Financial Management

With team-level plans and reporting, the Quarksoft executive team decided to track the monthly profit contribution of each engineering project. They then developed an EBITA[1] measure that showed each project's contribution to corporate profit. They first determined how to calculate a project's contribution to EBITA from that project's schedule and labor-hour status against plan and then allocated the other related direct and indirect expenses to give a complete project-level profitability picture.

By tracking project EBITA on a monthly basis, they could tell when and why some projects were not as profitable as others. They also found that project-level EBITA varied as much as 5%

---

1. EBITA is a widely used corporate measure for earnings before interest, taxes, and amortization.

per month. While this level of precision was far better than traditional quarterly measures, the one-month interval between EBITA reports did not allow them to identify problems in time to prevent them. On many projects, just a one-month delay in problem identification could cause significant extra expense.

Their current goal is to improve project-level EBITA tracking to once a week. To do this, they plan to derive and track each project's EBITA from that team's weekly earned-value (EV)[2] status report. This is possible because the TSP teams use daily EV measures to manage their own work. They then report EV status to management every week. This gives the executive team the data they need to derive the weekly EBITA project measures, and it guides the teams in quickly identifying and recovering from the small daily schedule slips that are common in development projects. With this level of precision, the management team expects to recognize project EBITA problems in time to take timely action.

R&D Improvement

In the R&D area, Carlos is principally concerned with ensuring that the development teams are using the latest and best technical practices. This, in part, is why he is the executive with responsibility for recruiting, training, and personnel development. He also has the goal of having every team operate at CMMI level 5, the highest CMMI level. While the TSP has enabled Quarksoft to achieve very high levels of project performance, the TSP is a team-level complement to the CMMI and not a

---

2. Earned value (EV) is a standard way to measure a project's status against its plan. Each task has a value based on its percentage of total planned project effort, and when that task is fully completed, that value is earned. There is no credit for partially completed tasks. EV is a standard TSP team measure.

replacement. Therefore, the CMMI includes some additional and useful organization-level process-improvement actions.

Carlos's goal is to close this gap. His plan is to adopt the CMMI level 5 continuous improvement practices as a way to assist the company in continuing to improve its product quality and project predictability. Carlos then plans to use the TSP measures for defect injection and removal, project cost performance, and the component quality profiles to establish and monitor team-level improvement goals.

People Evaluation and Motivation

For people evaluation and motivation, Quarksoft uses a 360-degree people evaluation tool. With this, each employee is rated by his or her peers, customers, subordinates, and boss. The company also has a bonus system where everyone gets a bonus that is a percentage of his or her annual salary, based on current company and project profitability. For example, every team has a profit objective, and if the team can beat that objective, part of the extra profit is distributed to the team as a bonus. In the future, the company will also establish links to the team's EBITA performance so that individual team members can see how their personal performance impacts corporate profitability and work so as to maximize their personal and team EBITA performance.

MANAGING THE BUREAUCRACY

As organizations grow and mature, they have many potential advantages over their smaller and less established competitors. Larger organizations have the resources to explore new ventures, and a larger pool of people with potentially innovative ideas. These organizations also have a broad customer base and a reputation on which to build. Some may even have dominance in a large part of their traditional market. With all of these advantages, one would think that these larger businesses would consistently outperform their smaller competitors. However, history shows that, in aggregate, small businesses have consistently outperformed their larger brethren both in adding new jobs and in creating new and innovative products.

While there are many potential reasons for large business inefficiency, managing the bureaucracy is almost certainly an important one. The routine parts of the bureaucracy should normally be managed in a traditional way using either a 360-degree rating system or some other way that gives priority to user service and customer satisfaction. However, those aspects of the bureaucracy that involve the core activities of the business should be viewed as scar tissue that was established to prevent the recurrence of prior problems. Like Brandon's review system, such bureaucratic procedures may be necessary for short periods, but they should be replaced by some less onerous mechanism as soon as it is practical. The longer such procedures remain in force, the more likely they are to be misused and the more they will limit the organization's speed and flexibility. Like the TSP methods described in this book, there are other more effective and less intrusive ways to achieve the same result.

SUMMARY AND CONCLUSIONS

This chapter describes the first of the two problems raised in Chapter 1: managing organizations as they grow. The seven key points made in this chapter are the following:

1. As organizations grow, they must build bureaucracies to help run the business.

2. The parts of the bureaucracy that run such routine activities as the cafeteria, payroll, or building maintenance are rarely a problem.

3. Where bureaucratic procedures are used to enforce standard procedures on the core parts of the business, however, they can become intrusive.

4. When bureaucratic procedures are used to prevent the repetition of prior disasters, they can, like bodily scar tissue, reduce speed and limit flexibility.

5. The use of bureaucratic procedures also suggests that management does not trust their knowledge workers to do their jobs correctly.

6. While such bureaucratic procedures may occasionally be needed to solve a major problem, they should be quickly replaced with less intrusive ways to achieve the same result.

7. The TSP methods described in this book provide data that management can use to efficiently manage their organizations as they grow.

Chapter 3 addresses the second key problem raised in Chapter 1: making knowledge work productive. It starts the discussion of knowledge work and knowledge workers, which is the principal focus of the balance of the book.

3
Knowledge Work

This chapter addresses the second challenge raised in Chapter 1: making knowledge work productive. Before delving into the details of knowledge work, however, we need to explain why executives and senior managers should care about knowledge work and the productivity of knowledge workers. There are four reasons why this is an executive-level issue:

1. Knowledge work is now an important part of your business and will be much more important in the future.

2. The current performance of knowledge-working groups in most organizations is unsatisfactory. The most common and obvious examples of these problems are software groups.

3. The solution to these knowledge-working problems requires a significant change in the management culture and style in most organizations.

4. Management culture and style cannot be changed by lower-level managers; they must be changed by senior executives and managers.

While we say more about these points in this and subsequent chapters, the reason that this chapter is here and why it covers some team-level issues in more detail than you might expect is because of the importance of making knowledge work productive. This chapter first defines what knowledge work is, discusses why knowledge work is so troublesome today, and explains who knowledge workers are. We next give an example of a knowledge-working team and show how highly productive knowledge-working teams actually work.

The description of this example team provides a snapshot of how knowledge workers behave and the kinds of troublesome management issues knowledge-working teams can often resolve quite easily. In closing this chapter, we describe why knowledge work has become so important in modern industry and the reasons why it is destined to become even more important in the future. The rest of the book then describes how to make the cultural and managerial changes needed to improve the productivity and effectiveness of your knowledge workforce.

THE NATURE OF KNOWLEDGE WORK

When Peter Drucker first discussed knowledge work, he defined knowledge workers as people who work with, use, or develop knowledge [Drucker 1957]. Unfortunately, this definition seems to encompass almost everyone in modern business. With few exceptions, every job in the modern industrial world involves some kind of specialized knowledge or skill. However, in Drucker's view, what separates knowledge workers from other workers, and what makes them a truly special breed, is that they use their specialized knowledge and skill to work on knowledge itself.

Knowledge workers take what is known, and after modifying and extending it, they combine it with other related knowledge to actually create new knowledge. This means that knowledge workers are working at the boundary between what is known and what is unknown. They are extending our total storehouse of knowledge, and in doing so, they are creating economic value.

Even this definition, however, is very broad and covers many jobs that seem to be perfectly productive and effective today. One could even say that the ancient Egyptian priests who forecast Nile floods and the Pythagorean philosophers of ancient Greece were all knowledge workers. In fact, people have been doing knowledge work for millennia. What makes today's knowledge-working problem so different is that it is no longer done by a few especially skilled and motivated individuals; it is now done by masses of talented workers who must cooperate to produce a creative and coherent result.

WHY KNOWLEDGE WORK IS TROUBLESOME

While we didn't originally call it knowledge work, software development was the first truly large-scale knowledge work. When developing software, knowledge workers work almost entirely with their minds. They typically record their conclusions on a computer, but the real creative activity is done in their heads and in brainstorming and negotiating sessions with their peers and users. Then, after these knowledge workers have produced their first product drafts, they typically modify, extend, test, and revise them to produce final running programs.

Many software developers work by themselves and produce relatively small products, but the truly troublesome projects are those that involve dozens, hundreds, or even thousands of developers working together to produce the larger programs needed for modern businesses. It is these larger projects that have typically been most troubled and that have resulted in the generally poor performance of software organizations.

The question, of course, is: "Why are software projects so troubled?" The simple answer is that from the very beginning of the computer era, software products have been delivered much later than planned, have cost much more than expected, and have been highly defective. While there have been exceptions and the quality of software products varies enormously, the problem stems from the fact that the practices of the entire software industry have been quite different from those of companies in other industries.

With few exceptions, software organizations rarely make firm product delivery commitments, write fixed-price development contracts, or provide meaningful product quality warranties. This has led to a general industry attitude that defective software products are a fact of life and that the customers must bear the cost, expense, and inconvenience of recovering from the poor quality of the software products they buy. These problems lead to three rather obvious questions:

1. Why do software customers put up with such shoddy performance? After all, no other industry treats its customers in such a cavalier way.

2. Why haven't these problems been solved before? Many other businesses deliver quality products with predictable costs and schedules, so it must be possible.

3. Is there a way to run software and other knowledge-working activities in a more businesslike way?

WHY CUSTOMERS TOLERATE SHODDY SOFTWARE WORK

The principal reason that customers tolerate shoddy software work is that they have few, if any, alternatives. Because essentially all software organizations have similar problems, the customers have nowhere else to go. Suppose, however, that some company or companies figured out how to do software work in a more customer-friendly way; what would happen then? While it is impossible to predict exactly what would happen, the general outlines are almost certainly what Schumpeter predicted: creative destruction [Schumpeter 1942]. As we described in Chapter 1, when a competitor comes up with a newer and better way to do business, the old industry leaders are ultimately replaced, sometimes surprisingly quickly.

This, for example, is how Toyota overtook GM to become the worldwide leader in vehicle sales. Just ten years after registering its first vehicle in the United States in California in 1958, Toyota's U.S. sales reached 71,000. Then, by 1988, the company started producing vehicles in the United States. Because it had participated in the Japanese quality initiative inspired by W. Edwards Deming [Deming 1982], Toyota was producing the highest-quality cars in the industry, allowing the company to introduce a 36,000-mile/3-year bumper-to-bumper warranty in 1988. By 2000, just 12 years later, Toyota's U.S. sales topped 1.6 million vehicles. Today, Toyota sells more vehicles than GM, both worldwide and in the United States.

Toyota has recently stumbled, but that is not surprising. According to Schumpeter, industry leaders always get complacent. They begin to believe that they are successful because they are so good, and because they are so good, they don't need to listen to outsiders or change their tried-and-true formula for success. Then, as history has amply proven, problems are inevitable.

Toyota is an example of how a small, innovative company can overtake a seemingly invincible industry leader and how, once it is a leader, it too becomes complacent. In fact, Toyota management now blames its recent problems on its drive to become the world's largest automobile company. This can happen to anybody. As soon as customers have an alternative to shoddy work, they will move. It may take a few years, but industry leadership will then almost certainly change. This, then, is the first reason why software's problems have persisted for so long: The customers have had no alternative. The second reason is that software, and in fact all knowledge work, is a new kind of work, and traditional management methods are not effective for knowledge work of any kind.

WHY SOFTWARE'S PROBLEMS PERSIST

The reason these software problems have not been solved before is, of course, that the cause has not been recognized and addressed. Merely trying to manage software or any other knowledge work by changing managers or tightening up on rules and procedures will not work. These strategies have all been tried before with little success. People also have tried all kinds of new fads and gimmicks to fix software's problems. A new magic answer appears every five years or so, such as CASE tools, RAD (Rapid Application Development), or the software factory. A tour of a Japanese software factory some years ago revealed that the engineers all wore white smock coats as if they were in a semiconductor clean room, and they all sat at rows of workstations. It looked just like a typical factory production line. This kind of superficial change may make management feel that it is doing something, but it won't accomplish much, if anything.

IS THERE A BETTER WAY?

Because none of the methods people have tried have addressed the fundamental problems with software management, none of them has been terribly successful. As noted in Chapter 1, the problem with managing software development is that software development is knowledge work, and the problems of managing knowledge work can be resolved only by senior executives and managers who understand the nature of this kind of work and establish the management style and culture needed to facilitate and motivate such work. The following example shows how knowledge-working teams behave and how they can address many of the problems that have plagued software work for decades.

A KNOWLEDGE-WORKING TEAM

Two geographically separated companies that do highly classified work for the U.S. Department of Defense (DoD) contracted with their mutual customer to jointly develop a complex, new safety-critical software system that both would use to support their development and manufacturing work. These companies were the only two organizations that produced a critical weapons system component for the U.S. military, and they had been competitors for years. Because the companies had different design and manufacturing support systems, however, the DoD had set up parallel logistics systems for their products.

These duplicate logistics systems were expensive and caused delay and confusion. While the government program manager had long urged these companies to establish a common support system, and the companies had tried to do so, they had been unable to get their people even to agree on a plan for doing the work. They had formed joint planning teams, established design committees, and set up steering groups. But because the two competing organizations had different histories and cultures, they had no basis for agreement.

Finally, at the request of the government program manager, the company executives agreed to sign a contract to develop the desired system. The company executives then asked the SEI at Carnegie Mellon University for their help. An SEI team explained to the executives the principles of managing knowledge work and described how the TSP could guide them in applying these principles to their project.

While the TSP was originally designed for software teams, it has proven to be useful for knowledge work of all types. In fact, some of the hardware design teams in these two companies are now using the TSP to develop weapons systems hardware, even when no software engineers are involved in the projects.

The Project Launch

After the executives agreed to try the TSP, the first step was to agree on a joint plan of action. SEI personnel briefed the two companies' executive teams on an overall strategy, and then they trained the managers and engineering teams in the TSP methods. After this brief training, SEI coaches guided the two companies' teams in producing a joint plan. This was done using the TSP launch process, which consisted of a series of meetings that brought all team members from both companies to one location to participate in a joint planning effort. The engineering staff was divided into three smaller unit teams, and a leadership team was established. Each of the two engineering teams, team A and team B, was assigned one of the system's two major components. The members of team A were all from one company and one location, and those on team B were all from the other company and location.

Another team, team C, was formed from employees of both companies, and its job was to establish a common set of requirements for the work. At the beginning of the first day of the team launch, the members of team C were sitting together in company groups and taking company positions. By the second day, however, this team had spent several hours discussing and agreeing on the team's goals, and once they agreed on goals, they began to act like one team. They no long stressed their companies' positions but started focusing on the team's goals, and the actions to best achieve them.

The leadership team was formed of the leads from the engineering and requirements teams plus an overall executive from each company. At the end of the first day, the leadership team was also acting like a single team and not a collection of corporate representatives. In contrast, each of the engineering teams built the rapport needed to do their own work, but they stayed in company teams and never built the intercompany relationships needed for a cooperative total development effort.

At the final launch meeting, the leaders of the engineering and requirements teams presented their overall plans to senior management and the responsible DoD acquisition executive. Everybody was nervous because the team's plan would require three years to deliver the functions the companies had contracted to deliver in one year. While the plan did produce an initial minimum-function release in one year, the teams saw no way to produce all of the desired functions in that time. At the end of the meeting, the acquisition executive said, "This is the best plan I have ever seen," and accepted the team's plan.

Without the guidance of the TSP, this team would not have been able to make a detailed plan, and it would not have known how long the project would take. Then, as is usual for software projects, the engineers would not have had the courage to confront management with the schedule facts, and their project would have had all the typical problems of traditional software projects.

Design Problems

When the two development teams started designing their parts of the overall system, they found that the management-defined system structure didn't work. The leadership team had divided the system into two parts so that one company team could develop one component at that company's location, and the other company team could develop the other component at its location. In doing this, they allocated system functions to components based on the expertise of the engineers at the location that would handle that component. As the teams started on the design, however, they found that the functions did not divide neatly into these two components, so they reallocated the functions to produce a more efficient system structure. This, however, meant that each of these new components had functions that would have to be developed by engineers at both of the companies' locations.

After about three months of work, the high-level design for both components was nearly completed and some of the detailed design work started. As the two teams tried to work together to produce the component designs, however, they had many disagreements that they could not settle. As these disagreements festered, development progress slowed, and the teams found it harder and harder to work cooperatively. At that point, the teams convinced the leadership team that they had to update their plans. Everybody was then brought to one of the company's facilities for a team relaunch.

The Team Relaunch

In the relaunch, the teams started by reviewing their goals and strategies. In debating their goals, however, they realized that their existing company team structure would not work and that all the engineers from both companies who worked on one component had to work together to make that component's plan. They then formed two component teams, and over the next two days they reestimated the work and produced an updated task plan for each component. Then, when management told them to return to their company teams, the developers disagreed. They said that they had made so much progress in component teams that they should finish the launch that way. Once the relaunch was over and the plan updated, the developers decided to keep the component team structure for the development work, and they never did return to their original company-based teams.

This new team configuration meant that each of the A and B engineering teams had members from both companies and both locations. The A engineers were in two locations, but they were all working on one component and had a common plan and set of goals. Similarly, the B team was split geographically, but all of its members also worked on the same component and had common goals and plans. While working with distributed teams was initially a little inconvenient, the engineers found it much easier to work together as members of the same team with common goals and plans than to work on location and company teams where the team members worked to different plans and different goals. The teams continued to work in this way and they completed their design work on schedule.

The Leadership Team

By the time the teams were ready for the second relaunch, they had been working as component teams for nearly eight months and were about ready for release 1 testing. So far, the leadership team had been jointly run by two executives, one from each company. Now, during final implementation and testing, there were many more issues that needed management attention. The two-headed management structure had resolved problems and provided team direction, but it often took a week or more to agree on issues. Even though the managers usually ended up agreeing, the delay had started to affect the teams' schedules, and they had already missed some dates. The teams urged the management team to establish a single executive decision point.

By this time, the two groups had worked together for long enough and had developed enough trust and respect that the senior management of both companies would agree to a single program manager. They picked the leader of the requirements team. Under this new leadership, the teams completed their work and delivered all of their releases on schedule. The DoD was delighted with the team's results and has continued contracting with this group for the long-term maintenance and enhancement of the companies' common development and support system.

TEAM ACCOMPLISHMENTS

This example demonstrates some important lessons. While these teams were designing and developing a complex system, they also managed to resolve several management problems that have plagued software development work for decades.

First, they withstood strong management pressure for an overly aggressive schedule, and they negotiated a date that the team members were all convinced they could meet. Software development groups typically do not do this for two reasons: They don't know how to make accurate plans, and they typically view management's originally stated schedule as nonnegotiable. This team, however, was asked by management to produce a plan for the job, and its members had been trained and practiced in the TSP's planning methods. With their newly learned planning abilities, they were confident about the accuracy of their plan and had the self-confidence to convince management and to negotiate a realistic and achievable schedule for the work.

The second lesson from this example is that even though they started with two competing groups encompassing a wide range of skills and working in different cities, they were able to complete a demanding planning process and to work through all of their issues and differences to become a productive team. They could do this because the TSP launch process did more than just build a team plan; it built a cohesive team. Because these groups had worked through their issues and agreed on common goals and plans, they had built a bond of team loyalty that overcame their employment, location, and professional differences. This was further demonstrated by the experiences of the two engineering teams in the first team relaunch. While these engineers initially had not developed common goals and plans and had disagreed for several months, once they were put on component teams and had jointly worked through a planning process, they too became cohesive, productive, and cooperative teams.

The third lesson concerns this team's feeling of ownership and responsibility. When they realized that the original management-imposed design strategy was inefficient and cumbersome, they changed it. While they had little trouble getting management to agree, they recognized the need for the design change and took the initiative to make it happen. Then, in the relaunch, they again overrode management. They knew that they could be more productive and effective when working as component teams rather than as company teams. Even though their management believed that they should work as company teams, the single-company team approach had not worked for the previous development phase. Then their success in working as component teams during the relaunch convinced the engineers—and ultimately their managers—that they should continue this integrated-team approach during the next development phase.

The fourth lesson from this example is that knowledge-working teams often know a great deal more about their jobs and how they should be done than their managers. As we will discuss in the next chapter, the key to managing knowledge work is to empower knowledge workers and enable them to participate as partners with management in controlling and directing their own work. Because these teams will then be thinking and acting more like owners than employees, they are likely to come up with creative solutions to problems when, often, their management might not even know these problems existed.

THE FUTURE OF KNOWLEDGE WORK

The reason that knowledge work is important today and that it will be increasingly important in the future concerns the nature of modern technology and what will likely happen in the future. In the course of industrial history, the sophistication and complexity of products and services have steadily increased. The reason for more complexity, of course, is to make products and services more convenient, flexible, and useful to their final users. Increased complexity used to lead to increased manufacturing costs, but that is no longer the case. The principal reason is the advent of modern computer technology. Starting with the microcomputer era, engineers found that they could implement complex functions far more economically with computer software than with mechanical gears and levers. This cut manufacturing costs sharply, because while producing gears and levers costs money, producing copies of software products costs essentially nothing.

Now, when powerful microcomputers can be obtained for a few cents and manufacturing costs for the programs that drive these microcomputers are essentially zero, just about all logical functions are handled with software. This means that more and more of the time of product designers is spent either writing programs or producing logical designs with methods that look very much like those used by programmers. This increased demand for programming-like work also extends to the manufacturing sphere where the production floor itself is heavily automated and much of the monitoring, adjustment, repair, and reconfiguration work involves software skills.

Even beyond product development and manufacturing, modern economies are increasingly service-oriented. For example, IBM used to be primarily a hardware company that manufactured and sold computing equipment. While it still sells computer hardware, over three-quarters of its business is now software and services. The employees doing this work are either programmers or analysts whose job is to solve customer problems. This, in fact, is increasingly the nature of modern work: defining and specifying complex problems so that they can be solved by computers. This is knowledge work, and, like IBM, most companies will soon find that it is the highest-value part of what their people do. That is why knowledge work is important, and it is why Peter Drucker stated that the principal challenge of this century will be making knowledge work productive.

SUMMARY AND CONCLUSIONS

This chapter addresses the second key challenge raised in Chapter 1: making knowledge work productive. As Peter Drucker has said [Drucker 1997],

> The productivity of knowledge workers will not be the only competitive factor in the world economy. It is, however, likely to become the decisive factor, at least for most industries in developed countries.

The following seven points are made in this chapter:

1. Knowledge work is now an important part of your business, and it will be much more important in the future.

2. The current performance of knowledge-working groups in most organizations is unsatisfactory. The most common examples of these problems are the software groups.

3. The solution to knowledge-working problems requires that most organizations significantly change their management culture and style.

4. Management culture and style cannot be changed by lower-level managers; that must be done by senior executives.

5. When properly guided and motivated, knowledge-working teams can resolve some business issues more quickly and effectively than anyone else in your organization.

6. When properly trained, led, and motivated, your knowledge-working teams can be highly creative and productive partners in running your business.

7. Your knowledge-working teams soon will be your most important single asset; treat them as such.

REFERENCES

[Deming 1982] W. Edwards Deming, *Out of the Crisis* (Cambridge, MA: MIT Center for Advanced Engineering Study, 1982).

[Drucker 1957] Peter Drucker, *Landmarks of Tomorrow: A Report on the New Post-Modern World* (New York: Harper & Row, 1957).

[Drucker 1997] Peter Drucker, "The Future Has Already Happened," *Harvard Business Review* 75, no. 5 (September–October 1997): 20–23.

[Schumpeter 1942] Joseph Schumpeter, *Capitalism, Socialism and Democracy* (New York: Harper & Row, 1975 [orig. pub. 1942]).

4

Managing Knowledge Work

Management, as an orderly discipline, had its start only about 100 years ago when Frederick Winslow Taylor published his landmark book, *The Principles of Scientific Management* [Taylor 1911]. Taylor, who lived from 1856 to 1915, was an American mechanical engineer who started studying manual labor in England as a young man. He originated the idea of breaking tasks into small steps, studying how best to perform each step, and then training workers to work in just that way. He looked at every aspect of the job from the most efficient tools, methods, and materials to the way the steps should be combined to accomplish the total job.

Taylor's work led to the time-and-motion studies that are a common practice of industrial engineers today, and that enabled U.S. industry to out-produce the rest of the world to win World War II. He applied his principles to bricklaying, bicycle manufacturing, steel making, and many other activities with dramatic results. He worked with Henry Ford in setting up the River Rouge production facilities for the Model T Ford, and he was the guiding force behind most of the management advances made in the first half of the twentieth century. In fact, Drucker says that Taylor's methods were largely responsible for the 50 times improvement in labor productivity over the last 100 years. Drucker adds, "On this achievement rest all of the economic and social gains of the 20th century" [Drucker 1999].

TAYLOR'S MANAGEMENT PRINCIPLES

In *The Principles of Scientific Management*, Taylor describes what managers must do when using scientific management. In his words, these four things are:

- They develop a science for each element of a man's work, which replaces the old rule-of-thumb method.

- They scientifically select and then train, teach, and develop the workman, whereas in the past he chose his own work and trained himself as best he could.

- They heartily cooperate with the men so as to insure all of the work being done is in accordance with the principles of the science which has been developed.

- There is an almost equal division of the work and the responsibility between the management and the workmen. The management take over all work for which they are better fitted than the workmen, while in the past almost all of the work and the greater part of the responsibility were thrown upon the men.

While this does not sound authoritarian, Taylor's description of how to apply these principles in the case of bricklaying makes his fundamentally top-down management strategy completely clear:

- First. The development (by the management, not the workman) of the science of bricklaying, with rigid rules for each motion of every man, and the perfection and standardization of all implements and working conditions.

- Second. The careful selection and subsequent training of the bricklayers into first-class men, and the elimination of all men who refuse to or are unable to adopt the best methods.

- Third. Bringing the first-class bricklayer and the science of bricklaying together, through the constant help and watchfulness of the management, and through paying each man a large daily bonus for working fast and doing what he is told to do.

- Fourth. An almost equal division of the work and responsibility between the workman and the management. All day long the management work almost side by side with the men, helping, encouraging, and smoothing the way for them, while in the past they stood on one side, gave the men but little help, and threw on them almost the entire responsibility as to methods, implements, speed, and harmonious cooperation.

Stated in this way, these rules sound totally inappropriate for today's workforce. They were, however, very effective in Taylor's time because both the work and the workforce were quite different from what they are today. Professions, such as medicine, law, and finance, were quite limited; the bulk of the population engaged in farming or ranching, trades, or manual labor. Taylor's work was focused on improving the productivity of unskilled laborers. The work that Taylor studied could be characterized roughly as follows:

- All jobs could be broken into steps.
- These job steps could be individually studied and analyzed.
- Each job step could be designed to minimize the time required to complete it.
- The individual job steps could be combined to produce the total job specification.
- When scheduling the work, suitable rest periods had to be included to enable workers to work productively for a full day.
- The supervisors could watch the work and ensure that it was done precisely as specified.

The people making up the manufacturing workforce of Taylor's day were also quite different:

- The workers were mostly uneducated.
- They were principally motivated by money.
- They had limited and largely interchangeable skills.
- Unless carefully supervised, the workers would not work as hard as they could.
- They could not be trusted to work hard even when they were supervised.

This last point refers to the common practice factory workers adopted when working under job quotas and piecework payment scales. They would never exceed their management-defined standard rates because they knew that management would then raise the rates but not increase their pay. In fact, workers were so united in this practice that they would threaten workers who exceeded the standard rates. This form of worker-management animosity was and remains a common feature of many production management systems.

THE MODERN TECHNICAL WORKPLACE

Today's technical workers typically know much more about their jobs than do their managers, and most professional workers are highly motivated and work hard whether or not their management is watching. Furthermore, with today's complex technologies, there are often many ways to do a job, and the job steps are often interdependent. This is particularly true of the balance among the development and quality-management steps in software engineering. Rushing through early requirements and design steps or skipping quality reviews and inspections might save some time in the short run, but it greatly extends time later in testing. In today's high-technology work, attempts to sub-optimize a job by minimizing the time spent in some single steps could result in an inefficient overall job. Finally, although pay is always an important motivator, today's professionals also seek other rewards such as interesting work, a cohesive and collabor-ative working environment, and an appreciative and supportive management.

While it seems obvious that today's work and workers are dif-ferent from those of 100 years ago, the unsuitability of today's management methods has not been as well recognized. Many business scholars are becoming increasingly aware that today's typical top-down hierarchical management structures are effec-tive only in a Taylor-like workplace. Once the workers know more about their work than their managers, it makes no sense to have managers tell the workers how to do their jobs. This means that today's management system must be redesigned, and we must start that redesign by redefining our assumptions about the work and the workers.

MODERN TECHNICAL WORK

The fundamental difference between the work of today and that of 100 years ago is as basic as the difference between things and concepts. Tasks were straightforward and linear in Taylor's time because the work typically concerned things rather than ideas. Every action had a reaction, and parts had to fit in place and be interchangeable. Things stayed in one place and where you put them, and the work was made up of separate and distinct steps. One job step followed another, and you could watch such work and tell how well it was being performed and when the worker was likely to finish.

Today's world is totally different, and every aspect of daily life is more complex. This is true of the work and the workers. You cannot tell what a computer is doing by looking at it, and you cannot tell what computer designers are doing by watching them work. Modern large-scale knowledge work is unlike any kind of work people have ever done before. For many modern technologies, products must be considered as systems with myriad interdependent parts, and the work needed to produce such products must also be considered systemically with many interdependent steps. Commonly, in fact, no single part by itself can do anything; it has utility only as a part of an entire system.

Similarly, the job steps to produce products often are interdependent and iterative. This is why modern technical work is nonlinear. For example, designers work at the highest conceptual level for a while, and when they hit some puzzling question, they burrow down to the lowest and most detailed design level [Curtis 1988]. Then, when they have worked out how that smallest part must behave, they return to the highest conceptual level to continue refining the overall system design. Most modern technical work is iterative, nonlinear, and widely varied. Typically, only the workers can know what they are doing, why they are doing it, or how they are doing it.

MODERN TECHNICAL WORKERS

While modern work is completely different from that of 100 years ago, today's workers are, if anything, even more different. Many are highly educated and often capable of working at the very forefront of their technical fields. They generally care about money, but that is not their principal motivator. They seek interesting and exciting work, a cohesive and rewarding working environment, and the recognition of their peers and management. They typically find their greatest rewards in building challenging products that work precisely as they intended. Experienced engineers are rightfully proud of the thrill and joy they feel when a complex system they created works for the first time.

Today's workers often have highly individualized skills and talents. The performance difference between highly skilled and average developers can be modest or almost infinite, depending on the task and the environment. Most creative ideas are accidents of environment, opportunity, and talent. When creative people face a challenging and important problem, their minds work on that problem even when they are sleeping, eating, or working on other tasks. Then, some seemingly unrelated comment or event triggers the inspiration needed to devise a solution. There is no way to compare the performance of this knowledge worker with one who is just putting in time to earn a paycheck.

What is surprising about knowledge workers, however, is that there is no way to tell in advance who will be creative and who will not. Furthermore, almost all knowledge workers, when properly motivated and challenged, are highly creative and productive. Finally, when skilled and motivated knowledge workers are teamed with an eclectic mix of peers and motivated by common challenges, they stimulate each other so that the team's collective creativity often far exceeds that of any individual member. Such knowledge workers are typically highly motivated and work hard whenever they have challenging, interesting, and rewarding assignments. In Taylor's day, supervision was required to make workers productive; for today's knowledge workers, close supervision often reduces or inhibits their motivation.

THE PRINCIPLES OF MANAGING KNOWLEDGE WORK

Knowledge workers and knowledge work seem almost unmanageable, so how can we possibly manage them? The team described in the example in Chapter 3 shows that knowledge-working teams can do great work, even under the most adverse conditions. That team had members from competing companies who were located in two widely separated locations. They were able to complete a challenging job with which their managers had struggled for many months without even being able to produce a project plan. How was this team able to succeed when most software teams fail under far less stringent conditions? The answer is that they followed a process that was designed for knowledge work. The inspiration for this process was an idea that Peter Drucker described in 1999: "Knowledge workers have to manage themselves. They have to have autonomy" [Drucker 1999].

To perform at their best, knowledge workers must be motivated, and they must have the skills, knowledge, and resources to do their work. In addition, they must do their work in a responsible and businesslike way. This means that they must work to defined and approved plans and processes; meet their cost, schedule, and quality commitments; and keep management informed of their status and progress. While the knowledge-working team described in Chapter 3 did this, it is not something that other teams normally do. This kind of team behavior is generally viewed as a management responsibility, and the team leaders and managers typically do it while the knowledge workers concentrate on their technical tasks.

However, as Drucker pointed out, managers can't manage knowledge work. This means that they cannot plan knowledge work, they cannot monitor and track such work, and they cannot determine and report on job status. While the managers could ask the knowledge workers how they plan to do their jobs and where they stand, the knowledge workers of today typically do not work to detailed plans and do not know their project status.

They may guess, but their guesses are rarely accurate. It is not that they are being difficult; it is that they have not learned how to plan, measure, track, or report on their own work.

Today, knowledge workers typically view all management tasks as their manager's responsibility, and they are not interested in managing themselves. Drucker did not explain how to get knowledge workers to manage themselves, but it is not that difficult once you consider the principles for managing autonomous knowledge workers and teams:

1. Management must trust knowledge workers and teams to manage themselves.

2. Knowledge-working teams must be trustworthy. That is, they must be willing and able to manage themselves.

3. The management system must rely on facts and data (rather than status and seniority) when making decisions.

4. Quality must be the organization's highest priority.

5. Management must provide knowledge workers and teams with the leadership, training, coaching, and support they need to manage themselves.

The remainder of this chapter explains why these principles are necessary to implement an effective management system for knowledge work. It also includes references to subsequent chapters where the principles are described in greater detail.

TRUSTING KNOWLEDGE WORKERS

The first of the five principles for managing knowledge work, trusting knowledge workers to manage themselves, requires a trusting relationship between management and the workers. However, establishing such a trusting relationship is a challenge for two reasons. First, there is a long record of mistrust between management and workers, and this has been true throughout human history. The reason is that bosses have been getting people to do their bidding for millennia, and for most of this time, the principal motivator was fear. Slavery was common and the most prevalent form of persuasion was a threat. However, during the industrial era, managers started to use greed as the principal motivator. While greed is a crass way to describe salary, bonus, and quota systems, such systems assume that people would always like more pay for their work. They can therefore be viewed as greedy. Thus, traditional payment systems are based on conflict: The bosses want more work for less pay, and the workers want more pay for less work. Because conflicts breed distrust, there is a natural level of distrust between workers and managers.

This motivation issue is important because recent studies have shown that traditional motivational methods are not effective for knowledge work. For example, some things that should obviously work, don't, and other methods that seem nonsensical are actually quite effective. An example of the latter case is open-source programming. Why would skilled people put in long hours to produce high-quality products for no pay? But this is now a common way to develop some kinds of software, and many people spend a lot of their time working for nothing.

A similar question about the effectiveness of bonus payments was raised by a recent study conducted by economists at MIT, the University of Chicago, and Carnegie Mellon University [Ariely 2009]. The researchers studied the effect of various bonus-payment levels on the performance of several kinds of simple tasks. Some of these tasks included modest intellectual effort and others did not. They even examined various kinds of intellectual effort such as memory, reasoning, and creativity. The tasks were very simple. For the purely physical tasks (PT), the job was to alternately press the *v* and *n* keys on a keyboard as rapidly as possible. For one of the mental tasks (MT), the job was to add a series of numbers. The performance measure was the percentage of the maximum possible earnings achieved in each case.

What the study found was that except for purely mechanical tasks, performance declined with increasing incentives. This was true regardless of the type of intellectual effort involved. To see if this effect depended on the magnitude of the incentive, the researchers performed similar experiments in the United States and rural India. In India, the rewards for superior performance were a significant percentage of a worker's typical annual wage. In all cases, the results were the same: Performance was less with larger incentives. The difference, in fact, was quite significant, as shown in Figure 4.1. One of the fundamental precepts of modern

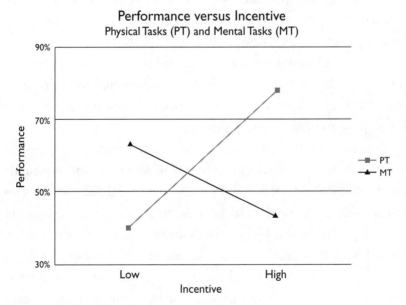

Figure 4.1 The effect of bonuses on performance

management is that better pay produces better performance. This is clearly not true for intellectual tasks like knowledge work. We discuss this motivation issue further in Chapter 5.

THE BLAME CULTURE

The second reason that building trust is a challenge is today's common culture of placing blame. When something bad happens, the first question is usually "Who did it?" Whether it is an improperly set valve, a damaging software defect, or a broken cookie jar, somebody obviously did something wrong, and it seems natural to find out who it was. The search for culprits, however, is rarely productive. It is better to view mistakes as process problems and to make an objective search for what happened in order to determine how to prevent a recurrence. Whether changes are needed in training, procedures, or job assignments, the underlying problems cannot be prevented unless the causes are understood. The key is to recognize that all people make mistakes and that our processes must be designed to minimize mistakes and to find and fix these mistakes before they cause serious harm. Until organizations learn to correct mistakes without affixing blame, the fundamental trust problem will continue, and workers will attempt to hide problems instead of helping to identify and fix them.

Suppose, for example, that a software defect in an automobile control system resulted in thousands of accidents and hundreds of deaths; does it matter who made the initial software design error? While the superficial answer might be yes, investigation would probably show that the software had been extensively tested and that hundreds to thousands of defects had been found and fixed. Many of these defects could have caused similarly serious problems, but the quality management system appears to have caught all but this one. To find any similar problems that might remain and to prevent any future ones, the entire quality management system must be reviewed and corrected. Disciplining or retraining one developer would not likely do much good, and it would probably make it more difficult to truly understand the problem and to devise an effective fix.

THE NEED FOR TRUST

To build trust, we must start with the assumption that everybody would like to do his or her job properly. With knowledge work, trust is a key part of making improvements, fixing problems, and doing great work. Often the knowledge workers themselves are the only ones who know enough to do any of these things. An untrusting culture is threatening. When their livelihoods and careers are at stake, people are often reluctant to take risks or to step out of line. Unless your people are willing to be different and to challenge the status quo, they are unlikely to make creative innovations, champion revolutionary changes, or produce great products.

This means that unless your people trust management not to punish them for mistakes, like the child who broke the cookie jar, they are not likely to speak up or take risks when they have creative ideas or see something they feel should be changed. A blame culture is often the key reason for lack of trust. While changing this culture may seem difficult, it is remarkably simple. All you need to do is to emulate what Admiral Rickover did when he established the U.S. Navy's Submarine Service. He directed his officers and crew to investigate all safety incidents on all nuclear submarines, to determine their causes, and to report the corrective actions to his office. Thereafter, every safety-related incident on every U.S. nuclear submarine was investigated by a captain's mast in which all involved officers and crew members participated. Everyone knew that a nuclear incident at

100 fathoms would likely be fatal, and everyone strove to be objective and to find and fix whatever problems they could.

Rickover established an objective fact-based culture throughout the nuclear fleet, but it took leadership from the top. While he insisted that his people take responsibility for their own work, he also recognized that all humans make mistakes and that the need is to objectively understand why problems occur and to fix the causes and not to fix the blame. To this day, the U.S. Submarine Service has a remarkable safety record. A retrospective analysis of the Submarine Service's contributions to the cold war said the following [Sieff 2007]:

> U.S. submarines far outperformed the Soviet ones in the crucial area of stealth, and Rickover's obsessive fixation on safety and quality control gave the U.S. nuclear Navy a vastly superior safety record to the Soviet one. This was especially crucial as in a democratic society, particularly after the Three Mile Island nuclear power station crisis in March 1979, a host of nuclear accidents or well-publicized near misses could have shut down the nuclear fleet completely.

An achievement like that of Admiral Rickover's Submarine Service can be made only by people who work in a trusting environment. Once you establish the proper management culture, the second part of building trust is helping your people to become trustworthy.

TRUSTWORTHY KNOWLEDGE-WORKING TEAMS

Unless your people are trustworthy, it would be irrational to trust them. Today, unfortunately, few knowledge workers or their teams can be trusted to meet their cost and schedule commitments or to consistently deliver quality products. While many would argue that this is a *management* problem, and it certainly is, it is not a *manager* problem. For knowledge work, the difference between *management* and *manager* problems is fundamental. Because managers cannot manage knowledge work, the knowledge workers must manage themselves.

Fortunately, however, the skills required for people to manage themselves are quite straightforward and easy to teach. While managers must ensure that knowledge workers are willing and able to manage themselves, convincing them to do so is a much more difficult challenge. This is critically important, however, for unless the knowledge workers truly want to manage themselves, there is no way that their managers or anyone else can make them do it. The TSP addresses this challenge in two steps.

The first step is to show knowledge workers how and why to manage themselves. This step, however, must do more than merely transfer knowledge; it must also build conviction. The need is to convince knowledge workers that once they start managing themselves, they will do better work and will have more satisfying and successful careers. Unless they truly believe this, no force on Earth could make them manage themselves. Knowledge work, after all, principally concerns how people think, and that is something over which the workers alone have control. The way the TSP addresses this challenge is described in Chapter 5.

Once knowledge workers understand how to manage themselves and have at least been convinced to try doing so, they are ready for the second step: participating on TSP teams. Chapter 6 describes how to get teams to consistently apply these knowledge-working methods to their projects.

USING FACTS AND DATA

Thus far, we have addressed the first two principles for getting knowledge workers to manage themselves: a trusting management environment and trustworthy workers. The third principle is for management to rely on facts and data rather than status and seniority when making decisions.

The way you make decisions is, in some respects, another aspect of trust. Upon what sources of information do you rely when making decisions? In the traditional management culture, the flow of information is hierarchical, just like the management pyramid. This means that you typically hear what your most senior managers believe, and their beliefs are based on what they have learned from their lieutenants. Information from the lowest levels of the organization has thus been filtered through many layers of management before it reaches you. However, as even a simple parlor game will show, it is nearly impossible to communicate accurately through multiple people.

In a knowledge-working organization where the working-level troops have the deepest understanding of technical issues, the information pyramid is inverted. You and your top executives and managers know the least and the workers themselves are best informed. While management has vastly more knowledge and experience on most business issues, many of the key decisions that currently affect modern businesses involve technical judgments. Unless you can base your judgments on the best available information from all sources, your decisions are unlikely to be sound. This topic is discussed in Chapter 7, where we describe how the TSP can help you and your management team make the best use of the facts and data potentially available from your working-level knowledge professionals.

QUALITY MUST BE THE TOP PRIORITY

You might wonder why quality is listed as one of the principles to consider in managing knowledge work. The answer is that it is fundamental. In fact, after the cultural issues of trust and decision making, it is the first and most important consideration in managing knowledge work. The reason is that knowledge work concerns ideas and concepts, and the difference between superior and poor-quality ideas is like night and day. A poorly conceived design, if not promptly corrected, can waste months of time and millions of dollars before it is corrected and the initially defective products replaced. Chapter 8 discusses why and how to make quality your business's top priority.

TEAM LEADERSHIP AND SUPPORT

The fifth and final principle for managing knowledge work is that leadership and support are required to help your people consistently manage themselves. This is critical because, like all of us, knowledge workers are human, and humans are not consistently disciplined. They make mistakes; they take shortcuts; and they skip or defer tiresome, difficult, or time-consuming tasks. While observing the workers and monitoring the quality of their work were practical for factory supervisors, it is not possible to do these things with knowledge workers. With such work, management must supply the knowledge workers with the leadership standards and team environment needed to make disciplined work normal and natural. Chapter 9, the book's final chapter, describes how the TSP addresses this issue, and it also discusses the steps required to establish a knowledge-working management culture in your organization. The book's appendices then describe in more detail what your management team must do to introduce and sustain this culture.

SUMMARY AND CONCLUSIONS

This chapter provides an overview of the principles and challenges you and your team must address to make your knowledge workers productive. The following key points are made in the chapter:

1. The management principles commonly used today were first defined by Frederick Winslow Taylor in 1911.

2. Today's work and workers are totally different from those of 100 years ago, so Taylor's management principles are no longer appropriate.

3. Peter Drucker described the fundamental principle for managing knowledge work: "Knowledge workers have to manage themselves."

4. The five principles to consider in managing knowledge workers are the following:

   a. Management must trust knowledge workers and teams to manage themselves.

   b. Knowledge-working teams must be trustworthy. That is, they must be willing and able to manage themselves.

   c. The management system must rely on facts and data (rather than status and seniority) when making decisions.

   d. Quality must be the organization's highest priority.

   e. Management must provide knowledge workers and teams with the leadership, training, coaching, and support they need to manage themselves.

REFERENCES

[Ariely 2009] Dan Ariely, Uri Gneezy, George Loewenstein, and Nina Mazar, "Large Stakes and Big Mistakes," *Review of Economic Studies* 76 (2009): 451–69.

[Curtis 1988] Bill Curtis, Herb Krasner, and Neil Iscoe, "A Field Study of the Software Design Process for Large Systems," *Communications of the ACM* 31, no. 11 (November 1988).

[Drucker 1999] Peter Drucker, "Knowledge-Worker Productivity: The Biggest Challenge," *California Management Review* 41, no. 2 (Winter 1999).

[Sieff 2007] Martin Sieff, "BMD Focus: O'Reilly Moves Up—Part 1," *UPI Energy*, October 4, 2007.

[Taylor 1911] Frederick Winslow Taylor, *The Principles of Scientific Management* (New York: Harper and Brothers, 1911).

5
Motivating Knowledge Workers

This chapter is about motivating knowledge workers to manage themselves. However, because these workers are generally highly motivated, the principal thing we need to do is to provide them with self-management skills and convince them that managing themselves will help them to better do what they already want to do. Also, of course, we must consider what you want them to do. The key, then, is aligning your objectives and those of the workers and then guiding and supporting them as they strive to meet these common objectives.

MANAGEMENT AND WORKER OBJECTIVES

In simplest terms, you want your knowledge workers to do high-quality creative work on predictable schedules and for minimum costs. Because these workers also typically participate on project teams and work for a manager, you also want them to be cooperative and effective team members, to consistently meet their personal and team commitments, and to keep management informed of their progress. Unfortunately, this is not what knowledge workers typically want to do.

One study of programmers concluded that management's and knowledge workers' objectives are actually in conflict [Linberg 1999]. Typically, the knowledge workers felt that their projects were successful if they were technically challenging, the final product worked the way it was supposed to work, and the team was cohesive and high-performing. Cost or schedule commitments simply were not a primary concern.

Conversely, managers viewed projects as successful if the teams met their cost and schedule objectives, whether or not the project was technically challenging or the team was cohesive and high-performing. Because these views are in conflict, the key question is, "Can we somehow align management's and the knowledge workers' objectives?" While the short answer is yes, the ways to accomplish this are not obvious.

THE NATURE OF TEAM MOTIVATION

Linberg's study underscores the widely held perception that knowledge workers don't care whether or not they meet their cost and schedule commitments. But this is not what we saw with the team in Chapter 3. That group of over 30 professionals overcame all kinds of challenging problems to deliver a quality product on schedule. Similarly, the Softtek and Quarksoft teams that were mentioned in Chapters 1 and 2 have been consistently delivering quality products on schedule for years. What is different about them?

The difference is team goals. Think of a basketball team. There is nothing particularly exciting about putting a ball through a hoop, but these teams make extraordinary efforts to do just that. Their energy, excitement, and enthusiasm are infectious, and they electrify entire arenas with thousands of cheering fans. What is infectious is meeting a team goal. Exactly the same thing is true of knowledge-working teams. The key to motivating such teams is to have them establish a challenging and motivating team goal and then work hard to meet it.

The reason that most software developers don't seem to get excited about meeting cost and schedule commitments is that these usually are not team goals. Although management may think that cost and schedule are important, typically no one ever tells the team why these goals are important, and the team isn't involved in making the commitments. As far as typical software teams are concerned, management makes the cost and schedule commitments, and the teams meet them if they can. In fact, the teams often think that management's requested commitments are totally unreasonable, but because they are paid to do what management asks, they give it the old school try.

Typical software teams get excited about delivering great products and having a cohesive team experience because these are the tacit goals of every member, and the team doesn't even have to discuss them. In fact, teams rarely discuss goals at all; most knowledge-working teams just start working. There is no team-building effort, no discussion of team goals, and in fact no real discussion of management's goals. The team is just told, "Here is your next job and it has to be done in nine months." Many knowledge workers find out that they are on a project team by getting an e-mail message or being told by their manager: "Your next job is Project XYZ; call Pete." Like so many cattle, they are just herded into one project chute or another.

The way to get your knowledge-working teams excited about and committed to meeting your goals is to empower them to set their own goals and, while doing this, to adopt your goals as part of their team goals. This is an executive and senior management issue because empowering people is a culture question, and an organization's culture can be changed only from the top. Other people can teach the required techniques and methods, but it is up to you to make this empowerment culture a corporate goal and to lead your management team in building and maintaining it.

THE KNOWLEDGE-WORKING CULTURE

The fundamental reason to change the organization's culture concerns the first of the five principles for managing knowledge work that we described in Chapter 4: Management must trust knowledge-working teams to manage themselves. This is essential because of the fundamental nature of knowledge work and knowledge workers:

- Only the knowledge workers know exactly what they are doing and how they are doing it.

- Because knowledge work is invisible, no one else, including the managers, can understand what the knowledge workers are doing or how they are doing it.

- Because it is impossible to manage effectively work that you do not understand, no one but the knowledge workers can manage knowledge work.

- Therefore, if the knowledge work is to be managed, the knowledge workers must manage themselves.

- When the knowledge workers do not manage themselves, their projects generally are troubled or end up as total failures.

You may accept these facts, but many managers would not. They would say that they can and do manage the knowledge workers in their organizations. While these managers may assign jobs, set schedules, and report to higher management, they do not do the one thing that you really need them to do. They do not get their teams to consistently produce quality products on committed schedules and for their planned costs. These managers can tell the knowledge workers what to do, but they have no way to know whether or not the workers actually did what they were told to do.

Assuming that you don't want your critical projects to continue being troubled or failing, you and your management team must do something different. We suggest that you teach your knowledge workers how to manage themselves and trust them to do so. The appendices to this book will guide you and your people in accomplishing that objective.

THE ELEMENTS OF TRUST

There is a big difference between trust and blind faith. President Ronald Reagan had an apt description for how he dealt with the Russians: "Trust but verify." There is another line from W. Edwards Deming that says much the same thing in a way that applies more directly to technical work: "In God we trust; all others bring data" [Davenport 2007].

For people to be truly trusted, they must be trustworthy. Unfortunately, with knowledge workers, this is a nontrivial challenge. After all, as demonstrated by the dismal history of software engineering, these knowledge workers have consistently failed to meet their commitments, so how can they possibly be trustworthy? The TSP addresses this problem by guiding, coaching, and supporting knowledge workers in consistently managing themselves.

A decade of experience with the TSP shows that when they manage themselves, knowledge workers can consistently deliver quality products on schedule and for their planned costs. However, before they can manage themselves, they first must be trained in the skills of self-management. They must also want to manage themselves. Therefore, the management challenge is to convince the knowledge workers that they want to manage themselves. This is difficult because knowledge workers are skeptical and will not truly believe that self-management will help them until they have tried it and found that it actually works.

This presents us with a chicken-and-egg problem. Knowledge workers will manage themselves only if they believe that doing so will help them to do better work. However, they will not believe that managing themselves will help them to do better work until they have actually tried managing themselves. So our challenge is to convince skeptical and very smart knowledge workers to try doing something they initially do not believe will help them.

THE START-UP PROBLEM

Once an organization has used the TSP on several projects and word of its benefits has spread, knowledge workers will be more receptive to the idea of managing themselves. Many may even ask to be trained in the TSP methods. Initially, however, and until the TSP becomes standard industry practice, all organizations will face the start-up problem. One approach to this problem is to put the knowledge workers in a course where they learn to manage themselves while doing a project. However, because projects typically involve several people and take a substantial amount of time, this is rarely practical.

The other strategy is to break the convincing process into two steps. The first step is to teach the knowledge workers the basic skills needed to start managing themselves, and the second step is to have them use these skills on a real company project. This strategy has one big advantage. It means that most of the training time doesn't cost anything because the knowledge workers are learning while they are doing their regular jobs. However, this strategy also has two potential issues.

The first issue is that the knowledge workers must spend enough time in training to learn the basic skills of self-management. Not only must they be willing to spend this time, but their managers must also be willing to invest the time and money to get them trained. The required training time is only about a week or two, so this objection can be overcome easily once you decide to adopt these knowledge-working methods.

The second issue is that after training, you can't use unimportant throwaway projects as training vehicles for the knowledge-working teams because such projects are usually canceled before they finish. Furthermore, even if the projects were not canceled, nobody would take the results seriously. Therefore, the training must be done on real projects that will serve as useful examples, not just for the knowledge workers but also for the rest of the organization.

To address these issues, we suggest that you convince yourself that the possible outcomes are worth the risks. The best way to do this is to review the results that other organizations have obtained from using the TSP and then determine if it would be a sound business risk for your organization. Appendix A provides data on the results many organizations have obtained through using the TSP.

SELF-MANAGEMENT TASKS

The TSP strategy for convincing knowledge workers to manage themselves is to put them on teams that actually manage their own projects. This means that they must make their own plans and schedules; negotiate their cost, schedule, and quality commitments with management; track and manage their work; and regularly report project status to management. To provide them with the skills to do these things, knowledge workers are given basic training in the Personal Software Process (PSP).

Basic PSP training teaches professionals the fundamental skills they must know to participate on a TSP team. Advanced PSP training can also be helpful but it is not required. The skills that are required are the following:

1. Make cost, schedule, and quality plans.

2. Gather and record data on the work.

3. Use an operational process.

4. Track and report on project progress.

The PSP provides knowledge workers with the ability to make accurate plans for doing their work. The PSP estimating strategy is to first estimate the size of the product to be produced and then to divide it by a productivity rate to get the total time required. However, because the productivity of individual knowledge workers can vary by a factor of ten or more, making accurate plans is not as simple as it sounds. The TSP strategy for addressing this issue is to show knowledge workers how to make accurate plans for their personal work. Once they can make accurate personal plans, they and their teammates will be able to make accurate project plans and to negotiate realistic commitments with their management. Then they will be able to consistently meet their commitments and can be trusted to manage themselves.

While learning how to perform these tasks sounds simple, it is actually not that easy. The required knowledge and skills are not complex, but the discipline required to perform these tasks consistently and accurately is much more demanding. This chapter discusses the training problem, and subsequent chapters address the discipline issue.

MAKING COST, SCHEDULE, AND QUALITY PLANS

If knowledge workers are to plan a project accurately, they must estimate the sizes of the products to be produced, estimate the time needed to do each part of the job, devise their strategy for producing a quality product, and define the process they will use to do the job. PSP training requires developers to write a small number of programs, and while doing this, they follow the defined PSP process that guides them through all of the steps required to build self-management skills.

In advanced engineering work, even though we are developing new products, much of our work is similar to things that we have done before. This means that if we know how long a previous job took, we should have a pretty good basis for estimating how long the new job will take. However, this is where the wide variation in knowledge-worker productivity comes in. Performance data from one knowledge worker is not of much help in estimating the performance of another, so each knowledge worker must have data on his or her personal work. With such productivity data and an estimate of the product size, each developer can easily calculate the estimated development time for his or her part of the project.

For example, if a developer has a historical productivity rate of 20 lines of code per hour and estimates that the new product will have 1,000 lines of code, the work will likely take about 50 hours. This is a pretty good estimate because productivity rates for individual knowledge workers remain relatively constant for similar work. The problem, however, is that size estimates are typically much more prone to error.

Estimating Product Size

Few knowledge workers have learned how to make size estimates or have much experience making such estimates. When they must make estimates, they merely guess at the size of the overall product. Although all estimates are guesses, simplistic size-estimating practices tend to overlook functions, judge other functions to be simpler than they actually are, or omit key things like error detection and recovery.

To address this problem, PSP provides developers with a statistically based estimating method called PROBE (PROxy Based Estimating). PROBE teaches developers to consider their products as composed of parts and to estimate the size of each part. The part estimates are then added together to produce a size estimate for the entire product. PROBE also requires developers to measure the actual sizes of these parts after they have been developed. With data from just a few products, developers have enough size data to make accurate estimates for new parts. There are three reasons that PROBE estimates are more accurate than just guessing:

1. Breaking their products into parts and estimating the size of each part reduces the likelihood that developers will omit key functions.

2. Using historical data increases the likelihood that estimates are unbiased. That is, the estimates are just as likely to be high as low. PSP training sharply reduces estimating bias.

3. When multiple unbiased estimates are combined, their errors tend to cancel each other, providing a more accurate total.

The third reason is somewhat helpful for individual estimators, but it can substantially reduce the overall error in team estimates, assuming that all team members use the PROBE method.

Making a Quality Plan

When knowledge workers have data on the quality of their work, they can also estimate how many defects their finished products are likely to contain. A project's quality plan specifies the number of defects that knowledge workers think they will inject and remove from the product in each step of the process as well as the number that are likely to remain in the finished product. During PSP training, developers learn how many defects they typically inject during various project phases, and they also learn that no matter how hard they try, they will always make at least a few mistakes.

Although defect injection and removal rates vary widely among developers, the rates remain relatively constant for individuals as long as they continue following the same practices. In PSP training, developers also learn three very important things. They learn that their defect-injection rates are relatively constant, allowing them to make reasonably accurate quality plans. They also learn about the kinds of mistakes they make most often, enabling them to better find and fix the defects in their own products. Finally, and most important, they learn how to rapidly and efficiently remove defects from their products. We discuss this topic in Chapter 8.

Developers can use the project's size estimate and their own personal defect data from prior projects to estimate how many defects they are likely to inject and remove in each development step and to calculate the number of defects that are likely to remain in the finished product. A development team can then combine the individual estimates to produce an overall quality plan for the project.

RECORDING DATA

If they are to earn management's trust, knowledge workers must master the first skill required to manage themselves: making accurate cost, schedule, and quality plans. However, to do this, they must have personal data. This means that they must master the second of the four skills needed for self-management: accurately recording data on their personal work. Knowledge workers need these data, not to give to management or anyone else, but to use in making personal plans and for managing and tracking their personal work.

This is the key factor that motivates knowledge workers to gather data. Once they know how to plan and are convinced that accurate planning is important to them personally, they also know that they must have data. Once knowledge workers are motivated to gather data, all they need is a clear definition of the kinds of data to gather and a support tool to make data gathering reasonably quick and efficient. In PSP training, developers learn how to define, gather, and use the time, size, schedule, and defect data they need to make accurate plans, and they gain experience using a basic data-gathering tool.

USING AN OPERATIONAL PROCESS

The third of the four things that knowledge workers must do to be trusted to manage themselves is to use an operational process. This is essential, for without the guidance of an operational process, people are rarely able to do complex tasks consistently and correctly. Then the knowledge workers would not likely gather and use all of the required data, they would be unable to make accurate plans, and management would not trust them to manage themselves.

Organizational Processes

There is a great deal of confusion about what a process is and why an organization, a team, or an individual should follow one. The two principal kinds of processes in the software field are organizational processes and operational processes. The most common organizational processes in software have been developed to satisfy the CMMI level criteria [Chrissis 2007].

These processes can be very helpful, but we saw in Chapter 2 that they can also cause problems if they are not properly implemented. Brandon established a clear set of checkpoints for measuring and managing project progress, and this helped him to gain control of his large software organization. But the approach he used had two drawbacks:

1. First, the way Brandon managed the organizational process resulted in a cumbersome and ultimately counterproductive enforcement bureaucracy.

2. The second and more general drawback is that when people are required to follow any demanding process, they are tempted to take shortcuts.

CMMI provides an example of the pitfalls of taking shortcuts. Because many organizations had to be rated at CMMI level 3 or above to compete for U.S. Department of Defense business, there was a strong temptation to focus on process compliance rather than on process performance. An organization might find it easier to produce data that showed that the process was being used when it was not being used effectively. This approach is ultimately self-defeating because, although the organization may get some additional business in the short term, it will have wasted a lot of time, effort, and money in implementing the organizational process without realizing the potential performance benefits. Ultimately, the organization's customers will recognize that the company's specific CMMI rating was not providing the desired benefits and switch their business to a competitor.

Operational Processes

While organizational processes are typically used to guide the management of an enterprise, operational processes are used to guide people as they do their work. Many of the larger organizational processes are also intended to guide individuals' work, but they are often contained in cumbersome procedural documents that are filed away and consulted only occasionally. As a consequence, organizational processes generally are followed only when some enforcement procedure like Brandon's phase review system requires that they be used.

Conversely, an operational process is meant to guide people when they are doing their work. These processes are designed to guide very specific tasks, such as using PROBE to make a development plan, and they are written in action-oriented language that is easy to understand and follow. Furthermore, while the larger and more cumbersome organizational processes frequently contain a lot of tutorial and explanatory material, operational processes do not. When properly designed, an operational process assumes that the users understand the job, know how to do it, and just need the process as a tool to help them do every step properly and in the correct order.

The Benefits of Operational Processes

The best-known operational processes are those used by airline pilots for doing preflight checks. Another example is checklists used by some hospitals to guide medical procedures. Dr. Peter Pronovost of the Johns Hopkins Medical Center ICU traced the source of an infection problem to a failure to properly perform the IV procedures every time they were used [Henig 2009]. He devised a five-step IV checklist and charged the nurses with ensuring that it was always followed. He also made sure that the hospital administration supported the nurses whenever they got into disagreements with the doctors. This operational process was credited with cutting infections from 11% to 0%, eliminating 43 infections, preventing eight deaths, and saving $2 million. The results of using a checklist to guide surgical procedures at eight hospitals were even more dramatic [Gawande 2009]. This process was more complex, so the checklist had 19 steps. In this case, surgical complications dropped by 36%, and deaths were reduced by 47%.

When people perform even a simple task, they tend to forget or skip steps, and their results are often substandard. As processes become more complex, process discipline is generally poor, so it is not surprising that for larger and more extensive processes like software development, poor process compliance is almost inevitable. That is, it is inevitable unless the practitioners know precisely what to do, have a well-designed operational process to guide them, and are motivated and supported to precisely follow this process.

Although it may not immediately be obvious why software engineers should precisely follow a defined process, it is the only way that they can consistently produce quality products on their committed schedules and for their planned costs. The discussions in subsequent chapters make it clear why having and precisely following a well-designed operational process is essential to the success of knowledge-working projects.

TRACKING AND REPORTING PROGRESS

The fourth and final thing that knowledge workers must do to be trusted to manage themselves is to accurately and regularly track and report their project's progress. This is an important part of building and maintaining trust. Because software developers, or any knowledge workers for that matter, generally have no clear or precise measures of project status, they usually have nothing to report. As a result, they typically don't say anything, at least not until they are in trouble and need help.

What this means is that most knowledge workers don't see their management until their projects are in trouble, which they typically don't know until it is too late for management to help them. This means that when the managers don't hear from their people, they soon become nervous and start asking questions. When the knowledge workers can give them only vague answers, the managers become even more nervous. As this cycle continues throughout the project, it becomes almost impossible for the managers to trust their knowledge workers, and the knowledge workers become increasingly reluctant to openly and honestly share information with the managers.

Before managers can trust their knowledge workers, they need free, open, and clear communication with them. In turn, this requires that the knowledge workers do four things:

1. Track project status.

2. Measure project status.

3. Describe project status.

4. Report project status.

Tracking Project Status

For many types of work, it is fairly easy to check on project status. This is because most jobs consist of multiple steps that must be done in a prescribed order. When building a house, for example, you must complete the foundation before you can start framing. Then, after framing and enclosing the structure, you must install the wiring and plumbing before you complete the walls and painting. To check on project status, you just need to look at what has been done. Likewise, the simplest way for knowledge workers to determine their project's status is to compare the tasks they have completed with the tasks that were supposed to be completed at a given point in the project.

Measuring Project Status

However, to know and describe their project's status with any precision, knowledge workers must have detailed plans. If, for example, their plans are like those for most typical software projects, they have only four steps:

1. Complete the requirements.
2. Produce the design.
3. Write the code.
4. Test the product.

While the developers may do their work in this order, each of these tasks typically takes many months to complete, and the tasks generally overlap. For example, on a one-year project, the original plan might have been to complete the requirements in one month, but the requirements typically change many times and are not actually completed until final testing starts or even later. As a result, the developers usually identify aspects of the job that have reasonably firm requirements and start designing them after the first month or so of requirements development.

Similarly, the coding work often starts well before the design is done, and testing starts before coding is done. Often, in fact, none of these four typical tasks is completed until the final few months of the job. This means that to have any idea of where they stand, the knowledge workers need much more detailed plans. These detailed plans should contain tasks that have precise completion criteria and can be done in a relatively short amount of time. Examples of such tasks are

- Module XYZ design completed and submitted for team inspection

- Module XYZ inspection completed and defects corrected
- Module XYZ coded and unit-tested

These are specific and measurable tasks, but they may not be precise enough to give a good picture of project status. The reason is that each of these tasks could take several weeks to a month or more to complete, depending on the module's size. This means that knowledge workers would know the task's status within the range of a month or more. To address this issue, the PSP shows knowledge workers how to measure the time they spend on their personal tasks in minutes, and the TSP calls for the tasks in detailed plans to be broken into subtasks that take no more than 10 hours each. This means that knowledge workers who are using the TSP can tell their job status to within 10 hours.

Describing Project Status

Describing job status for knowledge work is much more difficult than for, say, home construction. The reason is that knowledge work is far more varied and flexible. On a software project, for example, the developers may start on the high-level design and then find that they must know precisely how some function will work before they can proceed. So, they switch to detailed design, coding, and testing to complete this module and get the needed information. Then they switch back to high-level design work [Curtis 1988].

This means that the tasks in the project plan are often completed in an order that is quite different from what was originally planned. To account for this variation, the PSP shows knowledge workers how to use earned value (EV) to describe their project's status. With EV, each project task is given a value based on the hours that the task is planned to take as a percentage of the total time planned for the project.

If, for example, a planned task is supposed to take 8.5 hours on a project with a total estimate of 100 hours, the task's planned value would be 8.5. When the task is completed, the worker earns the EV credit of 8.5. EV is awarded only after each task is fully completed, and there is no partial credit for tasks that are nearly done. Also, the EV would be 8.5 whether the task took 2, 8.5, or 20 hours. By using the EV measure and a plan that shows how much EV was planned for each week, knowledge workers can tell if they are ahead of or behind schedule and by how much. This would be true regardless of the order in which the tasks were completed.

Reporting Project Status

By using the precise EV measure to determine their progress against the project plan, knowledge workers have the information they need to report their status in clear and understandable terms. The challenge is to ensure that they do so regularly, even when the project is not in trouble. To ensure that they do this, the TSP process guides knowledge-working teams in making regular management reports. The TSP process helps to ensure that teams review their status every week and then promptly report that status to management. This helps to maintain an open, informed, and trusting relationship between management and the knowledge workers, further reinforcing the benefits of self-management.

One additional advantage of precise project status measures is that managers can then see when their people are having trouble. Because new and inexperienced developers often lack the knowledge and skill to do complex development work, and because with knowledge work managers cannot determine how well these developers are doing their work, such skill problems can go undetected until very late in a project. The availability of precise status measures enables the managers to detect these problems earlier and to either reassign these developers or get them the help they need to improve their skills.

SELF-MANAGEMENT TRAINING

Because the majority of university programs currently do not teach their graduates self-management skills, essentially all knowledge workers must be specially trained before they can participate on a TSP team. The PSP course was developed to enable professionals to effectively participate as members of self-managed teams. This course addresses three objectives:

1. The first and simplest objective is teaching basic process management skills. These are the four topics that have been the principal subject of this chapter:

    a. Making accurate cost, schedule, and quality plans

    b. Recording data on the work

    c. Using an operational process

    d. Tracking and reporting on project progress

2. The second objective is building the discipline knowledge workers need to actually follow an operational process and to perform all of the required steps properly and consistently. While a brief course can provide the needed knowledge, discipline is a lifelong challenge for all professional workers, and even the most experienced occasionally are tempted to skip steps or take shortcuts "just this one time." Self-discipline is one of the principal subjects addressed by the TSP process, and it is discussed in more detail in the following chapters.

3. The third objective of self-management training is motivation. Knowledge workers need to understand the importance of consistently using their self-management skills. There are two parts to this objective:

   a. Convincing knowledge workers that planning, measuring, and tracking their work will actually help them do their jobs

   b. Convincing knowledge workers to use these new and unfamiliar methods on a real project where they will be under intense pressure to do a challenging job on an aggressive schedule

PSP training helps to address the first part of this objective, and the TSP process described in Chapter 6 addresses the second part.

OVERCOMING SKEPTICISM

When the PSP was first developed, only the method's inventor, Watts Humphrey, had used it. Nobody else believed that this self-management approach could work for software engineers. The method used to overcome this initial skepticism is to put knowledge workers in a course where they use the PSP self-management practices to write 10 small software programs. These exercises provide the students with personal data on how the methods work for them. This strategy has proven to be effective in getting developers to use disciplined self-management techniques.

The initial PSP course had 10 example programs that took nearly three weeks for most developers to complete. Because many organizations were reluctant to make this much of a time investment for all their developers, transition to the PSP and TSP methods was initially slow. Then, after the SEI had trained teams from a number of organizations, it had data on over 30,000 programs written by experienced industrial software engineers in PSP training. This volume of data was so convincing that the original skepticism about PSP's effectiveness largely disappeared, and it became possible to shorten the PSP training. Now, knowledge workers can learn basic PSP skills and gain the necessary motivation to start managing themselves after only a week or two of PSP training.

SUMMARY AND CONCLUSIONS

This chapter describes how to motivate knowledge workers to manage themselves and to align their objectives with those of their management. The chapter makes the following seven points:

1. Teams can be motivated to meet their own and management's goals by following a goal-setting process.

2. To use this goal-setting process, the teams must be trusted to make their own plans and be held responsible for meeting them.

3. To build the required trusting environment, a culture change is required, and this must be initiated and sustained by the organization's senior executives and managers.

4. Before they can be trusted, knowledge workers must be trustworthy. This requires that they consistently meet their cost and schedule commitments with quality products.

5. The best way to get knowledge workers to consistently meet their commitments is to convince them to manage themselves.

6. Before they can manage themselves, knowledge workers must be trained in basic self-management skills and be motivated to use these skills on their projects.

7. PSP training is the primary method for providing the basic skills and motivation needed to participate on a TSP team.

REFERENCES

[Chrissis 2007] Mary Beth Chrissis, Mike Konrad, and Sandy Shrum, *CMMI: Guidelines for Process Integration and Product Improvement, Second Edition* (Boston, MA: Addison-Wesley, 2007).

[Curtis 1988] Bill Curtis, Herb Krasner, and Neil Iscoe, "A Field Study of the Software Design Process for Large Systems," *Communications of the ACM* 31, no. 11 (November 1988).

[Davenport 2007] Thomas H. Davenport and Jeanne G. Harris, *Competing on Analytics: The New Science of Winning* (Cambridge, MA: Harvard Business School Press, 2007).

[Gawande 2009] Atul Gawande, *The Checklist Manifesto* (New York: Metropolitan Books, 2009).

[Henig 2009] Robin M. Henig, "A Hospital How-To Guide That Mother Would Love," *The New York Times*, December 24, 2009.

[Linberg 1999] Kurt R. Linberg, "Software Developer Perceptions about Software Project Failure: A Case Study," *Journal of Systems and Software* 49 (1999): 177–92.

6
Motivating Knowledge-Working Teams

This chapter discusses how to build, motivate, and manage teams of knowledge workers. The first step in the team-building process is having these teams manage themselves while they work on real company projects. Then, after they have completed just one project and seen how effective self-management can be, they will be motivated to continue managing themselves. Subsequent chapters describe how to use these knowledge-working skills to improve business performance. To illustrate how TSP teamworking methods work, we describe Beckman Coulter's experiences with the first of its growing number of TSP teams.

BECKMAN COULTER

Beckman Coulter develops, manufactures, and markets products used in biomedical testing and research. It has over 200,000 clinical and biomedical research systems in use by doctors and research centers throughout the world. The company has over 10,000 employees and 35 facilities, and it operates in more than 120 countries.

Beckman Instruments acquired the Coulter Corporation to form Beckman Coulter in 1997. Scott Garrett was made Chief

Executive Officer of Beckman Coulter in 2005 and then Chairman of the Board of Directors in 2008. He set a corporate goal of being the industry leader in biomedical testing. This meant that Beckman Coulter would hold the number-one or number-two position in all major product areas and major geographic markets, quality would be its key differentiator, investment capacity would be expanded significantly, a number of high-risk and high-reward programs would be funded, and its employees would be acknowledged as the industry's best.

In addressing Scott's directive, Rick Marshall, Beckman Coulter's VP of Software Platforms, and Carl Wyrwa, the Director of Quality, convinced management to launch a TSP program. They followed the standard TSP introduction strategy outlined in the appendices of this book to train and launch their first TSP team. This introduction program started in the normal way with a senior management briefing, management training, and TSP team-member training. John Hetzler, a functional area manager, and Larry Whitford, a quality engineer, were trained as the first TSP coaches, and Tim Lancaster was selected to lead the first TSP team.

BECKMAN COULTER'S FIRST TSP TEAM

Tim Lancaster and his team of 15 developers were asked to develop the software for the prototype of a very complex new system. The project also included a hardware engineering team, a chemistry team, and a firmware team that developed the microcode for the hardware. Tim's team was the only one that was to use the TSP and the only one to start the project with a TSP launch. This launch was coached by Larry Whitford with the support of experts from the SEI.

During the opening launch meeting in May 2009, Humayun Qureshi, VP of the Instrument Systems Development Center, told Tim and his team that their job was to develop the software for the initial prototype of this new system, and to do so in three months. Tim and his team spent the next week making the most aggressive plan they felt they could possibly meet, but they still were unable to meet Humayun's date. In the final launch meeting, when Tim presented the team's plan for a September 1 delivery date, the hardware and chemistry teams argued that the software would be too late for them to meet their schedules. Humayun also was unhappy with the team's date, but, after considerable debate, he accepted Tim's plan.

Based on his previous development experience, Humayun did not believe that any of the teams would finish when they said they would, but he had followed his customary strategy of pushing for an aggressive date in the hope that the teams would deliver earlier than they otherwise would. In this case, however, he was so impressed with the plan Tim and his team produced that he decided to accept their date instead.

Tim's team then started work, and within a few weeks they had fallen two weeks behind their plan. That meant they would miss their September 1 commitment by at least three weeks. One of the developers pointed out that all the other teams were late, so they could just ignore the problem and nobody would notice. Tim didn't like that idea, however, so he asked the rest of the developers what they thought. After some discussion, they all agreed that they had committed to meet a September 1 date and they intended to do so. In making their recovery plan, they found that they could meet the committed date if each of them worked just five more task hours per week. Although they also had to defer a couple of nonessential functions, they followed this plan and finished on time. All the other teams were late.

In the September project relaunch, Humayun gave the entire project a six-month schedule objective for a more complex and complete prototype of the same system. However, Tim and his team again found that they could not meet Humayun's date with the resources they had. In the final management review meeting, they presented four alternate plans with different combinations of delivery dates and resources. The plan they recommended would meet the requested schedule but would require five more software developers.

The other teams again objected to Tim's plan. They said that they needed the software sooner. Humayun told them, "I believe they will deliver on time with the highest quality. That overall should help everyone with their schedules." He then agreed with Tim's plan and gave him the five additional developers.

By managing themselves, Tim's team adopted a new working style and attitude. This not only affected what the team did; it also changed how management viewed them and their work. This had important consequences for the team's feelings of commitment and ownership and further enhanced their credibility with management.

TEAM COMMITMENT

The software team's attitude started to change during the launch. When Humayun gave them a three-month target, they would traditionally have said, "OK, boss, we'll try." But the three-month delivery date would have been Humayun's commitment, not theirs. While they would have tried to meet it, they would not have known what date would be realistic and they would not have been personally committed to meeting it. By working through the TSP launch process, however, the team made a careful estimate of the work and produced a detailed plan for getting everything done. In doing so, they found that they couldn't quite meet Humayun's date. They then had a choice: They could confront Humayun, who they knew was a tough and demanding boss, or they could just cave in the way they always had and accept his date even though they knew they would be late.

The team made the responsible choice and decided to deal with the issue head-on. They had made a good plan and they were confident that they could meet it. If they agreed to the three-month schedule, however, they knew they would run into trouble. Rather than put off the inevitable problem, they decided to trust their executive and tell him the facts. While they knew that Humayun would not believe them, they thought their plan was sufficiently detailed and complete to be convincing. Tim and his team also had to defend their plan against attacks from the other teams, but they had done a thorough job of planning and had the self-confidence and conviction to stick to their story. In the end, their decision to trust in Humayun's judgment paid off, and they ended up with a plan to which the entire team was committed.

Project Ownership

After Humayun approved the plan and they had worked for about a month, the team found they were falling behind schedule. Even though they knew that all of the other teams were also behind, they had committed to a date and they intended to meet it. It didn't matter what everybody else did. Without complaining or asking for help, they took responsibility for solving their own problems. They then developed an action plan, which they followed, and they finished on schedule. This wasn't just a team of employees doing what they were told. This was their project and they felt responsible for its success.

In advanced technical work, this is a critical attitude. No matter how good a plan a team makes, there are always surprises and unexpected problems. When teams are truly committed, they attack their problems and work their way through them. Even though it took extra effort, Tim's team was committed to meeting its delivery date, and everybody did his or her utmost to succeed. When teams have this win-at-all-costs attitude, they usually win, and when they don't have this attitude, they often fail.

Credibility

Tim's team did one other thing that turned out to be very important. They reviewed their progress every week and gave management a status report that showed precisely where they stood on the job. Their initial reports showed that they were falling behind, but they honestly reported the facts. Then, after they had adopted the recovery plan, their reports showed them gradually catching up.

Management could see what the team was doing, and they could tell that the team was taking the initiative to solve its own problems. This open and honest communication showed that the team members trusted management with the facts, and that they were capable of managing their own work. Once teams have established this kind of credibility, management will be willing and able to help them if they later run into problems that they truly cannot solve.

These management reports were a big change. Previously, the teams had no way to measure project status, so they could not provide useful reports to management. As a result, they never talked to management unless they were in trouble. This meant not only that management did not want to see them, but that management was in the dark on job status and problems. Under these conditions, management soon started to worry and suspected that the team was in trouble. This kind of all-news-is-bad-news situation does not make for a trusting relationship.

MANAGEMENT BEHAVIOR

While the changes in team behavior were important, the changes in management's behavior were even more important. The principal management changes concerned trust, motivation, and confidence.

Trust

Humayun didn't initially trust Tim's team's plans. The software teams had never met their schedule commitments before, so there was no reason for him to trust them now. However, Tim and his team had done such an impressive job of making a plan, and they had presented such a clear and convincing case, that he decided to accept their plan. While he was convinced that they would miss their commitments, he knew that they would never meet an earlier date even if he insisted on it. Once the team had started work, however, Humayun was pleased to get their weekly status reports, and he found that the detailed information and data in the reports were better than anything he had gotten before.

The early reports showed that the team was falling behind schedule, but he saw that the team was catching up without his intervention and that they then were able to complete the project on the date to which they had committed. This was a team with which he could negotiate, and he could use their plans to make sound business decisions. If he could get all of his teams to perform this way, he would be able to make more accurate business plans and be confident that his people would be able to implement them.

Motivation

Humayun saw that Tim's team was highly motivated and that they had done their absolute best to meet his needs. He was surprised, however, at how important the team's planning process turned out to be. In the first team launch, when Tim presented the team's plan and explained why they could not meet the requested delivery date, their commitment was obvious and they were clearly convinced that a shorter schedule was impossible. Humayun also realized that by making the team defend its plan and then trusting Tim and his team to deliver, he had played a key role in building their energy and motivation. He knew that the key to a successful business was a motivated workforce, and he now had a way to build a similar level of motivation and capability for all of his development teams.

Confidence

One further factor involves confidence. Executives and senior managers must make many trade-offs in deciding how to manage their resources to best meet corporate objectives. A key part of any decision-making process concerns the facts used to select among the most promising choices. Some of the most important of these facts are the time and money required to produce a product.

Time and money are independent variables. Once the total project resources are known, the schedule usually can be adjusted by adding or reducing the project's staff. Once Humayun knew that Tim's team could be trusted to meet an overall cost commitment, he knew that adding five more developers would not change the project's cost. After all, either 20 developers working for 12 months or 15 developers working for 16 months would expend 240 development months and cost about the same amount of money. If the four-month schedule difference was important, he could just take qualified resources from lower-priority jobs and assign them to Tim's team.

Although the choice to add resources was always an option, until Humayun could trust the team members to do what they said they would do, it would have made no sense to add more resources. After all, software teams had always demanded more resources, but they had never before made their committed dates. Adding more resources under those conditions would not have been a sound business decision.

BUILDING SELF-DIRECTED TEAMS

Development organizations have been plagued with delays and cost overruns for decades, and the most extreme examples of these problems have been the software teams. However, as Tim's team showed and as the Softtek and Quarksoft organizations have also demonstrated, self-directed teams do consistently make and meet aggressive quality and schedule commitments, and their performance enables their managers to make rational decisions with the confidence that their people will do what they have committed themselves to do. Once it is clear to senior management how powerful self-directed teams can be and what a difference such teams can make in the predictability and manageability of a technology-based business, the next challenge is to spread this capability across the entire organization. The key question, then, is how to introduce these methods to all of the development teams.

As we have shown in this chapter, it is relatively easy to form self-directed development teams and to show them how to manage themselves. This, however, is the simplest part of introducing the TSP. Developers love to work in teams, and they like to build complex and sophisticated products. With a little training and guidance, developers will find that managing themselves is actually quite easy and that it greatly improves their performance and quality of work life. However, although training developers is relatively straightforward, the key issues in the broader transition process are those involving management.

MANAGEMENT ISSUES

The appendices of this book describe the methods that the SEI has found most effective for introducing teamworking development practices into entire organizations. We have now been honing and improving these methods for several years and have shown many teams how to consistently produce quality products on their committed schedules and for their planned costs. We know that the introduction process works, and we have never had a case where the developers, when properly trained and led, have failed to do superior work. When there have been problems, they have always been with management. The management issues with TSP adoption have typically been of three kinds: management understanding, management dynamics, and management style.

Management Understanding

In traditionally managed organizations, the lowest-level managers must plan and guide the work, establish and maintain the teams, supervise the team leaders, and handle all of the personnel issues for their people. These are typically very hands-on managers who are used to doing technical work themselves, are just learning to delegate, and are most focused on and comfortable with the technical aspects of their jobs.

With self-directed knowledge workers, however, the development teams take over much of the hands-on management work, and the first-line managers are deprived of the one part of their jobs with which they feel most comfortable. These managers have not yet adjusted their behavior to the more sophisticated executive-like actions of delegation, negotiation, and people development required for managing knowledge-working teams, so they generally object to the TSP until they understand its underlying concepts.

When the management team is properly introduced to these methods, however, there is an opportunity to significantly broaden the organization's span of control and to keep more of the often superior engineers involved in technical work instead of making them first-line managers. In fact, as we discuss in Chapter 9, the roles of team leader and coach can provide excellent training grounds for future executives and senior managers.

Management Dynamics

Because management structures and styles vary widely among organizations, there is no simple and repeatable process for changing an organization's management style. The process used for guiding and informing management about TSP introduction is based on the assumption that managers are generally smart and motivated people. Once they understand why and how to manage knowledge work, see how effective self-managed teams can be, and appreciate their responsibilities for making their teams effective, they can generally figure out the best ways to manage their own responsibilities.

We have, therefore, developed an introduction program that requires that all managers above the TSP teams attend brief training sessions that explain the methods for managing knowledge workers and that provide examples of the management actions required when managing this kind of work. This introduction strategy has been effective and has resulted in very successful programs in a great many organizations.

In some organizations, particularly where the program initially is introduced at a low management level, we encounter reorganization problems. Although reorganizations are often necessary, they disrupt the management chain, and even after a standard TSP introduction process, such organizations often end up with several levels of managers who have never heard of self-directed teamwork, don't know why it is important, and don't understand how to manage it. Because, in most of these cases, management has made no provision for training newly assigned managers, the TSP teams end up being managed with traditional management methods. This disrupts team dynamics and soon reduces team performance to its prior unsatisfactory state. The only antidote that we have devised for this problem is to insist that TSP introduction start at a sufficiently high management level to ensure some level of stability. While senior executives and managers also get moved, they are typically more concerned about long-term organizational performance and are more likely to have taken steps to maintain the program's effectiveness.

At Beckman Coulter, Rick Marshall and Carl Wyrwa were themselves senior managers, and they had the support of Scott Garrett, the company CEO. Consequently, they supported the way John Hetzler and Larry Whitford addressed this issue. John and Larry would contact immediately any untrained manager who was assigned responsibility for one or more TSP teams, give him or her a brief TSP overview, and enroll the manager in the next planned manager or executive TSP course. This strategy was very effective in maintaining the needed level of management understanding and support for the TSP teams.

MANAGEMENT STYLE

The style of management that is most appropriate for a knowledge-working environment is much closer to the typical behavior of executives and senior managers than to that of first-line managers. This style follows the five principles for managing knowledge work enunciated in Chapter 4:

1. Management must trust knowledge workers and teams to manage themselves.

2. Knowledge-working teams must be trustworthy. That is, they must be willing and able to manage themselves.

3. The management system must rely on facts and data (rather than status and seniority) when making decisions.

4. Quality must be the organization's highest priority.

5. Management must provide knowledge workers and teams with the leadership, training, coaching, and support they need to manage themselves.

While these principles are relatively clear and every management level must understand and adhere to them, it is the first-line managers who are responsible for ensuring that the principles are followed. That is why it is essential to introduce knowledge-working concepts to *all* managers over *all* TSP teams, and to train *all* of these managers in their new responsibilities. Because every inadequately trained manager will likely cause one or more teams to perform poorly—or even to fail—inadequate management training can be expensive.

The management responsibilities for self-managed teams fall into three areas: maintaining team cohesion, providing professional coaching support, and recognizing and rewarding superior work. The first of these topics is covered in this chapter, and the other two are described in Chapter 9 and the book's appendices.

Maintaining Team Cohesion

Until one has worked on a cohesive and high-performing team, it is hard to appreciate its value. Such teams typically do extraordinary work, and they often set more challenging goals for themselves than their managers would dare to set for them. Then, when they make their own plans and manage themselves, they often surprise their managers and even themselves by how well they perform. Such teams break world records and routinely produce superior work. However, building and maintaining effective teams requires that management knows how to establish and maintain team cohesion. The two most common issues are team-member participation and effective team leadership.

Team-Member Participation

Although most knowledge workers fit comfortably into a cohesive team environment, a small number do not. Most of these people are skeptics who, once they honestly try the TSP methods, will ultimately be convinced. However, there is a small minority that are not able to work with others in a team setting. Whatever the reason, these people do not cooperate with their teammates and often refuse to follow the team's processes and plans. Even on large teams, the presence of a single uncooperative member can destroy team cohesion and seriously damage team performance. Typically, removing the one uncooperative member significantly improves the team's overall performance, even if that team member is not replaced.

First-line managers must be sensitive to this issue, regularly check with the team leaders and coaches on cohesion issues, and look for odd behavior in meetings and other team settings. Because it is difficult for teams to solve these cohesion problems by themselves, managers often have to step in to make the needed changes. After asking the team leader, the coach, and the team members for their views, the manager's next step should be to remove the troublesome team member. While personnel intervention may be required for counseling, the manager's first responsibility is to fix team cohesion. The personnel issues can be handled more easily when these difficult members are not under pressure from their teams to perform.

Ensuring Effective Team Leadership

The team leader's job is to use the team's resources to build superior products. He or she sets and maintains the team's standards and is responsible for providing an environment that supports the TSP's quality-first strategy. Most engineers want to do excellent work and will if they are provided appropriate support. To be effective, team leaders must be sensitive to teamworking issues and ensure that the members stay focused on the highest-priority tasks, maintain process discipline, and measure and manage the quality of their work.

If the team leader does not perform these responsibilities regularly and competently, team performance will suffer. The team coach or a team member can bring such issues to the team leader's attention, but the team leader must resolve them or they will continue to fester. In turn, a big part of a manager's job is to ensure that all of his or her team leaders are handling team-cohesion issues properly and are setting and maintaining the high standards needed in all important areas of the team's work. If not, the manager should counsel or replace any underperforming team leaders.

Great leaders get great results, and while not all of your team leaders will be great leaders, a surprising number will rise to the challenge and perform better than you or they expected. One of the most important parts of a first-line manager's job is to identify potentially great team leaders and then to guide and nurture their development.

SUMMARY AND CONCLUSIONS

This chapter describes how great teams are built, and it gives an example of a Beckman Coulter team that followed the team-building process described in this book. It also describes several of the issues commonly encountered during team building and teamworking. The key points made in the chapter are as follows:

1. For building knowledge-working teams, the TSP provides a launch process that guides teams in making plans to do the jobs they have been assigned.

2. During this launch, teams often cannot meet all of management's goals on the schedules and with the resources that they have been given.

3. By negotiating rational and businesslike plans with their knowledge-working teams, management plays a key role in building the teams' cohesion, motivation, and commitment.

4. When knowledge-working teams are properly trained and led, they strive to meet their commitments. Experience shows that they generally succeed.

5. By meeting their commitments, knowledge-working teams establish their credibility with management.

6. Management can run the business more predictably and effectively when they have confidence that their knowledge-working teams will meet their quality, schedule, and cost commitments.

7. Management leadership is key to the success of the TSP's team-building and teamworking process:

   a. Senior management must require and support a development strategy that emphasizes quality first.

b. Senior management must ensure that all managers understand their responsibilities for motivating and guiding their teams.

c. First-line managers must aid and support their team leaders in building and maintaining team motivation, discipline, and cohesion.

d. First-line managers must be willing and able to identify, nurture, and develop superior team leaders.

7
Managing with Facts and Data

Now that your knowledge-working teams are managing themselves, they should be doing quality work for predictable costs and on their committed schedules. Before they can do this, these teams must have data, and these data can be a valuable management tool. However, to be useful for you and the teams, the data must be of high quality. Furthermore, experience shows that the single most important indicator of superior TSP team performance is the accuracy and completeness of its data. This demonstrates that the team is highly disciplined, which in turn correlates with superior team performance. This suggests two questions:

1. How can you use the TSP data to help manage the business?

2. How can you know that the TSP teams are doing quality work?

We discuss the first of these questions in this chapter and the second one in Chapters 8 and 9.

AUDITABLE DATA

Asking how you could use TSP data is a little like asking how you could use financial data. The reason is that TSP data, like financial data, are auditable, and you can use your existing auditing staff to assure yourself that the data truly represent what is going on in the business. When the data do show what is going on, they, combined with financial data, will give you a precise and comprehensive picture of operational status and performance. While using these data, however, it is wise to remember what Samuel Clemens (Mark Twain) once said: "Figures don't lie but liars figure" [Kirkman 1996]. This means that people must be motivated not to fake or "adjust" their data. If they do, the data will not be trustworthy and could even be misleading.

Personal Data

The motivation to gather and use data is particularly important for knowledge work because the data concern how these people do their jobs. To be useful, TSP data must cover every aspect of the work: the time that the developers spend on each activity, the mistakes they make, and the defects they find and fix. With these data, their managers can quickly determine which workers are most productive, who is making the most mistakes, and who may not be producing much useful product. The first reaction of many managers to these data is: "Wow, now I can really clean house!" They visualize ranking their people, identifying those who are most productive, and dumping everyone else. However, not only would this be counterproductive; it would seriously damage your organization's ability to do creative work. There are two reasons for this.

First, using data to evaluate the people who gather that data would make those data threatening to those people. At the first hint that management is using their data as a performance assessment tool, your knowledge workers would either stop gathering data, or the data they gather would be so "adjusted" that the data could not be used to accurately evaluate anyone who gathered them. Not only would using data as an assessment tool destroy the effectiveness of the TSP; it would also likely destroy the engineers' motivation to cooperate with management. In short, management would become the enemy. Because the knowledge workers are the only ones who can gather these data, it would be difficult for anyone but a trained auditor to tell whether the data were accurate and complete. As noted in Chapter 5, the only way to ensure the quality of the data is to convince the knowledge workers that they need accurate and complete personal data to do high-quality personal work.

The second reason that management misuse of TSP data would be a bad idea is that all data, even TSP data, represent a simplistic one-dimensional view. Some engineers are superb coders and others are first-class designers. The most effective and creative teams include a mix of skills and talents, and most people are good at some tasks but not so good at others. The challenge for the teams is to know who is best suited for each kind of job and then to balance the team's workload so that the team's overall performance is maximized. This means that most team members must occasionally do some tasks for which they are not best suited. It is not that they want to work at less than maximum efficiency but rather that they were the best people available at the time.

Handling Poor Performers

While most managers understand that few employees excel at every task and are willing to make allowances, they generally rebel at not being able to use TSP data to identify and discipline their poorest performers. The reason this is unrealistic is that the poor performers know they are poor performers, and they rarely gather accurate data. These, in fact, are often the very people who strenuously object to using the TSP in the first place. They know that the TSP data could expose them, and they will do everything in their power to conceal their poor performance. In short, the poorest performers will view the TSP data as threatening, no matter what management does.

So, assuming that these poor performers did manage to make it onto a TSP team and that they did actually gather some data, their data would be so inaccurate as to be useless for evaluation purposes. In fact, the data would probably show that they were high performers, and if management tried to use the data for an evaluation, the data would likely show that these people were much better than they actually were. This would make it difficult for management to take disciplinary action.

While it is important to identify the poor performers and to remove them from their TSP teams as quickly as possible, these people usually have attitude problems and can be identified without using their data. The team members will know who is uncooperative and who is unwilling to work with and support the rest of the team. While the other team members are gathering and using their data and measuring and managing their work, the poor performers are not. Team performance then suffers, and the rest of the team members resent it. When properly coached and led, disciplined knowledge-working teams can help management identify and discipline the poor performers. As long as management is sensitive to the team's needs, they will learn who these problem team members are, and the team will be relieved to have them rehabilitated or reassigned.

Removing poor performers is always a problem. Poor performers are generally adept at concealing their failings, and their poor performance may not be recognized even by the other members of their teams. When they start to use the TSP, however, they must work to detailed plans and visibly track their progress. Then they will have no place to hide.

- Do they have detailed plans?
- Are they following these plans?
- Are they gathering data?
- Are they accomplishing their planned tasks?
- Are they helping and supporting their teammates?

If they are not, the whole team will know and resent it. Then, one way or another, the team will devise some way to let management know. Management will then be able to take action more rapidly than they ever could have before. As long as management doesn't use any team member's data to evaluate anyone, there will not be any problems.

AUDITING TSP DATA

The single most important performance indicator for a TSP team is the accuracy and completeness of the team's data, and the second most important indicator is the way the team uses these data. That is why team leaders, coaches, and management should treat the quality and use of team data as a high-priority item. This topic is discussed further in Chapter 9.

To keep teams focused on data quality, the company's financial auditors should regularly audit the quality and use of the TSP data. This will assure you that these data are accurate and complete, and that they can be relied upon to properly portray the organization's performance. This also means that you must treat unsatisfactory audits of TSP data just as seriously as you treat unsatisfactory financial audits.

TSP data audits must treat all personal data as confidential to the person who gathered it, and all audit reports should contain only team-level data and above. Of course, either the financial auditors would have to be trained in how to audit and evaluate

TSP data and in observing the privacy of personal team-member data, or some TSP-qualified group should be trained in professional auditing practices.

USING TSP DATA

Once you have auditable data from the knowledge-working teams, you will have a powerful tool for managing and improving the business. You also will be able to communicate rapidly and precisely about the operational aspects of the business, even through several layers of management.

TSP Data

The TSP data will enable you to understand operational costs and identify improvement opportunities in all areas that use the TSP. To appreciate these opportunities, consider what your people know. For every project, they know how much time was spent on each activity, the sizes of the products produced, and the numbers and types of defects that the developers injected and removed. They also know how the project's results compared with the original plans and which support tools and methods were used. To visualize the kinds of analyses you can perform using TSP data, consider the following 11 examples.

Productivity Analysis

Team productivity is generally not a useful means for comparing team performance because productivity is affected by so many variables. For example, productivity generally varies by as much as a factor of six depending on the type of product, the percentage of new or modified product elements, and the size of the product [Flaherty 1985]. However, with the TSP there is a very useful measure that directly correlates with team productivity. It is called the task-hour measure. Task hours are the hours that engineering teams spend actually working on tasks that are in the team's project plan. Because the percentage of time that developers can spend on project tasks directly influences the cost of the work, task-hour performance is an important though rarely used productivity measure.

On TSP teams, the task-hour measure provides a precise way to determine how much of a team member's time is spent on planned project tasks and how much on other activities. For example, typical TSP teams find that the amount of time they can actually spend on planned project tasks is between 15 and 18 hours out of a standard 40-hour workweek. The balance of their time is spent in meetings, handling e-mail, helping coworkers, talking with managers, taking training courses, or dealing with interruptions and questions.

When they first use the TSP, most teams find that they had been achieving only 10 to 12 task hours a week before they started measuring and tracking their task time; one large organization ran a study and found that its engineering teams were averaging fewer than five task hours per week before they started using the TSP. With the TSP, knowledge workers can quickly improve their task time.

Figure 7.1 shows how one team at Allied Signal improved team average weekly task hours from about 10 hours per week to about 16. That is a 60% increase in project time at no increase in cost. Most first-time TSP teams have similar results.

Benchmark Analysis

Your people can identify other organizations that are using the TSP and establish benchmarks on task-hour rates, quality performance, employee satisfaction, customer satisfaction, and many other measures. If such groups are local, they can even

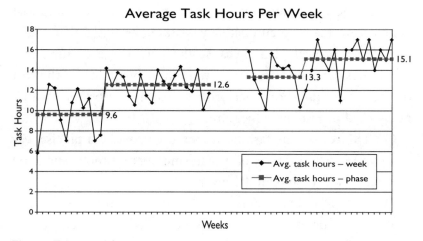

Figure 7.1 Allied Signal weekly task hours

arrange for occasional lessons-learned meetings or brief improvement workshops. They can also work with industry groups or the SEI to establish benchmarks among competitive organizations. Benchmarking is a powerful tool that can be most effective at the team level because the data show what other teams have produced. This shows your teams that improvement is possible and can help to motivate them to meet or exceed the benchmarks.

Analysis of Coaching Support

In Chapter 9, we discuss coaching support for TSP teams. Few technical organizations use coaches to guide and motivate their engineering teams, but the experience with TSP teams is similar to that with professional sports teams: The quality of the coaching determines the quality of the team. To assess the value of team coaching, your organization can experiment with various levels of coaching support and analyze the performance of the teams to determine the costs and benefits of each level of support.

In doing coaching analyses, ensure that all of the TSP coaches have similar qualifications and that they are actually coaching teams. The direct costs of coaching will be obvious, but determining the benefits requires a comparative analysis of your engineering teams. There are many ways to measure team performance, but the most useful measures concern schedule performance, quality performance, and task-hour performance.

When comparing projects, it is also essential to consider team experience. First-time TSP teams need more coaching support than experienced ones; however, the quality and task-hour benefits of professional coaching should quickly become obvious even with beginning TSP teams. With information about the effectiveness of coaching support, your management team can make informed decisions about the optimal level of coaching resources.

Cost-of-Quality Analysis

As noted in Chapter 8, the time and money wasted by poor-quality software work often exceeds 50% of total project costs. By using TSP data, your people can determine the quality costs for each project and identify the highest-priority areas for improvement. Then, by addressing the highest-priority areas, they can sharply reduce life-cycle costs. Because 70% to 80% of the costs of final testing and customer support are typically due to poor product quality, and because these costs often exceed the total cost of product development, showing the developers how to improve product quality can save large amounts of money (see also Appendix D).

Development groups are rarely considered responsible for the post-development costs of their work, so it is important to make these quality costs visible to them. Then, when they start new projects, they can establish cost-of-quality improvement goals and define plans to help them meet these goals. Your management team will then have the data to monitor team performance and to establish appropriate ways to recognize superior work.

Customer Satisfaction Analysis

Customer satisfaction studies can be particularly instructive for all kinds of development work. Customer satisfaction typically improves sharply as a reaction to better cost, schedule, and quality performance. For custom development work, team responsiveness and frequent, open, and honest communications between the customers and the engineering teams can be a major source of customer satisfaction and loyalty.

For large-volume proprietary products, IBM ran satisfaction surveys for all of its large-system customers using a five-level rating, from very satisfied to very dissatisfied. The results of each survey were then presented to senior corporate management, and any project manager who had a very-dissatisfied customer rating was required to attend and explain his or her resolution plan to this executive. Any product manager who had not already visited every very-dissatisfied customer and resolved his or her problems was severely criticized.

Development managers are often surprised to find that many aspects of their work that they had largely ignored are very important to their customers. Examples are product documentation, installation complexity, fix quality, and the user interface. Customer satisfaction surveys can focus development attention on these often-ignored details and quickly turn very dissatisfied customers into loyal supporters.

Employee Satisfaction Analysis

Employee turnover can be a major cost in technical organizations. Because the best people are often the ones most likely to leave, the costs of replacing them can be substantial, particularly considering lost skills and project disruption. Because dissatisfied employees often have low task hours, poor data-gathering practices, and product quality problems, an analysis of team performance data can often identify possible satisfaction problems before they cause turnover problems.

Facilities Analysis

While many organizations have experimented with various workplace configurations for their knowledge workers, few have any data to support their actions. Poor facilities arrangements can sharply reduce team task-hour performance. In one case, a newly hired developer was found to have much lower weekly task hours than anyone else on the team. The team leader considered replacing her until he learned that her desk was in an open area beside the copying machines. Whenever people were waiting for an available copy machine, they would stop and talk to her. When they moved her desk, her task hours came up to the team average. Without the task-hour measure, the team leader would have had no way of knowing why this developer's performance was substandard.

Financial Performance Analysis

Financial performance is one of the most promising and profitable areas for using TSP data. As noted in Chapter 2, Cesar, the CEO of Quarksoft, initiated a program to track the profitability of every engineering team on a weekly basis. By assigning a profit target to each team based on its planned effort and schedule, the company could calculate the percentage of the work done each week and compare it to the percentage of planned effort expended. Then management could determine the profit earned to date. The company found that although these weekly profit earnings fluctuated considerably, they provided a valuable early warning of potential project problems. As Carlos, Quark-soft's VP for R&D, said, using TSP "is important for us because it shows on a weekly basis the financial viability of the organization." Previously they got this information only monthly.

Organization Structural Analysis

One question on which there is little agreement and even less data concerns management's span of control. How many people should one manager supervise and how deep an organizational pyramid is optimal? The normal considerations in this decision concern the ability of managers to provide adequate personal guidance to their people. A countervailing consideration for which organizations typically have no data concerns the task time that the managers consume talking to their people or asking them for reports, feedback, or special assignments.

In the case of one organization that uses TSP, senior management noticed that after a steady average of 16 task hours per week, the teams jumped to over 20 task hours for one week before dropping back to 16. When they looked for the cause, they found that there had been a management off-site that week. With no managers to interrupt or distract them, the developers had more time to devote to their project work. The obvious conclusion: While some level of supervision and guidance is essential, with self-directed teams, more managers mean fewer task hours and lower engineering productivity.

Staff Support Analysis

Some organizations are proud to have what they call a "lean and mean" organization. By this they mean that they have minimized the size of their support staff. While the size and effectiveness of the support staff should always be monitored, few organizations have the data to evaluate the trade-offs. When management minimizes the size of the support staff, they are forcing the knowledge workers to do their own clerical work. Developers become very high-priced clerks when they have to make their own copies, complete expense reports, file documents, and the like. Some simple experiments with various levels of clerical support coupled with an analysis of team task-hour performance could help to determine the optimum level of staff support. Because few developers know how to use staff support effectively, some brief training sessions would likely help them improve their use of staff and improve their task time.

Tool Support Analysis

Tool support is an obvious area for study. When many projects are doing similar work, it is often possible to compare the task-hour and quality performance of teams using different kinds of support tools or engineering methods. However, because human performance varies far more widely than the likely impact of any tool or method selection, a substantial number of projects should be studied to get statistically meaningful results. While such studies can be interesting, the principal surprise will be how small a difference tools actually make. The team members will object strenuously to inconvenient or poorly performing tools, but any new tool's actual measured impact on team performance is likely to be less than 10%. The single exception is tool support for data gathering, which can have a bigger payoff. The payoff would not be in cutting the modest amount of time required for data gathering but in increasing the quality and completeness of the data.

COMMUNICATING WITH DATA

Organizations often have communication problems, particularly between the executives and senior managers and the working-level developers. These problems generally occur in two areas: communication accuracy and the communication hierarchy.

Communication Accuracy

When people communicate verbally, there are often misunderstandings, particularly if the subject is either complex or urgent. People generally hear what they are listening for, and our words often poorly represent what we intend to say. This is why the financial controls in most businesses are far more precise and reliable than those for any other aspect of the business: They are based on auditable data that are precisely defined and commonly understood at all levels of the business. With the TSP, you will have precise, well-defined, and auditable data on development operations. This will provide an equally accurate and reliable way to communicate about the major operational aspects of your business. One key challenge, however, is to listen.

The Communication Hierarchy

Hierarchical communication problems concern the credibility that people typically gain by attaining a senior management position or a high level of seniority. This typically makes it hard for junior people to be heard, even when they have an important message. In his book *The 7 Habits of Highly Effective People*, Stephen Covey gives a wonderful example of the hierarchical communications problem [Covey 1990]:

> Two battleships assigned to the training squadron had been at sea on maneuvers in heavy weather for several days. I was serving on the lead battleship and was on watch on the bridge as night

fell. The visibility was poor with patchy fog, so the captain remained on the bridge keeping an eye on all activities.

Shortly after dark, the lookout on the wing of the bridge reported, "Light, bearing on the starboard bow."

"Is it steady or moving astern?" the captain called out.

Lookout replied, "Steady, captain," which meant we were on a dangerous collision course with that ship.

The captain then called to the signalman, "Signal that ship: We are on a collision course, advise you change course 20 degrees."

Back came a signal, "Advisable for you to change course 20 degrees."

The captain said, "Send, I'm a captain, change course 20 degrees."

"I'm a seaman second class," came the reply. "You had better change course 20 degrees."

By that time, the captain was furious. He spat out, "Send, I'm a battleship. Change course 20 degrees."

Back came a flashing light, "I'm a lighthouse."

We changed course.

Sometimes junior people know critical things that you really need to hear. The advantage of focusing on facts and data is that it can cut through all the prestige and status issues that befog most organizational communications and quickly guide you to the essence of the problem at hand. Then you can have the accurate and timely information you need to inform your decision making.

Once your working-level professionals understand the power of their data, they will have the ability to bypass the normal constraints and taboos of the organizational hierarchy so they can be heard. Then, like the battleship captain, your challenge will be to listen. This might sometimes force you to make an embarrassing change of course, but that would be better than stubbornly sticking with an untenable position and putting your organization on the rocks.

SUMMARY AND CONCLUSIONS

This chapter defines the steps required to ensure that the TSP data gathered by your knowledge-working groups are accurate and reliable, and it describes some of the opportunities you could have to use these data to maximize organizational performance. The key points made in this chapter are as follows:

1. Experience shows that the single most important indicator of superior team performance is the accuracy and completeness of its data. Superior data quality demonstrates superior team discipline, which typically correlates with superior team performance.

2. Before you can use TSP data with confidence, you must ensure that these data are accurate and complete, and that they are used appropriately. There are two aspects of doing this:

    a. If data are to be useful, they must represent accurately what is being done. That means that data must not be used to evaluate people, because the data would then be viewed as threatening and would not likely be accurately reported.

    b. Even if data are not used in a threatening way, people are rarely sufficiently motivated to gather their data completely and consistently. By using the financial auditing staff to check the quality of the TSP data, you can ensure that data gathering and use are consistently viewed as high-priority items.

3. Once you have high-quality data, there are many ways to use these data to improve business performance. The chapter briefly discusses the following 11 example areas:

    a. Productivity analysis

    b. Benchmark analysis

    c. Analysis of coaching support

    d. Cost-of-quality analysis

    e. Customer satisfaction analysis

    f. Employee satisfaction analysis

    g. Facilities analysis

    h. Financial performance analysis

    i. Organization structural analysis

    j. Staff support analysis

    k. Tool support analysis

4. With precise operational data on your business, you will be able to communicate far more rapidly and accurately than ever before. The two key aspects of this communication issue are as follows:

    a. With precisely defined and well-understood data, the likelihood of misunderstandings will be greatly reduced, making it possible to rapidly communicate important facts from the bottom to the top of even large organizations.

    b. With this data communication capability comes an obligation, particularly for senior executives and managers, to listen to the data, regardless of the prestige or seniority of the messenger.

REFERENCES

[Covey 1990] Stephen R. Covey, *The 7 Habits of Highly Effective People: Powerful Lessons in Personal Change* (New York: Simon & Schuster, 1990), p. 33.

[Flaherty 1985] M. J. Flaherty, "Programming Process Productivity Measurement System of System/370," *IBM Systems Journal* 24, no. 2 (1985).

[Kirkman 1996] T. W. Kirkman, "Statistics to Use," www.physics.csbsju.edu/stats/, 1996 (accessed March 7, 2010).

8
Managing Quality

At several points in this book, we have said that quality must be your top priority, but we have not yet explained why. This chapter explains why quality is critically important to you and to your business. It also describes several additional quality topics and shows how effective quality management impacts the bottom line. While much of this discussion addresses software quality, the principles, methods, and practices described here apply equally well to all forms of knowledge work.

MAKE QUALITY THE TOP PRIORITY

We develop two key points in this chapter:

1. An effective quality program can save a lot of money.
2. If the quality program doesn't save money, it is not being managed properly.

A third point, which is part of every topic we discuss in this book, concerns measurement. If you don't measure something, you cannot manage it, and if you don't manage something, it will not improve. Because few people measure quality, most quality improvement programs are just motivational talk and produce no meaningful benefits. This is why any serious quality program must start with measurement.

The Cost-of-Quality Measure

For most businesses, the principal reason for managing quality is economic; poor-quality work is enormously expensive. Dr. J. M. Juran, one of the all-time greats of the quality movement, defined a businesslike way to measure quality [Juran 1999]. It is called the cost-of-quality (COQ) measure, and it provides a way to measure what poor-quality work costs a business. According to the COQ measure, quality costs have four components:

1. Internal failure costs—the costs of fixing defects during product development

2. External failure costs—the costs of fixing defects after product delivery to customers

3. Appraisal costs—the costs of reviewing or inspecting products to find and fix defects before testing

4. Prevention costs—the costs of identifying the causes of defects and changing practices or procedures to eliminate those causes

Few businesses measure the costs of poor-quality work. This is unfortunate because these costs are typically very high, and the costs of an effective quality program are modest. When organizations do not have an organized quality program, their costs of poor quality generally are 40% or more of the total cost of sales [Juran 1999]. Organizations typically view their quality costs as highly confidential, but experience shows that failure costs can usually be cut to less than 10% of sales. Cutting the cost of sales by 20% to 30% would give an enormous boost to the bottom line of any business.

The only way to achieve superior quality is to motivate the people who do the work to personally dedicate themselves to producing defect-free products. Quality work is not done by mistake, and it is not done by unmotivated or disgruntled employees. The developers must care about their work, strive to consistently improve, and be proud of what they produce.

Most development organizations have quality departments. While having such a group is essential, it can have the unfortunate consequence of making this department responsible for product quality. That is why typical software engineers feel that quality is a problem for the testing group. While testing is necessary, this chapter explains why knowledge workers must feel personally responsible for the quality of the products they produce.

Safety-Critical Systems

While cost is the principal reason to manage quality, some businesses market life-critical or business-critical products whose quality can literally mean the difference between life and death, both for people and for businesses. Examples of safety-critical devices include automobiles, medical devices, commercial aircraft, weapons systems, and nuclear power plants. Many businesses provide services that are now or will soon be critically important to their customers' operations. The reliability and trustworthiness of financial management, investment trading, and manufacturing control systems can make the difference between business success and failure. There have even been cases where the loss of a single key data-processing executive or senior manager has resulted in business failure.

Today, many of the systems on which our lives and livelihoods depend are run by software. Whether we fly in airplanes, file taxes, or wear pacemakers, our safety and well-being often depend on software. With each system enhancement, as the size and complexity of these systems increases, so does the likelihood of serious problems. Defects in video games, reservations systems, or accounting programs may be inconvenient, but software defects in aircraft, automobiles, air traffic control systems, nuclear power plants, or weapons systems can be dangerous.

All of us depend to some degree on the national transportation network, on hospitals and medical devices, on public utilities, and on the international financial infrastructure. All of these systems are run by increasingly complex and potentially defective software systems. And increasingly, particularly since the Toyota stuck-accelerator problems of 2009 and 2010, the public is realizing that software quality problems can be dangerous. In Toyota's case, the loss of life has been modest when compared with other automotive fatality statistics. For any company, the loss of public confidence would be embarrassing, and it could even be devastating.

There are technical solutions to these quality problems, but there are no known ways to quickly restore public confidence. If your business depends on public confidence in your products or services, you cannot afford the first high-profile disaster.

THE SOFTWARE QUALITY PROBLEM

For organizations that do a substantial amount of software work, quality costs are typically 40% to 60% or more of total development costs. And this doesn't even include the large and widely variable quality costs for customer support and service. For a software-intensive business, a large part of these support costs are due to the poor quality of the software development work. The software quality problem is like a perfect storm. Three counterproductive forces converge to create an almost totally dysfunctional technology. These three forces are an archaic management culture, an ill-prepared technical workforce, and an ineffective quality strategy. In the previous chapters, we have described remedies for the archaic management culture and outlined the skills that knowledge workers need to do superior work. This chapter is about software quality and the quality strategy required for knowledge work.

Software Quality Facts

Software is and must remain a human-produced product. Although we have tools and techniques that can automate the production of code once the requirements and design are known, the requirements and design must be produced by people. Furthermore, as systems become increasingly complex, their requirements and design grow increasingly complex. This complexity leads to errors that result in defects in the requirements, the design, and ultimately the code itself. Even if code could be automatically generated from defective requirements and design, that code would reflect the requirements and design defects and thus would still be defective.

When people design things, they make mistakes. The larger and more complex the designs, the more mistakes they are likely to make. From course data on thousands of experienced software developers learning the PSP, we have found that developers typically inject about 100 defects into every 1,000 lines of the code they write [Humphrey 2005]. The distribution for the total defects injected by 810 experienced developers at the beginning of PSP training is shown by the total bars in Figure 8.1. While there is considerable variation and some developers do higher-quality work, just about everybody injects defects.

Developers use various kinds of tools to generate program code from their designs, and they typically find and fix only about half of their defects during this process. This means that about 50 defects per 1,000 lines of code remain at the start of initial testing. The distribution of the defects found in initial testing is shown by the test bars in Figure 8.1.

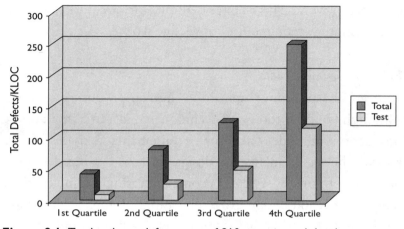

Figure 8.1 Total and test defect rates of 810 experienced developers

Developers generally test their programs until they run without obvious failures. Then they submit these programs to system integration and testing, where they are combined with other similar programs into larger and larger subsystems and systems for progressively larger-scale testing. As can be seen from Figure 8.1, developers remove about half of their defects before submitting their products to initial testing. The defect content of programs entering system testing typically ranges from 10 to 20 defects per 1,000 lines of code.

The most disquieting fact is that testing finds only a fraction of the defects in a program. That is, the more defects there are in a program at test entry, the more defects are likely to remain at test completion. The reason for this is the point previously made about extensive testing. Clearly, if defects are randomly sprinkled throughout a large and complex software system, some of them will be in the least-often-used parts of the system, and others will be in those parts that are exercised only under failure conditions. Unfortunately, these rarely used parts are the same ones that are most likely to be exercised when such systems are

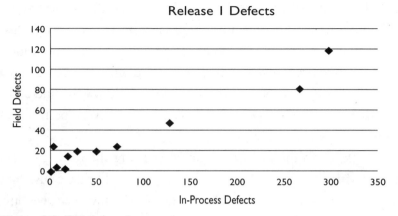

Figure 8.2 IBM defect data

subjected to stresses such as high transaction volumes, accidents, failures, or military combat.

IBM published data on the numbers of defects that escaped testing and ended up in the delivered version of one of its major products [Kaplan 1994]. Figure 8.2 shows the defects found in development testing compared to those found by customers. As is clear from this figure, the traditional logic for a test-based quality strategy is unsound: When more defects were found in process (by development), more were found in the field (by users). If the test-based strategy were sound, when more defects were found in testing, fewer should be found by the users. As this chart shows, this strategy is wrong. Unless the development process removes almost all defects before the start of testing, testing alone cannot produce a quality product.

The Defect Problem

A defect is an incorrect or faulty construction in a product. In software, defects generally result from mistakes that the designers or developers made as they produced the products. Examples are design mistakes, oversights, misunderstandings, and typographical errors. Furthermore, because defects result from mistakes, they are not logical. As a consequence, there is no logical or deductive process that can possibly find all of the defects in a system. They could be anywhere, and the only way to find all of the defects with testing is to exhaustively test every path, function, and system condition.

This leads to the next question concerning the testing objective: "Must we find *all* of the defects, or couldn't we just find and fix those few that would be dangerous?" Obviously, we only need to fix the defects that would cause trouble, but there is no way to determine which defects these are without examining all of the defects. For example, a complex design defect that produces a confusing operator message could pose no danger, but a trivial typographical mistake that changes a no to a yes could be very dangerous. Because there is no way to tell in advance which defects will be damaging, we must try to find them all. Then, after finding the defects, we must fix them, or at least all of the ones that could be damaging.

THE TESTING PROBLEM

Today's most common software quality strategy is based almost entirely on testing. This is unfortunate because testing is both a very expensive and an ineffective way to find and fix the volumes of defects that software developers typically inject in their products. Defects could be anywhere in a large software system, so the only way for testing to find them all would be to completely test every program function under every possible operating condition. The reason this is essentially impossible, at least for large and complex programs, is indicated in Figure 8.3.

The circle represents all of the possible ways in which a complex system could be tested. At the top is the range of possible

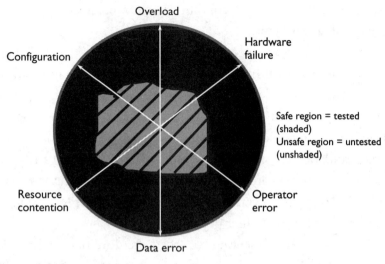

Figure 8.3 System testing

system workloads or data rates, and to the top left is the particular configuration being tested, such as the number of connected network ports, terminals, files, printers, and the like. The bottom left area, resource contention, concerns the number of things going on at the same time, such as printing while sending a message or handling a device interrupt while doing a calculation. At the bottom are data errors, for example, an excessively long message or an improper data type or value. To the right are operator errors or hardware failures.

As computing systems have grown larger and more complex, and as the users have interconnected more and more application areas such as payroll, sales management, and manufacturing scheduling, the number of possible operating conditions for these systems has grown astronomically. In Figure 8.3, the shaded area in the middle represents the portion of the system that has been tested and where all the defects have been found and presumably fixed. It is considered the "safe" area because of the unique nature of computer programs: As long as they are used under precisely the conditions that were tested, the programs will always work.

The key question, then, concerns the relative sizes of the circle and the safe area. In the early days of computing, applications were relatively simple and the computing systems were too small and underpowered to do more than one thing at a time. In those days, we could exhaustively test many of our simpler programs and be reasonably sure that they would always run. In such cases, the safe area would cover the complete circle in Figure 8.3. Today, however, as systems have grown larger and more powerful, this is no longer possible.

For example, in a meeting we asked the developers who were creating the Microsoft Windows operating system what percentage of this testing circle they thought could be considered safe. They concluded that it was probably around 1% or less. Although it would be extremely hard to make even an approximate calculation for this figure, the test-coverage percentage for Windows— or any other large and complex system—is probably far smaller than 1%.

This number is so small because a single test can cover only one system configuration, one set of data values, and one combination of operating conditions. Furthermore, a simple calculation shows that there are *millions* of possible configurations and *millions* of data values to test for *each* configuration. There are also many millions of possible normal operating conditions, plus many more millions of ways in which these systems can fail or be misused, and each of these combinations would have to be tested against every system configuration and data value. Only then could the testing be considered exhaustive. If it were even possible to conduct these millions and millions of tests in a reasonable period of time, the costs alone would be prohibitive. For both financial and feasibility considerations, it is impossible to produce large-scale high-quality software products through testing alone.

Conclusions on Testing

At this point, we can state several conclusions. First, today's large-scale systems typically have many defects. Second, these defects generally do not cause problems as long as the systems are used only in ways that have been tested. Third, because of the growing complexity of modern systems, it is impossible to test all of the ways in which such systems could be used. Fourth, when systems are stressed in unusual ways, their software is most likely to encounter undiscovered defects. Fifth, under these stressful conditions, these systems are least likely to operate correctly or reliably. Therefore, with the current commonly used test-based software quality strategy, large-scale life-critical systems will be least reliable in emergencies, and that is when reliability is most important.

Why Defective Systems Work

With so many defects remaining in systems, and with such a small percentage of program functions being tested, one might wonder why we don't have more software quality disasters. The reason is that the beta-testing strategy adopted by many organizations has turned out to be surprisingly effective.

When IBM encountered a system-testing problem with its early OS/360 operating system more than 40 years ago, it started a practice that is called beta testing. In beta testing, a system is thoroughly tested and then early copies are sent to selected users. Then, when these users find problems, the supplier produces fixes. Once all of these early users' problems are fixed, the supplier releases the beta-tested system for general use. This strategy is now widely used and has been quite effective. As long as the users' behavior is reasonably predictable and as long as the applications are not safety critical, this strategy usually results in fairly reliable systems. However, although this beta-testing strategy is helpful now, as systems get more complex, users' behavior is likely to be much less uniform and beta testing will be much less effective. And, even though your users may be reasonably satisfied now with the quality of the software that beta testing produces, the beta-testing strategy is expensive and typically delays product release by at least a year. Clearly, an alternative will soon be needed to replace the current beta-testing approach to software quality management.

SOFTWARE QUALITY ECONOMICS

The arguments in favor of a new software quality strategy are certainly compelling for complex or life-critical systems, but the economic arguments are even more persuasive and apply to *all* types of software systems. The reason is that the cost of finding and fixing a defect in a software system increases exponentially the longer the defect is left in the product. This is illustrated by the Xerox quality data shown in Figure 8.4. These data were gathered by a Xerox TSP team during development of a software system.

To explain these data, we first must describe how defects are injected and removed during the development process. This process is shown in schematic form in Figure 8.5. At the start of development, the product requirements typically contain some defects. The developers should review and inspect the requirements to find any problems, but they typically just start using the requirements they are given, and these initial requirements are frequently wrong, or incomplete, or both. When the developers produce the designs and write the program code, they inject still more defects. After completing the design and writing

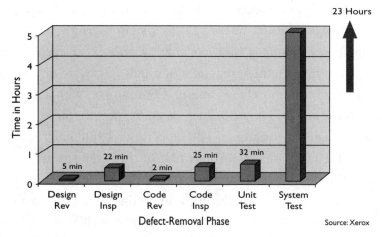

Figure 8.4 Xerox removal time per defect

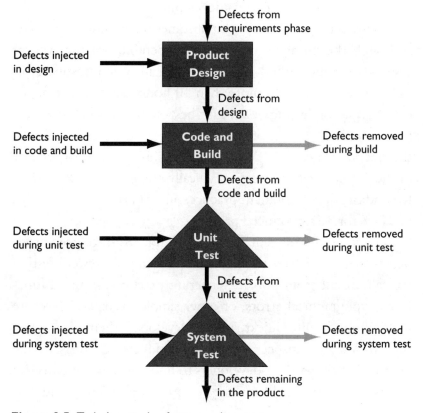

Figure 8.5 Today's typical software quality process

the code, the developers build and unit test the complete program or system before releasing it to system testing.

This process is very time consuming and expensive because the quality-management practices of today's software developers are based almost entirely on testing. For example, with a modest-sized program of 100,000 lines of code, development groups typically inject an average of 100 defects per 1,000 lines of code, or about 10,000 defects. About half of these defects are found during the build process at nominal cost, and half of the remaining defects are removed during unit testing at a cost of about half an hour each. Half an hour may not seem like much time, but if there are 5,000 defects in the product after build, removing only half of them would take about 1,250 hours of development time. That is over half a development year.

In system test, defect removal becomes much more expensive. Although the numbers vary widely depending on the type of system, the time to find and fix a defect in system testing typically ranges from 10 to more than 40 hours. And, as is true for other types of testing, even the best system-testing practices remove only a fraction of the remaining product defects. While this fraction varies widely with system complexity and the quality of the development process, it typically ranges from 50% to 75% for traditional development practices and can run as high as 95% to 100% for TSP-produced products.

The reason this percentage is so high for TSP-produced products is that the defects that are hardest to find in system testing typically result from poor engineering practices: omitted functions, typographical errors, or other simple mistakes. These are usually found quite quickly by the developers themselves when they review and inspect their own products. Conversely, the defects that are hard for developers to find in reviews and inspections are systemic problems like performance, usability, and synchronization, which usually show up quite quickly in system testing.

Thus, continuing with the above example, if 2,500 defects are left in the code after unit testing, it would take from 12,500 to 18,750 hours to find and remove a fraction of the defects left in the system during system testing. Furthermore, because the people fixing these system-test defects are rarely the product's designers, about 20% of the defect fixes will be in error. The 12,500 to 18,750 hours required to do all of this testing and fixing represent between six and nine developer years of work, assuming that these developers were physically able to do nothing but testing and fixing defects for 40 hours a week. And, even after all of this cost and effort, there would still be hundreds of defects in the finished product.

THE QUALITY TRANSFORMATION

To improve product quality, sharply reduce testing time, and cut costs, your software developers must follow a quality strategy like that shown in Figure 8.6. In each development phase, the developers perform an activity such as requirements development, design, or code and build. During the development part of each phase, they typically inject defects. Following this development step, each developer then personally reviews his or her work products to find and fix as many defects as possible. After completing this personal review, the developer asks a team of other developers to thoroughly inspect the product to find as many more defects as possible. Only after each product has been reviewed and inspected is it considered ready for the next development phase or for release to testing.

The economic benefits of this strategy are best illustrated by the experiences of TSP teams. For example, the defect-removal times for a Xerox team were shown in Figure 8.4. In that dia-

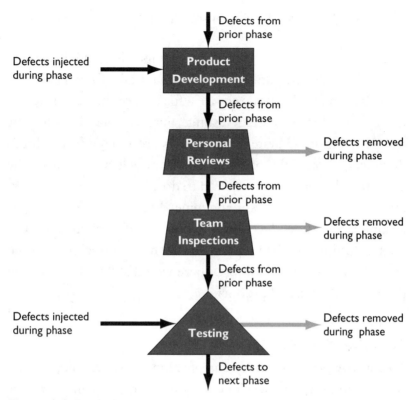

Figure 8.6 The TSP quality process

gram, we can see that it takes just a few minutes to find and fix each defect in the personal review steps, and the inspection steps take about half an hour per defect. By adding these review and inspection steps, TSP teams typically find and fix 95% to 100% of all the defects in a product before releasing it to system testing. The difference in product quality between TSP teams and non-TSP teams is due largely to improved development practices, personal quality ownership, team leadership, and the quality of the team's coaching.

If we apply review and inspection improvements to the example case cited above, there would be only 100 or fewer defects released to system testing instead of 2,500. The economic impact of improving product quality before the start of testing is substantial. System-testing time in this example is cut from 12,500 hours to 1,000 or fewer hours, producing savings of over 10,000 development hours. The cost of the reviews and inspections needed to accomplish these savings is only about 500 to 1,000 hours.

THE BECKMAN COULTER TEAM

As we pointed out in earlier chapters, knowledge workers such as software developers are very independent people. They will not follow any disciplined strategy unless they are convinced that it will help them to do better work. The effectiveness of the TSP process in motivating knowledge workers to manage the quality of their personal work is illustrated by the way Tim Lancaster's team at Beckman Coulter managed the quality of its work.

The job that Tim and his team were asked to do was described in Chapter 6. After the team relaunch, the team had completed much of the design work, and the members were in the code-and-build step when the hardware engineers asked them for an early copy of the system. The hardware work was on schedule, but the software engineers had found that the features they were building were larger and taking more work than they had estimated, so they were behind schedule.

Tim challenged his software team. He asked them for ideas and a plan to ensure that they could meet the desired schedule. In the ensuing discussion, the planning manager pointed out that they could cut a month off the schedule if they skipped the team inspections. The quality manager felt this would mean releasing more defects into system testing and that it could ultimately delay the work instead of accelerating it. The test manager then pointed out that this was only a prototype system that would not be released to customers and that testing would not exhaustively test all of the product's functions.

After some discussion, the team agreed to revise its quality strategy for this product release. After completing his or her personal review, each team member would have one other team member perform a second review in place of a larger and more formal inspection. After each set of reviews, they would meet with the quality manager to review their data and decide whether the component was of sufficiently high quality to release into test. If not, they would inspect the component. Everybody agreed with this plan. They followed this strategy and did the personal and peer reviews, and they also chose which modules to fully inspect. They delivered the system prototype on schedule. The hardware team was able to fully test their system with the software, and only one significant defect was found, which the software team quickly corrected. This kind of objective, business-like behavior is typical of knowledge workers when they have the skills to manage their own work and when management trusts them to do so.

SUMMARY AND CONCLUSIONS

This chapter describes the issue of quality in knowledge work, and it uses data from software teams to illustrate the enormous economic benefits gained from using a sound quality strategy. The key points made in this chapter are as follows:

1. The principal reason for adopting a measured and managed quality strategy is economic: Poor-quality work is very expensive.

2. If the quality program doesn't save money, it is not being properly managed.

3. For organizations that supply safety-critical or business-critical products and services, a sound quality-management strategy can mean the difference between business success and failure.

4. The software quality problem is caused by three simultaneous counterproductive factors:

   a. The current archaic management structure (discussed in Chapter 4)

   b. The poor preparation of the technical workforce (discussed in Chapters 5 and 6)

   c. An ineffective quality strategy (discussed in this chapter)

5. An effective software quality strategy must consider the nature of software work, the large numbers of defects involved, and the limitations of testing.

6. By striving to remove all defects before the start of testing, software developers can reduce development costs sharply, shorten delivery schedules, and improve product quality.

7. The key to achieving these benefits is a highly motivated and skilled workforce that feels personally responsible for the quality of its own work.

REFERENCES

[Humphrey 2005] Watts S. Humphrey, *PSP: A Self-Improvement Process for Software Engineers* (Boston, MA: Addison-Wesley, 2005).

[Juran 1999] J. M. Juran and Frank M. Gryna, *Juran's Quality Control Handbook* (New York: McGraw-Hill, 1999).

[Kaplan 1994] Craig Kaplan, Ralph Clark, and Victor Tang, *Secrets of Software Quality: 40 Innovations at IBM* (New York: McGraw-Hill, 1994).

9

Leadership

In this book we have talked about many things, but our primary objective has been to describe why and how to build a competitive knowledge workforce. As we noted in Chapter 1, Peter Drucker said [Drucker 1997],

> The productivity of knowledge workers will not be the only competitive factor in the world economy. It is, however, likely to become the decisive factor, at least for most industries in developed countries.

So, at least according to Drucker, a productive knowledge workforce is the key to the future. This is a leadership challenge, for, as he also said [Drucker 1969],

> To make knowledge work productive will be the greatest management task of this century, just as to make manual labor productive was the great management task of the last century.

Software is the first and most common form of large-scale knowledge work, so the methods for managing knowledge work were first developed for software projects. However, the principles and methods for building software capability apply to knowledge work of all kinds. This is important, for even if you are not in the software business or don't see software as a critical part of your operations, knowledge work is pervasive: It is the essence of the modern innovative workforce.

The organizations that excel at knowledge work will be the leaders of the future. This is why the Internet, the virtual disappearance of national borders, and the instantaneous availability of information are changing the nature of competition. Anyone anywhere can suddenly become a dangerous competitor. Physical plants and equipment are now much less important than human capital. As Thomas Friedman has said, the world is flat, and smart and motivated people, wherever they are, can instantly challenge your business [Friedman 2005].

If you are ahead of the curve, you must keep innovating and improving business performance, but if you are not a leader, change must be your top priority. With the accelerating pace of technological innovation and with capable competitors springing up almost daily, aggressive and enlightened leadership is more important than ever before. Fostering the skill, creativity, and motivation of your knowledge workers and forging them into a productive workforce must be your highest business priority.

This book has described the elements needed to accomplish this objective, but you and your executive and senior management team must provide the leadership to integrate these elements into a coherent change program that will enable your people to excel in this exciting but challenging future. The principal elements of this leadership are:

- Goals
- Support
- Motivation
- Standards of excellence
- Execution

GOALS

Perhaps, like Blanca Treviño of Softtek, your goal is to be the quality benchmark for your marketplace; or, like Cesar Montes de Oca Vazquez at Quarksoft, you will strive to offer the best and most profitable customer service. Similarly, Scott Garrett at Beckman Coulter challenged his people to be rated number one or number two in every line of their business. In each case, these challenging goals provided the impetus for these organizations to make dramatic improvements and to achieve or maintain strong leadership positions in their industries. But what is it that makes goals so important? After all, just naming a goal doesn't actually accomplish anything. What are the pieces and parts of goal setting that make goals effective in changing an organization?

To be effective, goals must motivate action. But this can't be just any action; it must lead to a productive and effective result. The following two examples illustrate both the dangers and the benefits of challenging goals.

Faster, Better, Cheaper

When Daniel Goldin took charge of NASA, he was concerned about the long schedules and high costs of NASA projects. He felt that the work was overly complex and could be greatly simplified. He then initiated a new strategy called "faster, better, cheaper," and NASA started launching new spacecraft in a fraction of the time and for a fraction of the cost of prior missions. It looked as if the new strategy was a success. Then along came the Mars Orbiter and Polar Lander missions.

On September 23, 1999, the Mars Climate Observer, which had been launched nine months earlier, crashed into Mars and was destroyed [Oberg 1999]. Because NASA had another Mars mission on the way, it conducted three studies to find out precisely what had gone wrong, wanting to prevent the next mission

from having the same problems. The studies found several problems, with one critical mistake in the software. Through a design
oversight, two separate parts of the orbiter used different measurement systems; one was metric and the other used inches and
feet. This meant that the software controlling the mission actually gave incorrect commands and caused the orbiter to crash
into Mars, destroying the $125 million mission.

After considerable study, NASA engineers thought that they
understood what happened to the Mars Orbiter and that the
Mars Polar Lander would not have the same problems. It didn't,
but it had other problems. On December 7, 1999, the Mars
Polar Lander also crashed into Mars and was destroyed. This
time, the problem was a spurious signal that, when misread by
the software, caused the lander's engines to shut off prema-
turely. It was another costly failure after a lot of expense and a
long space mission.

While both the Mars missions had different problems, the
problems had several common causes: design and testing errors
coupled with faulty management decisions. In the rush to get
the missions launched in minimum time and for least expense,
the engineering teams and their managers had not paid sufficient attention to quality. The management at NASA's Jet Pro-
pulsion Laboratory (JPL), which had developed and operated
these missions, failed to properly manage the "faster, better,
cheaper" charge from Mr. Goldin. The objective was noble; the
problem was in the implementation.

A standard management principle is that what gets measured
gets managed, and what gets managed gets done. However, what
does not get measured and managed often gets ignored. JPL knew
very well how to measure and manage "faster and cheaper," but
no one established a measurement and management plan for
better. As a result, by measuring faster and cheaper and ignoring

better, they actually got "faster, cheaper, worse." These multi-million-dollar missions were launched quickly, but they were total failures. So, by not measuring all three parts of the goal, "faster and cheaper" turned out to be very expensive in the long run.

It is clear from this example that to be effective, goals must be measured and tracked. However, measurement and tracking can't just focus on the obvious things like cost and schedule; they must also address the quality of the work. Are the people doing the right things, and are they doing them in the right way? These are questions of standards and execution, which we discuss later in this chapter. The next example concerns a successful goal-setting experience, and it also provides some important lessons.

Breaking World Records

Suppose you wanted to have the fastest product cycle in your industry. What would you do? You should first realize that you don't just want shorter schedules; you want faster deliveries. The schedule is the plan or template for the job. Shortening the schedule without also accelerating the work is a recipe for disaster. To actually speed up the work, your people must focus on defining how the tasks are done and what it would take to accelerate a project.

To see how to accelerate a job, let's consider a seemingly simple example. How would you set the world record for building a house? The San Diego Building Trades Council, in conjunction with many local builders and building trades, decided to do just that: They built a house in world-record time [BIASD 1983]. Starting with a dirt lot, two crews of 350 workers each raced to build, decorate, furnish, and landscape two nine-room houses in the fastest possible time. The winning team built and finished the house and had it passed by on-site building inspectors in just 2 hours and 53 minutes.

Because the normal time to build, inspect, and ready such a house for sale was 90 days, it is easy to dismiss this as a trick. However, if you watch a video of the actual construction, you will appreciate what was involved. They added chemicals to heat the concrete so that it would set in 45 minutes; they had parallel teams for every possible task; and they had all of the materials on hand and ready. Nothing was prefabricated; they started with raw lumber, pipes, and nails. They also planned every step to the minute, and they built two complete practice houses the week before to test the process and to ensure that everybody knew precisely what to do. There was no waiting around; they just did their jobs. These were highly motivated teams. You could see the excitement and hear the cheering. The teams did an extraordinary job and they loved every minute of it.

Although building a house and developing complex systems are very different jobs, we can learn a great deal from this example. Think about the challenge of getting 350 people to synchronize their work and to cooperatively carry out *any* complex task, let alone to do it in world-record time. First, to accelerate a job, the most obvious need is planning. Without a precise and detailed plan, 350 people could not possibly coordinate all of the tasks needed to build a house in 2 hours and 53 minutes. In fact, they probably could not have built the house in 90 days. These teams had detailed plans that showed what every worker would do for every minute of the job. So, the critical requirement is that the engineering teams make detailed and comprehensive plans. However, the engineers must make the plans, not the managers. Only the engineers know the job details, and only they can define all of the required steps. Also, the managers must ensure that all of the engineers are trained and able to make detailed and accurate plans, and the immediate managers must participate with their teams in making the plans. Finally, the more-senior managers must review these plans for detail and completeness. If the engineers, teams, and managers meet all of these goals, you can be pretty confident that the work has been adequately planned.

After planning, the next requirement is to have the teams use their plans to do the work. In fact, one of the major benefits of having detailed plans is that teams can do workload balancing. This is what teams do when some members fall behind schedule and others are ahead. The early members can help the late members or rearrange the team's tasks. Workload balancing is an essential part of teamwork, and high-performing teams do it instinctively. In the house-building example, the same teams took about six hours to build two practice houses the week before. During this practice, the workers learned how to better balance their work, enabling them to cut their building time for the same house from six hours to just under three. Think of that: With the same plans, workers, and materials, they built the identical houses in half the time! This is the power of workload balancing. It really accelerates the work. This leads to a key goal: to have the teams dynamically rebalance their workload and plans, even every day if necessary.

Another obvious need from the house-building example is quality. There simply is not time to do the job over; it must be done right the first time. In fact, of the two competing teams, the losing team was actually ahead until the inspectors found that the roof was incorrectly placed. Although the required adjustments were minor, they took long enough for that team to lose the race.

In addition to quality, these construction crews had a lot of support. Their management assembled them ahead of time and had them produce detailed plans. They also arranged to have all of the materials and supplies on hand precisely when needed and arranged for the building inspectors to be on hand during the job. Finally, both teams actually performed trial runs and mentored and coached team members on how to improve their performance. Because of this coaching and practice, both teams were able to cut their construction times in half between the trial runs and the actual competition.

After support, one more thing is needed: motivation. It is clear from the house-building example that every member of each team did his or her utmost to build the house in the shortest possible time. How do you get teams to work like this? Obviously, your developers must be motivated and your teams must provide a motivating and supportive environment. Clearly, this must be a crucial organizational goal: to have motivated knowledge-working teams.

As shown in the above example, the key elements required to make goal setting effective are support, motivation, standards, and execution, and providing these elements takes leadership.

SUPPORT

Support is one of the critical needs for every group that does challenging work, particularly work like software development that leaves little or no room for error. High-quality work is not done by mistake, and it certainly is not done by people who don't care. But everybody needs support, even people who are dedicated, know the best methods, and strive to do essentially perfect work. The key aspects of support are training, coaching, and recognition.

Training

Training is the simplest part of support; all it takes is time and money. While everyone knows that proper training is essential for surgeons and lawyers, they rarely feel the same way about software development or other kinds of knowledge work. As in any modern technical field, the most effective methods are not obvious; they have been learned through years of thoughtful practice and improvement. The elements of superior knowledge work involve self-management and teamworking methods. As described in this book's Appendix B, training is required for everyone involved in managing and performing knowledge work.

Coaching

Coaching support is a challenge for many organizations because they have never considered coaching to be important for knowledge-working teams. However, effective teamwork does not just happen. There are many elements required for building and supporting a team. This has been demonstrated by many years of experience with teams in sports and the performing arts. There also is a growing body of knowledge about how to coach military teams and aircraft flight crews. Although we now know a great deal about building and coaching teams, that knowledge is rarely used for knowledge-working teams.

Self-management and team-member participation are challenging for most teams because they are hierarchically organized; the boss, leader, or captain has ultimate authority. Without some way to ensure prompt, complete, and accurate communication, either subordinates are reluctant to speak up or the boss fails to listen. To consistently build productive knowledge-working teams, a qualified coach is needed to guide the team, the team leader, and management through a launch process. This launch process addresses the hierarchical authority problem and establishes effective communication both within the team and between the team and management.

Once the team has been built, the coaching focus then turns to establishing and maintaining the discipline with which the team members do their work. Undisciplined work leads to errors, and, at least for software, essentially all errors must be corrected before the finished products will work correctly, reliably, and efficiently. But correcting software mistakes in test can take tens to hundreds of times more work than it would take if the developers had followed modern software quality practices. Effective coaching improves development discipline, reduces defects, and cuts development time and cost. This is why coaching is an economic issue and why coaching effectiveness can be assessed in economic terms. The steps required to ensure effective team coaching are described in Appendices B and C.

Recognition

Superior work looks easy. If you watched Kim Yu-Na's flawless figure-skating performance in the 2010 Vancouver Winter Olympics, you might have wondered what the fuss was all about. It looked so easy. In any but the simplest fields, truly superior performance is hard to appreciate unless you have actually tried to do it yourself. One of the best definitions of expertise is from the book *Zen and the Art of Motorcycle Maintenance*: "If you want to paint a perfect picture, just make yourself a perfect painter and paint naturally" [Pirsig 1974]. This is what true professionals do. They learn their trade, build and practice their skills, and then just perform naturally. This is an enormously satisfying way to work, but it looks so easy that it is hard to appreciate.

In one example, a TSP team had striven for months to produce a high-quality product on schedule. Their efforts paid off when they got into system testing on time and the product sailed through with no defects found. When they presented their results to senior management, they did not mention this quality achievement until the very end. Then, when they said that they had completed final testing in only one week with no defects, the executives did not realize what an enormous achievement this was, and they didn't even compliment the team. What was most upsetting for the team was that another team had not followed sound quality practices and had been late getting into final test. They then spent several months working until late at night fixing defects in test. When they finally shipped the product late, they had struggled so hard that management gave them a party with a cake.

If you want superior work, you must recognize it and reward it. Superior work takes dedication and commitment. But championship teams have fan clubs and perform at their best before an appreciative audience. A key part of every manager's job is to be a fan and to recognize, applaud, and reward superior work.

MOTIVATION

In Chapter 6, we talked about team motivation and how teams can become highly motivated just by making a commitment to meet a common goal. Motivation is critical for superior team performance. The process used by the TSP to build this motivation is the launch process used to make a team plan. As long as your development teams are properly coached through the launch process and then effectively coached and led in doing their jobs, they will be highly motivated and will do superior work.

While motivating development teams is important, motivating management is even more important. One way to do this is to follow the TSP strategy for building team motivation: Have your management team develop the business plan to meet your goals. TSP teams are somewhat different from management teams because they are building products that management has convinced them are important to the business. However, even if your goals are corporate rather than product, the overall process is the same. You must decide what is important to you and to the business, and then you must sell your management team on the importance of meeting these goals. This management planning process should be the first step in executing any improvement program, and it is the subject of the final paragraphs of this chapter.

STANDARDS OF EXCELLENCE

People can accomplish things they never thought they could do. However, we and they often settle for just ordinary accomplishments and rarely challenge our people to do truly excellent work. The key is to establish a standard of excellence and then to motivate your people consistently to work to this standard. That is how world records are broken, and it is how some organizations consistently outperform the rest of their industry.

Defining Your Standards of Excellence

By defining and publishing your standard of excellence, you do more than merely set expectations; you establish the basis for making decisions, evaluating people, and recognizing and rewarding superior performance. The specific elements of an excellence standard should be defined for each organization; the definition should be clear and compelling, and it should be understood and endorsed by your entire management team.

In setting this standard, we suggest that you first define the elements that you believe truly constitute excellence, then meet with your senior management team to develop and agree on an organizational standard for excellence. Document and distribute this definition and make sure that everyone understands it. Finally, establish measures, track and review performance, and recognize and reward superior performance.

The dimensions of excellence that you define for your organization will necessarily be unique, but they should include elements of many if not all of the following categories:

- The customer: What would constitute product and service excellence in your customers' eyes?

- Product quality: What are the key quality attributes of your products and services?

- Product development and manufacturing: What would constitute excellent work by your people?

- Practices: Do your people consistently follow best known practices?

You may also want your excellence standard to address the topics needed for an effective knowledge-working environment such as people motivation and development and building a trusting, open, and honest organizational culture. Above all, you should consider addressing continuous improvement. This concerns complacency, or the tendency of people to become comfortable in a working routine and to just drift along. It takes effort and drive to maintain a sense of urgency, but without urgency, nothing much gets done. Many organizations just drift along and are then shocked when their more agile and energetic competitors catch them flat-footed. Do your people coast, or do they regularly look for better ways to do their jobs?

These standards of excellence should rank near the top of your leadership priorities. They apply not only to the organizational transformation program we discuss in this book, but also to all aspects of your business.

EXECUTION

Appendix B of this book describes the strategy that we have found to be most effective for building a productive and competitive knowledge-working organization. While we know that these methods work, and you might even be convinced of this by what we have said so far, many executives and senior managers are skeptical. Their typical reaction goes something like this: "What you say sounds convincing, but managing software has been an intractable problem for so long and your results look so extraordinary that I just can't believe them."

This is entirely understandable. Appendix A describes the experiences of many organizations, and it shows that these methods are doubling development productivity, improving product quality tenfold or more, and saving money at the same time. This seems almost too good to be true. However, these methods do actually work, and if you are still skeptical, talk to some people who have done what we recommend and see what they say. Then run a few pilot projects to see how these methods work for you. If, as we predict, the results are positive, get started; you have no time to waste.

SUMMARY AND CONCLUSIONS

This chapter concludes the body of this book by describing your role in implementing the changes we have described. Although the specifics of how to do this are described in the appendices, and your people can use these appendices to guide their implementation efforts, the key to making this happen is leadership. The principal points this chapter makes about leadership are the following:

1. Knowledge work is likely to be the decisive factor for business success in the twenty-first century.

2. Making your knowledge workers productive requires a change in the culture and management system of your organization.

3. There are four principal elements to the leadership challenge:

   a. Setting challenging goals and maintaining a sense of urgency in addressing them

   b. Ensuring that your executives, managers, and professionals get the training, coaching, and recognition required for superior work

   c. Building and sustaining the motivation of your knowledge-working teams, and establishing a trusting management culture

   d. Defining your standards of excellence, and insisting that your people strive to meet them in everything that they do

4. Nothing can actually be accomplished without an effective execution program. This requires that you do the following four things:

   a. Look at the evidence from teams that have used these methods and convince yourself that these methods will also work for you (Appendix A).

   b. Conduct several pilot programs to get the evidence needed to convince your management team and your knowledge workers that these methods will help them to do better work (Appendix B).

   c. Put a key executive or senior manager in charge of the change effort, and have your management team prepare and commit to a broad implementation plan (Appendix C).

   d. Monitor progress and insist that everyone establish and strive to meet aggressive goals.

REFERENCES

[BIASD 1983] Building Industry Association of San Diego, *Four Hour House* (videotape), San Diego, CA, 1983; also at http://video.google.com/videoplay?docid=5661470904690661035#.

[Drucker 1969] Peter F. Drucker, *The Age of Discontinuity* (New York: Harper & Row, 1969).

[Drucker 1997] Peter F. Drucker, "The Future That Has Already Happened," *Harvard Business Review* 75, no. 5 (September–October 1997): 20–23.

[Friedman 2005] Thomas L. Friedman, *The World Is Flat: A Brief History of the Twenty-first Century* (New York: Farrar, Straus and Giroux, 2005).

[Oberg 1999] James Oberg, "Why the Mars Probe Went Off Course," *IEEE Spectrum* 36, no. 12 (December 1999): 34–39.

[Pirsig 1974] Robert M. Pirsig, *Zen and the Art of Motorcycle Maintenance: An Inquiry into Values* (New York: William Morrow and Company, Inc., 1974).

A
Will the TSP Work in My Organization?

If you're reading the appendices for this book, you are likely considering using the TSP. The concepts make sense to you and the performance and other benefits are appealing, but you need to know more to make a decision:

- Will the TSP work in my organization? Who else is using it?
- Budgets are very tight today. What will it cost to implement the TSP?
- How long will it take? When will the investment pay off and how can I justify it?
- What are the critical factors for successful TSP adoption?
- How do I get started? What's involved? Where's the best place to start?

Perhaps you're considering the TSP but are still skeptical. You can see how the TSP might work for some companies, but your situation is really different or unique. You may have several questions or concerns:

- We're very busy and I don't see how we could stop and take the time to implement something like this, training every engineer, hiring coaches—it just doesn't seem practical today.

- We're already using CMMI (or Agile methods, or another methodology), and I just don't see how the TSP would work or provide benefit in our environment.

- Frankly, our maintenance contracts are an important aspect of our business, and there would be no financial benefit if we were to produce higher-quality products.

- The results are so good that they are hard to believe.

APPENDIX A OVERVIEW

The purpose of Appendices A through E is to answer the questions that you might have about the TSP, whether it will work for you, how to implement it, and what kind of results to expect. The appendices answer questions about cost, schedule, and return on investment (ROI). They describe who's using the TSP, the organizational settings where the TSP has been applied, and the benefits. Many other questions are addressed, including applicability, scalability, scope, and other project, product, and organizational factors. Finally, the appendices describe how to get started, how to build internal capability, and how to roll out the TSP across the organization: what has worked, what hasn't worked, and the factors that are critical to a successful implementation.

The appendices are organized as a roadmap for implementing the TSP, as shown in Figure A.1. Each appendix answers questions and provides information that relates to a milestone on your journey from awareness to a fully implemented capability (see Table A.1).

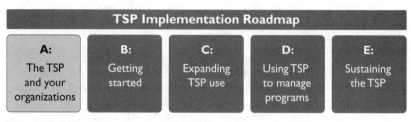

Figure A.1 Roadmap to the appendices

Table A.1 The Appendix Roadmap

Appendix	Topics
A	This first appendix answers the question "Will the TSP work in my organization?" Topics covered include a summary of some of the organizations that are using the TSP, characteristics of these organizations, the types of applications that have been developed with the TSP, project types and characteristics, and TSP implementation considerations. It also addresses cost and ROI issues.
B	Appendix B answers the question "How do I get started?" An important but often overlooked aspect of any new technology is the strategy for successful implementation. Implementing the TSP begins with planning, staffing, training, and trial use. This appendix describes the steps involved, the costs, training requirements, initial staffing plans, and other details required for a successful initial introduction.
C	Appendix C answers the question "How do I expand the use of the TSP and build internal capability?" After successfully piloting the TSP, you will need to develop a plan for broader adoption. This appendix describes an approach that has worked for other companies. It also describes how others have used the TSP to implement integrated product teams and to handle multidisciplined projects.
D	Appendix D describes how managers can use TSP data and methods to help them run their development programs. It covers the TSP methods available for precisely tracking project work, assessing project and program issues, and devising effective steps to promptly recognize and address program problems. Experience shows that with precise and timely information, most programs can be kept on schedule and within committed costs. The TSP methods can provide that precise and timely information.

(continues)

Table A.1 The Appendix Roadmap (*Continued*)

Appendix	Topics
E	Appendix E addresses how an organization can sustain the TSP effort once it is in place and how to use the TSP continuously to improve the performance of the organization's teams. If management does not provide the motivation to improve, performance won't level off; it will actually get worse. This appendix describes how to use the TSP data and methods to achieve even greater benefits.

WHO IS USING THE TSP?

One of the great benefits of being involved with the SEI is the community. The SEI's Partner Network has established a community of practice for any organization that is applying an SEI technology such as the TSP. The SEI Partner Network comprises organizations that are tested, monitored, and licensed by the SEI to provide our courses and services. It provides opportunities for sharing lessons learned, networking, and participating in the evolution of software technologies. For more information on the SEI, see the sidebar "The Software Engineering Institute."

Many of the organizations that are using the TSP belong to the SEI's Partner Network, and they routinely share their TSP data and experiences. From this rich source of information, and from the SEI's direct involvement in helping organizations adopt the TSP, we know a great deal about who is using the TSP, how they are applying it, and how it is working for them.

Several of the world's top computer software companies are using the TSP, including Adobe, Intuit, Microsoft, and Oracle. Within Microsoft, several IT groups for different business units reported a tenfold reduction in mean schedule error and the elimination of the "death march ending" that so often accompanies software development projects. Intuit reported reduced test schedules and a 30% increase in functionality delivered in each

The Software Engineering Institute

The Software Engineering Institute (SEI) was established in 1984 as a federally funded research and development center (FFRDC) at Carnegie Mellon University in Pittsburgh, Pennsylvania. It is a nonprofit organization charged with identifying and transitioning improved software engineering technologies and methods into general practice.

SEI Programs

The SEI has four principal programs:

- The Acquisition Support Program (ASP) works directly with key DoD acquisition programs to help them achieve their objectives.
- The Networked Systems Survivability Program (CERT) focuses on protection, detection, and response to attacks on networked computer systems and on improving the security of software products.
- The Research, Technology, and Systems Solutions Program (RTSS) develops and transitions improved methods for architecting and designing large-scale complex software-intensive systems.
- The Software Engineering Process Management Program (SEPM) develops and transitions improved methods for managing and developing software-intensive systems into widespread practice.

SEI Evaluation and Certification Services

With the increasing need for large-scale, high-quality software, a growing number of methods have been developed and marketed to help organizations improve their software practices. This has led to a requirement for objective and reliable ways to evaluate these methods. With the recent advent of quantitative software engineering methods, the SEI has developed a number of certification offerings that provide objective, fact-based evaluations of individual, team, and organizational capabilities. For example, to help ensure that the TSP is properly implemented and that the results match those described in this book, the SEI certifies TSP coaches, PSP developers, and TSP-using organizations.

release. Adobe and Oracle have reported similar results, citing improvements in predictability, productivity, and quality.

Many onshore, near-shore, and offshore business application developers are using the TSP to deliver software products in very competitive markets where cost and schedule advantage are vital. Two examples are Softtek and Quarksoft in Mexico. While success in the global outsourcing market involves many other factors, low costs, predictable schedules, and working software are important, especially for repeat business.

Softtek, a large custom software supplier, decided to implement the TSP as a next step after achieving CMMI maturity level 5, the highest and best of CMMI's five maturity levels. Softtek's objective was to use the TSP to improve its competitive advantage as a custom software house. The founders of Quark-soft, also a custom software developer, based their company's business model on TSP principles for the same reason.

Many industry and DoD organizations that produce embedded software or mission-critical software, where reliability, safety, or security is vital, are using the TSP. A key benefit in this setting is the substantially higher quality of the software produced by TSP teams. In these types of applications there may be no room for error, or the cost of repairing or replacing defective software may be prohibitive. Among the DoD organizations that are using the TSP for this advantage are the Naval Air Systems Command facilities at China Lake and Patuxent River, the Naval Oceanographic Office (NAVO) at the John C. Stennis Space Center in Mississippi, and the Software Maintenance Organization at Hill Air Force Base, Ogden, Utah.

One of the unique embedded software application domains where the TSP has been applied is the software game industry. One of the industry's top software game producers, Vicarious Visions, now part of Activision, uses the TSP to produce many popular software games such as Guitar Hero. When distributed in a game cartridge or DVD format, these software applications are like embedded systems. Quality and reliability are critical because the users of gaming software generally have a low tolerance for software faults, and so game developers must produce very high-quality products or face reduced market share and warranty losses.

A profile of these companies and others that are using the TSP shows that they range from very small companies with fewer than 25 developers to very large organizations with more than 2,500 developers. They include companies that develop software for internal use, for customers under contract, for embedded systems and mission-critical software, and, like Adobe and Vicarious Visions, for public distribution and sale.

WHAT TYPES OF APPLICATIONS HAVE BEEN DEVELOPED WITH THE TSP?

Many different types of systems and application software have been developed with the TSP, including new systems, enhancements to legacy systems, and engineering protoypes ranging in size from small applications of fewer than 10,000 lines of code (LOC) to large applications with more than 1,000,000 LOC.

Figure A.2 uses the North American Product Classification System (NAPCS) to show the types of software products built with the TSP. NAPCS classifies software into two broad categories, system software and application software, and subcategories within these major classifications, including those in the figure. Included in the chart are systems and applications software, games and entertainment applications, ERP systems, medical devices and health care systems, financial systems, IT services applications, various embedded systems, aircraft flight control software, factory automation software, mission-planning applications, modeling and simulation software, and communications software. These different product domains represent a broad spectrum of software applications, development tools, environments, and languages. In each category, the reported project performance and organizational benefits of using the TSP are essentially the same.

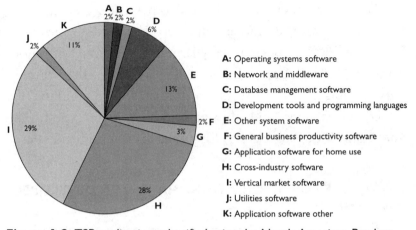

A: Operating systems software

B: Network and middleware

C: Database management software

D: Development tools and programming languages

E: Other system software

F: General business productivity software

G: Application software for home use

H: Cross-industry software

I: Vertical market software

J: Utilities software

K: Application software other

Figure A.2 TSP applications classified using the North American Product Classification System (NAPCS)

WILL THE TSP SUPPORT OUR PROJECTS AND TEAMS?

The TSP has been applied to a wide range of software project team configurations and settings. The TSP was initially used on colocated teams with 2 to 20 team members, working on either new development or enhancements to existing systems.

With time and experience, the application of the TSP to other project team settings grew well beyond these initial projects to include larger teams, larger and longer projects, geographically distributed teams, and other engineering domains and disciplines outside of software, as shown in Table A.2.

Table A.2 Characteristics of TSP Project Teams

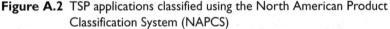

Project Team Characteristic	Experience
Team size	From 2 to 20 team members per team and multi-team projects up to 100+ developers
Team location	Colocated, geographically distributed, and even multi-team settings with more than one organization participating

Table A.2 Characteristics of TSP Project Teams (*Continued*)

Project Team Characteristic	Experience
Engineering domains	Software engineering, hardware teams, systems engineering, nuclear engineering, and IT services
Multidiscipline	Integrated teams consisting of many disciplines, such as software, hardware, test, quality assurance, business analysts, architects, game developers, artists, documentation specialists, and other engineering disciplines
Project duration	Very short projects of a few weeks' duration up to projects lasting a few years
Project development strategies	Mostly incremental or iterative development with periodic internal and external releases; cycle or sprint length ranging from a few weeks to a few months
Project mode	New systems, enhancements to existing systems, including very large legacy systems, pure maintenance, prototyping, system feasibility, system proposal teams, and projects or groups providing ongoing and request-based services

WHAT WILL IT COST TO IMPLEMENT THE TSP?

The cost of implementing the TSP is directly proportional to the scale of the implementation and the duration of the projects where the TSP is implemented. The most significant ongoing costs are the costs of training project teams and of providing coaching support.

Consider an example project with one project manager or team leader, one part-time coach, 10 developers, and a one-year schedule. The training for this team includes

- One day of pre-reading and a three-day training course for the team leader
- Two days of pre-reading and a five-day training course for each of the ten team members

This comes to approximately 75 days of training for this project team.

The team will also need coaching support, including

- Eight days for launch preparation and the initial launch
- Six days of support for each of three cycle postmortems and relaunches, or 18 days in all
- Another 25 to 30 days of ongoing coaching support

The coaching support for this project team is about 50 to 55 days, and with the addition of the training days it represents a cost of about 125 to 130 days.

While this may appear to be a large cost, it is offset by a much greater return. Among the many benefits achieved with the TSP, the easiest to quantify are increased productivity and improvements in product quality. Organizations using the TSP are reporting a typical first-project productivity gain of 25% or more, and a fourfold reduction in the number of defects found and fixed in system test, acceptance test, and post-release [Davis 2003]. Using these data, a project that would normally take one year will finish in about nine months with savings of about 13 weeks per developer or about 650 days total. Additional savings will accrue from reductions in post-release rework.

When you compare the 650 days' saving with the initial investment of 125 to 130 days, it's clear that the cost of implementing the TSP will be recovered on just about any project that has a planned duration ranging from one year to as short as eight months. In addition, once the initial investment is made, the ongoing coaching costs are all that is required for subsequent projects. This distinction between the initial costs of training the people involved and the costs of ongoing operations is made clear in the following discussion of return on investment.

TSP RETURN ON INVESTMENT

An ROI analysis can be useful in evaluating the relative benefits of various alternative improvement activities. In making such analyses, however, it is important to recognize that the costs of improvement efforts are much easier to estimate than the likely benefits and that the promised benefits are often highly speculative. Unless you have substantial data on current operations, we recommend that you not use sophisticated financial analysis methods. The simplistic ROI method used here should be appropriate for most cases.

For this ROI analysis, we assume an organization of 100 development team members with 10 team leaders and five executives. Of course, these costs can be scaled up or down to fit any particular case. The start-up investment costs cover those activities required to prepare the organization and its development teams for their first use of the TSP. The ROI analysis then compares the total start-up investment with the savings generated during ongoing operations.

In the previous section of this appendix, the costs of team coaching support were included in TSP implementation costs. While it is appropriate to consider these initial costs when deciding to pilot the TSP in your organization, these coaching costs are required for every TSP team and are not start-up investments. For an ROI analysis, the coaching costs must be included as ongoing operational costs and not as start-up investments. The TSP start-up investment consists entirely of training, and it is shown in Table A.3 for this hypothetical 100-developer organization.

Table A.4 shows the incremental added costs of operations with the TSP. These costs assume that there are 10 development teams with 10 developers each and that each team has one team leader. They also assume that each team will have one initial project launch and three project relaunches per year. The operational

Table A.3 TSP Start-Up Costs for a 100-Developer Organization

Activity	People	Days	People Days
TSP executive seminar	5	1	5
Team leader—preparation	10	1	10
Team leader—training	10	3	30
Developers—preparation	100	2	200
Developers—training	100	5	500
Total one-time start-up costs			745

Table A.4 TSP Operations Costs for a 100-Developer Organization

Activity/Team	Days/ Team	Times/ Year	Total People Days/Year
Initial project launch preparation	8	1	80
Cycle postmortem and relaunch	6	3	180
Ongoing coaching support	56		560
Engineering work	2,400		24,000
Total ongoing labor costs			24,560

savings from using the TSP typically derive from improved engineering efficiency, more accurate estimating and planning, and higher-quality products. Note that because the project launch is devoted to tasks that every project should normally perform, the launch time is not included as a TSP cost.

The savings shown in Table A.5 are based on data from organizations that have used the TSP [Davis 2003]. Experience shows that TSP teams are at least 25% more productive than non-TSP teams. These numbers can be readily checked in your organization by using the method Intuit used to make a similar calculation [Sartain 2007]. The Intuit data for more than 40 teams showed that the TSP teams, on average, spent 8% of their total project effort repairing defects after code complete. Con-

Table A.5 The TSP ROI Analysis—100-Developer Organization

Start-Up Costs	People Days
One-time start-up costs	745
Continuing Annual Costs	
Engineering work	24,000
Ongoing coaching support	560
Total annual labor costs	24,560
TSP Operational Savings	
Prior cost of doing one year of TSP work	32,000
Gross 25% saving due to TSP	8,000
Less one-year coaching cost	560
Net one-year savings from TSP	7,440
Return on Investment	
One-year ROI = Net savings/Investment = 7,440/745 = 10.0	

versely, the non-TSP teams spent 33% of their effort on defect repair work after code complete. Because the time the teams required to develop their programs was essentially unchanged, the productivity difference can be calculated as follows:

- The non-TSP teams spent 33% of their time fixing test defects and 67% of their time doing development.

- For every 100 engineer days of development work, these teams spent $100 \times (100/67) = 149$ days of work.

- The TSP teams spent 8% of their time fixing test defects and 92% of their time in development work.

- For every 100 engineering days of development work, the TSP teams spent $100 \times (100/92) = 109$ days of total work.

- Doing the same work in 109 days instead of 149 days means a productivity improvement of 27%.

While the TSP will also produce additional savings in reduced product maintenance and support, lower engineering turnover, and fewer canceled or delayed projects, the ROI analysis shown in Table A.5 considers only the direct team productivity savings from reduced test defects.

As shown in Table A.5, the total investment for this organization is recovered by only one of its ten teams in the first year. All the savings from the other teams and the savings in subsequent years are an added benefit. Finally, to determine the time required to recover the full costs for TSP implementation, add the first-year coaching costs to the total one-time start-up costs, giving 745 + 560 = 1,305 people days that would be recovered by only two of the 10 teams in the first year.

HOW LONG WILL IT TAKE TO IMPLEMENT THE TSP?

The time required to implement the TSP will depend on the pace of the implementation and the scope. The TSP is implemented on a project-by-project basis that allows the organization to establish the pace and scope and control the costs.

As shown in Figure A.3, the TSP is implemented in three phases. The details of each phase are provided in Appendices B, C, and E. In the initial piloting phase the TSP is applied to only two or three projects. After these projects have achieved the goals established for the piloting phase, the second phase can start the broad implementation effort. Soon after broad implementation is started, a third phase, focused on sustaining and improving performance, gets under way. These phases overlap and would be repeated in large organizations when moving from division to division across the entire organization.

The project-by-project implementation strategy used in the first and second phases includes a training component and a coaching component. The TSP is introduced by training project

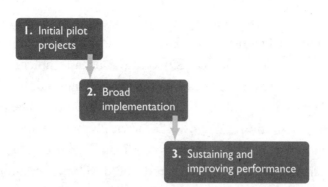

Figure A.3 TSP implementation phases

managers and project team members. Training is followed by a team launch and coaching support. To ensure consistent results, we recommend that an SEI-certified TSP Coach/Instructor deliver the training and coaching support.

The training, the launch, and the coaching support are required for successful implementation. The training is a prerequisite for the launch. Without the training, a team will not be able to complete the launch. The launch establishes the preconditions for using the TSP. Without the launch, the team will not be able to use the TSP. The coaching support is required to sustain TSP implementation. Without coaching, the team will not achieve its best performance and may abandon the TSP under the schedule pressure normally faced by most development teams.

How long will the implementation take? Some projects have completed the training and the launch in two to three weeks. The majority complete these initial steps in four to six weeks. During the two- to three-project piloting phase, the initial training and launch activities are completed within one to two months.

After the TSP is successfully piloted, broad implementation begins, using the same basic training and coaching support as in the piloting phase. During the broad implementation phase, organizations begin or continue to build internal training and coaching capability. The objective of the broad implementation phase is to increase the breadth of the implementation at a sustainable pace using internal coaches and instructors. The pace of the implementation can grow geometrically but is typically constrained by the availability of project teams or internal support. An organization with 20 teams and 200 developers could implement the TSP on all projects within two to three years. With added support, it could be done much faster. Until you have a reasonable base of TSP experience, however, it is best not to rush the broad implementation effort.

HOW DO I GET STARTED?

This is both the easiest and the hardest step. It just takes leadership. All that the senior managers must do is decide to implement the TSP and allocate the needed resources and management.

Where's the Best Place to Begin?

The details of finding the right place in the organization to begin, setting the initial scope, and selecting the best coaches, projects, managers, and team members are discussed in Appendix B. The short answer to this question is to start with projects that are important, that are representative of the organization's work, and that are managed and staffed by people who have shown an interest in trying the TSP. The best way to find these people is to hold an open forum for discussing the TSP and to select those teams that are open to the idea. Skeptics should be welcome but not those who are motivated to prove that the TSP won't work.

You will probably want to seek outside help to get started. An experienced external resource can provide the initial training and coaching, help develop your internal capability, help with the initial strategies and plans, and so on. These details are addressed in Appendix B.

What Can I Expect to Achieve with the TSP?

Perhaps the most important responsibility that you will have is establishing management objectives for the TSP. You will need to make it clear why you're taking this step, what you expect to achieve, what problems you are attempting to solve, and what success will look like.

The TSP provides many important benefits that can be directly measured and many less tangible benefits that also provide value. For most organizations, improved performance and more effective management practices are probably at the top of the list. Employee job satisfaction is another key objective.

Here are a few examples of the typical benefits. Most organizations have reported a dramatic improvement in cost and schedule performance. The typical TSP project delivers the full functionality promised at the beginning of the project with actual cost and schedule results that are within 10% to 15% of the team's commitments. Moreover, there are nearly as many projects that come in ahead of schedule or are under budget as there are projects that are late or over budget. In other words, cost and schedule variance is reduced and the mean variation is balanced around zero. This does not mean that TSP projects can achieve impossible schedules, but TSP projects can have aggressive but realistic plans that they are very likely to meet. TSP teams almost always deliver more features, with better quality, than similar projects that accepted impossible schedules.

Most organizations report productivity gains of at least 25% to 30%, from requirements through user acceptance test, and similar gains for design through system test or user acceptance test. Some organizations express the gain in team productivity, others as a reduction in cost and/or schedule, or as an increase in features per release.

The quality measure in the TSP is defects. Product quality is often reported as defect density in system test, user acceptance test, and/or the released product. The most common expressions of defect density are defects per thousand lines of code or defects per thousand function points. The quality management system in the TSP is so effective that most organizations are reducing defect density by 70% to 80% or better while also improving productivity. While there are many business benefits here that may not be obvious or may be difficult to quantify because of a lack of existing data within your organization, an 80% reduction in defect density will have a similar impact on rework costs, bug-fixing costs, testing costs, warranty costs, defect-tracking costs, and other costs. Although you might not have measured these costs, you would likely find that they are high—as much as 30% to 60% of your overall costs, and maybe much higher. A reduction in product defects of this magnitude will be noticeable to your users and your stakeholders.

All of these performance benefits can be directly related to business objectives and competitive advantage.

There are a few objectives that the TSP will not help you to achieve. It is important to understand what these are before beginning. No method will enable teams to meet costs or schedules that are truly impossible, including the TSP. Some managers believe that software teams just need to be driven harder and they will meet an impossible deadline. There is a belief, grounded in perception rather than data, that such a strategy has worked in the past. Another objective that must be avoided is the misuse of data. Again, some managers see the TSP as an opportunity to use personal data to micromanage teams. This has never worked. It will have the effect of killing the TSP effort with the complete loss of the investment already made. The principal message of this book is that the TSP is a way to motivate software and other knowledge-working teams to perform at their best. But it also requires that the entire management team trust, motivate, and lead them in doing so.

Finally, no process can compensate for poorly conceived products. However, the TSP allows your creative people to concentrate on building great products instead of spending much of their time testing and fixing defective work.

Organizational Considerations

The TSP changes the way software teams work, which may necessitate some adjustments to other organizational systems. Concepts such as the self-directed team management style and the coaching role are probably new to your organization. The interfaces between the project team and other groups, such as quality assurance, test, process improvement, or the project office, may also be affected. These items are briefly described below. Additional information can be found in the later appendices.

TSP Management Style

The TSP implements the concept of self-managed or self-directed teams, but not all elements of the self-managed work group are required. These are the notable differences between the TSP and a full implementation of the self-managed work group:

- TSP teams are self-organizing within limits. Teams are free to organize around the roles in the TSP, but the team or project leader is typically assigned by management.

- The TSP requires that team members determine, plan, and manage their own work; assume responsibility for product quality; track and report on project progress; and consistently improve their performance. Management still establishes the goals and objectives for the team.

- The TSP requires teams to negotiate their commitments with management. When a sound and reasonable plan suggests that management's objectives cannot be met, management has an obligation to work with the team to find a suitable alternative. Forcing a team to accept unreasonable commitments won't work. While the TSP will dramatically improve cost and schedule performance, it won't enable teams to achieve truly impossible commitments.

- The TSP does not require any special approach for performance appraisals. In most of the TSP implementations, performance appraisals are still conducted by management.

Here, we define an impossible commitment as one for which the team has been unable to build a plan to which all the members will voluntarily commit.

Organizing for the TSP: The Coaching Team

The role of coach will be a new role for most software organizations. It is an extremely important, value-added role in the TSP. Good coaching helps to ensure project success. Poor coaching will almost guarantee that a project will not achieve the performance that is expected of a TSP team. Because coaches are such a valuable resource, you should consider establishing a new group or team with responsibility for providing TSP coaching services. This topic is discussed further in Appendix C.

The TSP coaching team will be responsible for most aspects of the TSP implementation. Besides coaching, this includes planning, training, and many of the activities involved with transition and change management. Management must create, fund, and staff the coaching team; train the staff; and assign management responsibility.

The size of the coaching team will depend on the size and number of project teams, and the experience of the coaches and teams. Because coaches must be objective, the coaching team must have a reporting chain that helps to ensure objectivity. To get started, the best approach is to find one or two people with a desire to be TSP champions and train them to be coaches. Assign them to the manager who is sponsoring the TSP initiative.

Good coaches have management and technical skills, people skills, change management skills, and at least a few years of experience in software development. They are often recognized leaders and are respected within their organizations. SEI's TSP coach-training and coach-mentoring programs can help you develop many of the needed coaching skills. Finding people and giving them incentives to join the coaching team are important management responsibilities. A description of the most critical coach attributes and training requirements is in Appendix C.

Project Management Impact

The role of team leader or project manager in the TSP can be confusing. Terms like *project leader*, *project manager*, *team leader*, *engineering lead*, and *technical lead* carry many different meanings from organization to organization. The self-directed team management style used in the TSP adds the concepts of coach and team member/role manager to this list of "management-like" roles. With so much change to the project management system, it is easy to see why there are questions about management roles and responsibilities when implementing the TSP. If you have a project management office, this may add to the confusion.

The reality is that most of the confusion will disappear once TSP implementation begins. The new concepts introduced in the TSP will become clearer, and most of the organization's existing responsibilities will not change. The best advice is to follow the TSP guidelines for the pilot projects and wait until there is a better understanding of these roles before making changes. Appendices B and C cover this topic in more detail.

Process Improvement, Quality Assurance, and Test Group Impact

The managers or members of testing organizations might believe that the TSP will substantially reduce the size of their groups. This is a common initial reaction. The managers or members of the process improvement or QA groups may have similar concerns. In practice, organizations that have adopted the TSP have not experienced these problems.

The TSP pushes responsibility for project management, quality, and process improvement down to the level of the team and team member. On the surface it appears that the teams have assumed responsibilities that were in these other groups. However, most organizations find that the effectiveness of these groups improves after implementing the TSP. The principal reason for this is that the TSP creates an effective interface (or communication vehicle) between the project team and the test, QA, and process improvement groups.

In many organizations the relationship between the project team and the test, QA, and process improvement groups is workmanlike at best. Project teams are required to provide data to these groups, or are subject to audits or reviews for which the project team sees little or no benefit.

As shown in Figure A.4, when development teams use the TSP, the data and artifacts needed by the process group and QA are a natural output of the teams as they do their work. Because the teams provide more useful data, these groups are able to

Figure A.4 Project team context

provide better services, and the teams are in a better position to take advantage of those services.

The relationship between the project team and the test group also improves. With the TSP, testing is typically involved from the early requirements and design phases, and testing schedules aren't cut at the last minute because of development slips. In many cases, the testing team is even incorporated into the development team, and the role of testing shifts from finding defects to validating that the system meets its overall objectives. Time is now available for additional testing, such as performance, usability, or security testing.

Because every organization is unique and experience is the best teacher, organizations should wait until the TSP pilot projects are under way before making any changes to address these concerns. There is more information on the relationship between the TSP and these related groups in Appendices C and D.

Critical Success Factors and Barriers

As Fred Brooks said, "There is no silver bullet" and there is no magic potion or cure for the management problems in the software industry [Brooks 1987]. While the TSP has a very good management track record with documented, dramatic, and measurable improvements, it is not a silver bullet either. Yet many managers continue to look for the silver bullet. They often ask, "What's the one thing that makes the TSP so successful?" or "What's the secret to the TSP's success?" as if there were a silver bullet buried somewhere in the TSP.

There is no "one thing" or "secret" to the TSP's success. The truth is that the TSP is a system, with parts that were designed to achieve the outcomes reported by TSP users. It's not one thing; it's many things. It's the processes, measures, tools, training, coaching, management style, Personal Software Process, launch, inspections, estimating methods, implementation strategy, and other elements of the TSP that make it work.

Why is this important? It is important because you may be tempted to implement just the one or two things that look like silver bullets to you. The best advice is to resist this temptation. Start by implementing the TSP on pilot projects with minimal tailoring. Rely on experienced resources to guide you. Then, as you gain experience and understand the TSP system, you will be in a better position to adapt the TSP to your needs. Or, to quote a common adage from master chefs: "Don't change the recipe until after you have cooked the dish."

There are two other critical success factors that have already been briefly described, the coach and the team leader. A study of key success factors on dozens of projects at Intuit identified the team leader as the most critical success factor and the coach as a close second [Sartain 2007]. Also, a minimum level of executive support is required. This support includes setting an expectation that improving quality and efficiency are key priorities for the organization and that engineering leadership will be measured against these improvements as performance goals. The leadership team must also provide people, funding for training, and other resources as initial investments. More information on the roles of the coach and the team leader can be found in Appendices B, C, and E.

CONCLUSION

Will the TSP work in your organization? Most likely it will. Today there are many organizations that use the TSP. They range from small to large groups that work in many different settings and product domains, have many different business models, have small to large project teams, and have projects with very short to very long development and release schedules. A wide variety of development tools, languages, and other methods have been used with the TSP. With few exceptions the results across this broad spectrum are very similar. The conclusion is that the TSP works in many domains and settings and will produce great results when properly implemented, as described in the implementation roadmap found in Appendices B through E.

REFERENCES

[Brooks 1987] Frederick P. Brooks, "No Silver Bullet: Essence and Accidents of Software Engineering," *IEEE Computer* 20, no. 4 (April 1987): 10–19.

[Davis 2003] N. Davis and J. Mullaney, "Team Software Process (TSP) in Practice," *SEI Technical Report* CMU/SEI-2003-TR-014, September 2003.

[Sartain 2007] J. Sartain, "Critical Success Factors for TSP/PSP Adoption in a Consumer Software Company," European Software Engineering Process Group Conference, Amsterdam, sponsored by the Software Engineering Institute, the Netherlands, June 12–15, 2007.

B
Getting Started

This appendix describes how to get started with the TSP. As shown in Figure B.1, it describes the first steps needed to introduce the TSP and to motivate your knowledge-working teams to consistently follow the TSP process. Experience shows that they will then produce quality products on their planned schedules and for their committed costs. Once you have followed the guidelines in this appendix and have established a firm foundation of TSP experience, Appendix C shows you how to expand that capability across the organization, and Appendices D and E describe how you and your management team can use the TSP to manage and continually improve your organization.

APPENDIX B OVERVIEW

As with any major change program, there are many important elements of TSP implementation. However, the element that is most critical to the TSP's success is the energy and momentum

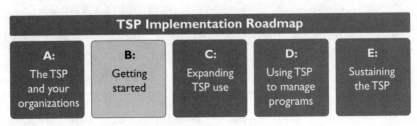

Figure B.1 Roadmap to the appendices

of the implementation effort itself. To build and sustain this energy, you must name a hard-driving and enthusiastic change champion, form a strong implementation team, and establish and follow an aggressive implementation plan. This appendix describes how to do this.

The appendix starts with a brief overview of the TSP implementation strategy. This provides a composite picture of the entire implementation effort. Subsequent sections then review change management principles, the TSP implementation team, and how the TSP is implemented for a project team. The TSP project cycle is next described, along with a discussion of management's role in the TSP process.

THE TSP INTRODUCTION STRATEGY

The TSP introduction strategy is project-focused. Implementation starts with three or four pilot teams and then proceeds project by project and team by team. Once installed and used by the first projects, TSP is implemented for the next ones. This process continues across all of the organization's projects and teams until the implementation goals are met. When following this strategy, it is most important to carefully select, implement, and support the initial TSP teams. Their performance will demonstrate to management and to the rest of the organization the benefits of introducing and using the TSP.

The success of the early pilot projects is crucial for several reasons. First, these initial projects will be examples of how the TSP works, and everybody in the organization will be watching how it works and whether the team members find it helpful to them personally. Second, early success will demonstrate to the management team how they can meet your standards of excellence (see Chapter 9). Third, the early adopters will likely become TSP promoters and advocate its adoption by other teams.

Finally, any unsuccessful teams will likely become outspoken and influential critics. That is why it is critically important to select initial adopters who are highly motivated volunteers.

The first step in TSP introduction is to identify someone to represent you in selling the TSP introduction program, to recruit the change agents, to develop the introduction plan, and to implement that plan. For most pilot programs, this initial effort will require only a few people, but for even small implementation efforts, you should use the TSP process to launch and guide the implementation program.

After forming the implementation team and approving its plan, the next steps are to select the initial pilot project teams and to train these teams and their managers in TSP and PSP concepts and methods. Then the teams begin following the TSP process under the guidance of a trained TSP coach. This process starts with a project launch where the coach guides the team in developing its project plan and in following that plan to complete its project.

The TSP training, the project launch, and the team coaching are all focused on the project team members and on how they are led, motivated, and supported. The objective is to quickly build highly disciplined teams that have leaders and managers who are proficient in leading self-directed teams. Their role is to motivate these teams to consistently follow their defined processes and plans, to regularly report their progress to management, and to strive to produce defect-free products.

This TSP implementation strategy contrasts sharply with many popular improvement programs that do not provide adequate training, skills development, operational support, or team buy-in. Such programs often fail to convince the knowledge-working teams that they need to change their personal behavior. Consequently, such programs produce only marginal and transitory changes in team performance.

After you have established broad executive support for the TSP, there are seven steps to follow in implementing the needed changes. Steps 1, 2, and 3 must be performed in order, but the other four steps should be performed together. All of these steps are important, and if you do not address every one of them properly, your program will either fail at the outset or will not become self-sustaining. The seven steps are as follows:

1. Recognize and follow the proven principles of effective change management.

2. Establish an energetic and assertive change implementation team.

3. Build a strong TSP coaching team. This topic is briefly discussed in this appendix but addressed more thoroughly in Appendix C.

4. Conduct and evaluate an initial set of TSP pilot projects.

5. Broaden TSP use throughout the organization. This is the topic of Appendix C.

6. Build TSP management capability. This subject is addressed from different perspectives in this appendix as well as in Appendices C, D, and E.

7. Establish the resources and practices needed to sustain the TSP. This is the principal topic of Appendix E.

THE PRINCIPLES OF CHANGE MANAGEMENT

John Kenneth Galbraith said, "Faced with the choice between changing one's mind and proving that there is no need to do so, almost everyone gets busy on the proof" [Galbraith 1971]. The software profession is no different; when confronted with a proposed change, we begin to construct a solid defense against it. The cost and time required are probably at the top of the objection list, followed closely by denials of the need to change. "We've always worked this way" and "In my experience" are certainly among the top objections. These common arguments are likely to be followed by highly technical and carefully crafted analyses that are designed to preserve the status quo.

Why is Galbraith's observation important? Introducing the TSP involves change, and managing this change is your responsibility and the responsibility of the team you assign to guide and manage the implementation. The TSP implementation strategy is guided by change management models, and the principles and concepts in these models are built into the TSP introduction strategy. This means that you do not need to create your own change strategy but that you should be familiar with change management principles. In case you are not, the following paragraphs summarize the key issues.

Rogers's model of adopter categories guides the selection of initial projects, teams, and managers, and it defines the actions needed to scale up across adopter categories [Rogers 2003]. Conner's model of commitment stages is a guideline for building commitment within the organization, the project teams, and for each individual participant [Conner 1992]. It describes the stages through which each person and group advances on the path toward widespread use. Training introduces the TSP principles and builds the skills needed to get started, and combined with data and a "self-convincing" learning model, it produces the behavioral changes needed to produce truly disciplined and sustained high performance. The TSP approach is designed to convince the knowledge workers themselves that this is a more effective and rewarding way for them to work.

Commitment to Change

The key elements of the Conner and Rogers change models are shown in Tables B.1 and B.2. In his book *Managing at the Speed*

Table B.1 Characteristics of Conner's Change Model

Degree of Support		Time Line
Preparation Phase	Succeed: Awareness	
	Failed: Confusion	
Acceptance Phase	Succeed	Positive Perception
	Failed	Negative Perception
Commitment Phase	Succeed	Institutionalization
	Failed	Abort

of Change, Daryl Conner defined the change process, change management roles, and the commitment stages that individuals and groups move through when committing to change. The stages are phases in the commitment process and indicate the level of commitment. The model describes the actions that lead to the next level of commitment and the failure modes that could terminate the process at any stage.

Table B.2 Roger's Change Model

Adopters	Number	Characteristics
Initiators	2.5%	Venturesome and daring risk-takers who are willing to accept substantial difficulty
Early Adopters	13.5%	Opinion leaders and role models who are respected by the early majority. They reduce risk by adopting the new idea and thereby "approve" use by others.
Early Majority	34%	Deliberate and slow to adopt a new idea but ahead of most, they provide the link in the network between early adopters and the late majority.
Late Majority	34%	Skeptical and risk averse, they adopt under peer pressure or necessity.
Laggards	16%	Suspicious of new ideas and favoring tradition, they are the last group to adopt a new idea.

In the *preparation phase* individuals have their first contact with and become aware of a proposed change. In the *acceptance phase* individuals gain an understanding of a proposed change and form a positive or negative perception of that change. If the perception is positive, they move to the *commitment phase* where they install and experiment with the new concepts, refine them, and move forward through the *adoption phase*, the *institutionalization phase*, and the *internalization phase*.

Conner's model defines the roles of the three key people in the organization who must be involved in the change process: the sponsor, the change agent, and the change target. The TSP implementation strategy includes defined actions and responsibilities for each of these people at each step of the change process. This includes you, the change sponsor; your management team; the change agents, who are typically TSP coaches; and the change targets, who are all of the managers and developers who will be adopting the TSP.

In his book *Diffusion of Innovation*, Rogers describes how new ideas or technologies advance through a group, a culture, or a social system. His research led him to conclude that successful diffusion of innovation depends in part on the network of communication that exists between different adopter types within the target group (Table B.2). He found that this network is central to establishing lasting change and commitment. When new ideas or technologies were introduced into a group without regard for this network, they generally were not successful.

Rogers's model shows that the successful introduction of a new idea or technology must start with the early adopters. Once successful with this group, the sponsoring managers and the TSP coach then enlist the early adopters as change agents and provide them the support they need to communicate the benefits of the TSP to the early majority. The early majority then help the later target populations through the remaining phases in the commitment process.

Conner's and Rogers's models are based on empirical studies, and they help with TSP implementation in three ways. First, they define the key change roles and responsibilities that must be staffed to have a successful change program. Second, they provide guidance in selecting the teams and groups for initial TSP pilot introduction. Finally, they provide overall strategic guidance for spreading TSP adoption across the organization.

Building Executive Sponsorship

Once the overall sponsor of the TSP effort has agreed to launch an improvement program, the next step is to build broad support across the entire executive team. This is typically accomplished with a one-day TSP Executive Seminar for the top management group. This seminar covers the principles behind the TSP, examples of the results that others have obtained, and a review of the actions required to put the TSP in place in this organization.

Wherever possible, you should have already identified potential candidate groups for initial TSP adoption and have invited one or two of their senior executives to attend this senior-level seminar. This will build local support and give you a head start for the later implementation.

Once this senior executive team agrees to proceed, the next steps are to establish an implementation team, to plan the overall effort, and to get started.

ESTABLISHING THE TSP IMPLEMENTATION TEAM

The TSP implementation team includes the management sponsors and the change agents. The size of the organization and the scope of the TSP implementation will determine team size and composition; in very small organizations or groups, you and a senior technical lead might be the entire team. Regardless of its size, all the members of this implementation team must fit the "early adopter" profile, and all of them should be respected, goal-oriented opinion leaders drawn from the ranks of management and development.

The TSP implementation team will act as TSP advocates and champions within their peer groups, and they must demonstrate an early-adopter attitude. The key characteristic here is a positive perception of the TSP and a personal commitment to making the change program successful. The TSP must make sense to them, they must be able to visualize how to use the TSP, and they must readily recognize its potential benefits. Their principal concern should be how to implement the TSP and not whether it will work.

Launching the TSP Implementation Team

The implementation team must start with a plan, and the best way to make this plan is to have this team follow the TSP process and conduct a team launch. To facilitate this process and to ensure its success, we suggest that you retain a qualified TSP coach to guide the effort. The TSP launch process consists of nine meetings; in meeting 1, the team first meets with management to understand the goals for the effort. Then the team meets privately with the coach to establish its team roles and strategy and to develop a comprehensive implementation plan. As with all TSP-produced plans, this plan defines the end products of the implementation effort, the time and resources required, the risks to be managed and/or mitigated, and any alternate plans that are deemed appropriate.

An important step in this planning process is for the implementation team to define measureable short-term and long-term goals, objectives, and success criteria. The detailed and timely data the TSP provides make it easy to measure TSP project results, but it will be difficult to make comparisons with the organization's prior performance because comparable baseline data on prior work are rarely available. To address this problem, the team should identify the data that are available for comparison and then attempt to define pilot program success criteria in terms of the available data. Example data could be measures of resources, costs, or schedules. Also, data on testing times, test defects, customer defect reports, or maintenance costs for existing projects could be used.

In designing these comparative measures, it is important to understand how the data are gathered, reported, and used. For example, time card or effort report data are not generally useful for measuring actual effort on a project. They typically do not include overtime and reflect only where individuals are budgeted rather than the hours actually spent on project tasks. Data on the sizes of previously developed systems can be used to normalize the project cost, schedule, and quality data. This will enable more realistic comparisons of before-and-after performance data.

Another concern involves timing. Evaluation data are usually needed early in the implementation effort, but final pilot project results will not be available until project completion. For projects of less than one year, this is rarely a problem, but when projects take longer, it is often necessary to use interim results. Possible ways to address this issue include using results from interim builds or development cycles or projecting results based on interim data such as cycle estimation accuracy, product quality, or process yields. Other potential benefits to consider are the availability of precise and timely project data and the ability these data provide to identify and correct project problems in time to prevent serious problems for the overall program.

The implementation team then follows the standard TSP launch process to define the transition process, to estimate the work involved, to produce a schedule with key milestones, and to evaluate project risks. As the final step in the implementation team's launch, the members produce a plan presentation and review it with you.

Reviewing the Implementation Plan

Here you will review the TSP implementation team's plan, including the schedule for the key implementation milestones, the cost of the effort, the key risks, and the proposed risk mitigation plans. You should also ask about the criteria and plans for selecting the pilot teams and their managers. Finding the right volunteers is the key to success.

The training plan is also critical, and that plan should give the participants enough advance notice so that they can arrange to handle all of their existing commitments and complete the reading required before the training. The plan for selecting the instructors must also allow them adequate time to prepare for and to deliver the training. This is especially important for the PSP training courses where the instructor must spend several hours each day grading the assignments.

The longer-term coaching plan is also important because the quality of coaching support is critical to project and team performance. For the initial teams, nearly two weeks of coaching support are needed before the launch and two more weeks are needed during and after the launch. Once you have reviewed and approved the implementation plan, the team gets started on implementing its plan. The first step is then to launch the pilot programs. This subject is discussed in Appendix C.

Motivating Participation

Before making any broad announcements of the TSP effort, consider how to motivate participation in TSP implementation. Some early adopters may have already volunteered, and others will follow once you communicate the strategy. The most important group to motivate is the middle managers who traditionally face the greatest risks. To them, the TSP will be seen as a cost and not as an opportunity. While some will recognize the value of the investment, many will be unwilling to commit time or resources because of the schedule and resource pressures of their current projects. Those who do readily agree to participate are probably the early adopters.

The motivational strategy that we consistently have found to be most effective is based on continuous improvement. This strategy, together with examples of how to manage it, is discussed in Appendix E. All of the involved people—the developers, the project and team leaders, and the middle managers—will look for evidence that the concepts are technically sound and that they personally will have some control over the implementation. That message is critical.

Communicating the Idea

After the implementation team has been staffed, the objectives defined, and the plan produced and approved, you are ready to make a broad announcement of the TSP effort. In doing so, there are a few TSP-unique things to consider:

- Connect the TSP and the implementation team's goals and objectives to the corporate vision and standards of excellence. One company had a stated goal of differentiating itself in the marketplace as the highest-quality provider. After evaluating many other software development processes and methods, the company chose the TSP because of its proven high-quality results.

- Describe carefully the purpose of the pilot projects and the expected results. Ensure that the people do not think of the TSP as a management ultimatum or of the TSP pilot projects as unimportant experiments. They must know that management is committed to implementing the TSP and that management needs their help to make it work.

- Be clear about changing the status quo and offer support as a "red tape cutter." An objective of piloting new methods is to find different and better ways of doing the work. Demonstrating your support for trying something new is an important message to give to the early adopters.

BUILDING A STRONG COACHING TEAM

The coaching team is critical to the success of the TSP effort. It is the coaches who guide the managers, team leaders, and teams in using the process properly and in producing truly superior work. They know how to motivate the teams to strive for excellence, and they understand the actions that management should take to ensure the success of the TSP effort. Without a strong coaching team, your effort will not likely start as rapidly as it could, and it may not become self-sustaining.

Identifying the Initial TSP Coaches

For the implementation effort, the change agents must be trained and qualified TSP coaches. While it is usually necessary to retain an external coach from the SEI or from an SEI transition partner to help you get started with the implementation, one of the first steps in the planning should be to identify one or two experienced managers to fill this coaching role. These managers should have development experience, be respected by their peers and senior management, and be early adopters.

At least one of the initial coach candidates should be part of the implementation team and participate in implementation planning. These candidate coaches should then be PSP-trained along with the first of the pilot TSP teams and attend the TSP team leader–training courses. They should then assist the external coach in conducting the initial pilot team launches and guiding and coaching the teams when they start their projects.

As soon thereafter as possible, these coach candidates should take TSP coach training and become qualified as coaches themselves. Then they can gradually take over from the external coaches and, along with any additional internal coaches that are needed, lead, guide, and support the TSP implementation process. The most important point is to identify these coach candidates at the outset so that they can participate in the initial TSP pilot efforts. This will provide them the background and experience to take full advantage of TSP coach training and to rapidly build the skills required to be effective TSP coaches.

The Coach Development Strategy

This coach development strategy is based on experience gained in training insurance agents. In an unpublished study, a large insurance company divided its new sales trainee hires into three groups. The members of group A were given complete sales training and then sent out as salespeople. The members of group B were trained and then assigned to work with experienced salespeople who mentored them for a considerable period. The members of group C were given brief initial training and then sent out on their own as sales trainees; after a couple of months, they were brought back in and given the full sales training course. Over the course of the 20-year study, the group A salespeople did worst, the group B members were next, and the group C members did best. They were more effective at the outset than their peers, and their superior performance persisted for the entire 20-year period of the study.

The conclusion is that early exposure to real-world problems provides a framework that makes the subsequent training relevant and enables the trainees to grow and develop most rapidly. That is why it is important to select your coach candidates as quickly as possible so that they can participate in all of the steps involved in initiating the TSP program. There will be many valuable experiences to be gained, and it would be a waste of time and money for your coach candidates to miss this important learning opportunity.

THE TSP PILOT PROGRAMS

Implementing the TSP involves the steps shown in Figure B.2. Implementation starts with planning for the installation and trial use of the TSP on a few pilot projects. Next, the managers, developers, and other involved participants are trained, and the project teams begin using the TSP, starting with the TSP launch. The teams are then coached and supported until the

Figure B.2 TSP team implementation cycle

projects are concluded. While the plan is being executed, performance data, project results, improvement suggestions, and other information are gathered and evaluated. The implementation approach is then assessed and refined and then repeated on the next project.

During TSP implementation you should also plan to hold regular reviews of progress. This will help to maintain the effort's initial momentum and ensure that it continues to receive the priority needed to succeed. If the implementation team is using the TSP to plan and track its work, similar review formats can be applied to their reviews. In the beginning, use the TSP weekly meeting format to review status. Later, the other meeting formats can be applied. If the team is not using the TSP, these same reviews can be adapted to the team's planning and tracking approach. As noted in Appendices D and E, you should then establish a regular quarterly review program to examine the status of the organization's overall improvement efforts, including the TSP.

Conducting the Pilot Projects

Running the initial pilot projects will be relatively easy once your people are properly prepared. At this point, you should have a TSP implementation plan, a clear statement of the problems to be solved, a description of the success criteria, and initial volunteer teams that are motivated to participate. Then, by following the steps defined in the following section, "Implementing the TSP for a Project Team," you conduct and evaluate the pilot projects.

Evaluating the Pilot Projects

Soon after launching the pilot projects, begin working on how to evaluate the projects against the goals and objectives established during TSP implementation planning (see Figure B.3).

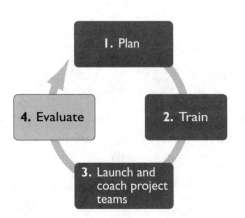

Figure B.3 TSP implementation: evaluate

Evaluation is the last step in the implementation cycle, but you cannot wait until the projects have been completed because you may then discover that some important evaluation criteria were not considered and the needed data are no longer available. Also, as in many organizations, you may find that the results from the first one or two cycles are sufficient and that you wish to accelerate the adoption pace. Organizations often decide to start looking for additional TSP introduction opportunities without waiting for the initial pilot projects to be completed, particularly when these pilot projects are expected to take a year or more to complete.

As TSP implementation gains momentum, you will soon want to start measuring TSP team performance and establishing benchmarks of excellence to use in motivating continuing improvement. To facilitate these later efforts, consider the following list of measures that TSP teams readily provide. To the extent that your existing project measures can produce comparable data, these measures will also help in the pilot program evaluations.

- A comparison of the actual resources expended to the resources planned for a particular project, project cycle, or phase

- A comparison of the actual time required to the planned time for a particular project, project cycle, or phase

- The amount of product produced per development hour compared to that planned (The typical TSP size measure is the number of new and changed LOC in the finished product, but other measures can be used.)

- The sum of the total time spent conducting all reviews and inspections during development compared to the time spent for testing and defect repair from the time the team completes developing the code (code complete) until the end of acceptance testing and compared to the total development time

- The total number of defects found and fixed per thousand lines of new and changed code from code complete through acceptance testing

- A comparison of the percentage of development effort expended from the project's start to code complete to the percentage expended from code complete to initial product shipment

- A comparison of the percentage of the project schedule that was used from the project's start to code complete to the percentage used from code complete to initial product shipment

Two other important evaluation measures are customer satisfaction and employee satisfaction. Your customers will probably not be interested in the engineering methods your teams use, and they will probably not have heard of the TSP, but they will be most interested in cost and schedule predictability, features delivered, post-deployment quality, and operational costs. Unfortunately customer satisfaction feedback data are rarely available in time for a pilot program evaluation. It would then be desirable to get some anecdotal feedback from a few customers if possible.

Employee satisfaction should improve as the TSP teams learn to manage themselves and to work together as cohesive teams. One indication of TSP success is when the pilot project team members recommend the TSP to their peers. Collect such information regularly throughout the project and use it to identify and address TSP implementation problems.

Another indication of employee satisfaction is reduced employee turnover. Softtek found that the turnover of its TSP team members was one-quarter that for the non-TSP team members. The benefits of reduced turnover can be substantial and should be considered whenever the required data are available. Unfortunately, this will probably not be for at least a year after the TSP implementation effort is fully under way.

IMPLEMENTING THE TSP FOR A PROJECT TEAM

As shown in Figure B.4, the process for implementing the TSP for a project team has four steps: planning, training, launching/coaching, and evaluating. With only minor changes, the same process is used for the initial pilot teams and for all subsequent teams.

Planning—Select Project Teams

The first step in planning TSP implementation is project selection. Starting with the right projects is very important. The selection criteria in Table B.3 are based on experience and represent factors that are most likely to lead to early success, such as choosing volunteers or early adopters. As adoption proceeds, these criteria can be relaxed or eliminated.

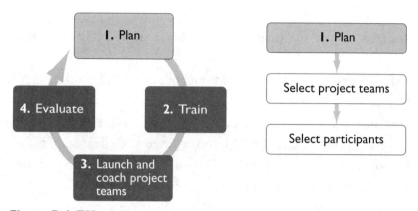

Figure B.4 TSP implementation: planning

Organizations should pilot the TSP on two or three projects to reduce risk. Choosing one pilot project could fail for reasons other than the TSP, for example, if the project were delayed or canceled. Starting more than three pilot projects could also be challenging for your staff and for any external consultants. Identify sufficient candidate projects to ensure having two or three pilot projects after reviewing them against the selection criteria and satisfying the logistics and timing requirements for training the teams and launching the projects.

Table B.3 Pilot Project Selection Criteria

Criteria	Desired Characteristics
Team leaders/ project managers	The most important project selection criterion is that the project manager or team leader be an early adopter and a willing participant.
	He or she should not be volunteered for the pilot project. In surveys of critical success factors at both Intuit and Adobe, the team leader or project manager was identified as the role most likely to influence the project outcome [Sartain 2007].

Table B.3 Pilot Project Selection Criteria (*Continued*)

Criteria	Desired Characteristics
Team members	The second most important criterion is that the project teams be early adopters and the team members be willing participants.
	They should not be volunteered for the pilot project. They should have early adopter characteristics, be opinion leaders, have been successful at implementing new ideas and technologies, and be interested in trying the TSP.
	Teams of people are not likely to have all these characteristics, but the central tendency should be there. Skepticism is normal, but a willingness to learn something new is necessary. If too many people on the team are convinced that TSP won't work, the TSP will probably not work for them.
Importance and relevance	The pilot projects should be important to the business and should represent the types of work or projects that are commonly undertaken.
	Important projects are more likely to proceed and finish. Choosing an important project reduces the risk that the investment in TSP training and support will be lost because of project cancellation or delay.
	A common mistake is to choose an insignificant project for piloting; the idea is to avoid the risk of failure on an important project. These projects make the worst pilots. They often fail or are canceled for other reasons. Even if they are successful, the results are typically viewed as unimportant.
Project type	The best projects for piloting purposes are projects involving new product development or projects that involve enhancements to existing systems.
	Projects with product goals and release dates are the best projects for the standard TSP. Because they have a common goal that the team can share, they provide the best team-building opportunities.
	Pure maintenance projects consisting of fixes to existing systems are suitable if that is a primary type of work for the organization. With such projects, it is usually necessary to define departmental or group goals for team-building purposes. An alternate version of the TSP for Functional Teams (TSPf) is recommended for such projects.

continues

Table B.3 Pilot Project Selection Criteria (*Continued*)

Criteria	Desired Characteristics
Project development phase	TSP implementation can begin at any phase, any development iteration, or any cycle, starting with requirements development through to implementation.
	If development has been completed and only testing remains, however, it is too late to achieve much benefit from the TSP.
Project team size	From 5 to 15 team members is ideal.
	Team members are working members of the team who are assigned work during the launch and participate in the team's weekly status meetings. Team composition may include members from other groups, but they must be working members with detailed plans, team member roles, and assigned tasks to qualify as TSP team members.
	The standard TSP process supports teams with from 2 to 20 members. Larger projects are implemented as teams of teams using the TSP-MultiTeam process that can support up to a few hundred developers.
Very large multi-team projects	Piloting the TSP on one or more teams of a very large multi-team project has been very successful. However, differences in the processes, project management styles, schedule commitments, and dependencies among the pilot teams and the rest of the teams will require some management adjustments.
	For example, the TSP is often introduced with those teams that are developing product features that are late in the development cycle and are among the last groups to start system testing. However, because of their higher product quality, these TSP projects are typically the first ones to finish system testing. Management must consider how to handle this or similar situations.
Single-site versus multi-site projects	Colocated, single-site project teams are easier to train and launch than teams from multiple sites. Multi-site teams can also make good pilot projects, but the logistics are more challenging. See Appendix C for more information on such projects.

Table B.3 Pilot Project Selection Criteria (*Continued*)

Criteria	Desired Characteristics
Project duration	Projects lasting from about 3 months to 18 months are ideal.
	The TSP supports projects of almost any duration, but projects lasting less than a few months may not provide enough data for evaluation. Projects of longer than 18 months' duration may not allow for a timely evaluation of pilot results. Projects that are too long can work if the project has interim versions or releases that can satisfy the pilot project evaluation criteria.
Product characteristics	Any software or software-intensive product will support the pilot project objectives.
	Products that involve other engineering disciplines—hardware, systems engineering, etc.—will have the same schedule challenges as multi-team projects, but the TSP team's schedule may not align with that of the other groups. Experience has shown that in most such instances, the TSP teams will deliver on the dates to which they commit and the other teams will not.
	The TSP has now been used with other engineering disciplines, but until more specific process support is available for these disciplines, the pilot projects should be restricted to the software engineering aspects of projects.
Languages, environments, operating systems, platforms	The TSP is independent of the languages, environments, operating systems, and platforms used by the projects. It has been piloted on many projects where one or more of the languages, environments, operating systems, or platforms used were new to the team.
	The only consideration for the pilot projects would be to incorporate an early calibration milestone in the team's plans to evaluate the effect of a new or different development context on the team's estimating accuracy.
Compatibility	Compatibility with existing processes and methods should not be a concern. The reason is that as part of the launch process, TSP teams customize the process they will use to the specific needs of the team, the project, and their working environment.

continues

Table B.3 Pilot Project Selection Criteria (*Continued*)

Criteria	Desired Characteristics
Tool support	The TSP has unique project management tool requirements, and a tool designed to support the TSP will be necessary. Tools are currently available from the Software Engineering Institute and from SourceForge.

Planning—Select Participants

After selecting the projects, identify the managers, team members, and other staff who will be involved in the pilot projects so that a training plan can be prepared. For a successful implementation, the project team, the team's manager(s), and their managers up the chain to the sponsoring executive need to complete the appropriate training courses. For managers, the objective is that each pilot project have a connected chain of sponsorship from the sponsoring manager down to the project manager or team leader. This is accomplished by providing training for each manager and then working with these managers to address issues, provide support, establish goals and objectives for the pilot, and create incentives. Management support is vital for success, especially from the direct manager of the project or the team leader. If a manager seems unable or unwilling to support the pilot, it may be necessary to create a temporary reporting chain that bypasses that manager or to select another project.

Sponsorship is also required from the managers of such groups as testing, quality assurance, technical support, or other engineering teams that are working on the same project. It may not be possible to get 100% support from all of these managers, but you should make clear that your intent is to have a fair evaluation and a successful pilot program.

Team members must also be selected for the pilot projects. Ideally, all the team members will be volunteers and early adopters who are eager to try the TSP and PSP. There are normally some skeptics among the team members, and these skeptics will need to better understand how TSP and PSP will affect them and their projects. The PSP training and the TSP launch should address most of their concerns, and with proper coaching, most of the rest of their concerns will be addressed during the first few weeks of using the TSP.

Informal estimates made by managers of organizations that are using the TSP suggest that a small percentage of software developers, approximately 5%, are not able to adapt to the TSP's self-directed team management style. With proper coaching and support from their team members and manager, many will work through this issue. However, there will still be a few developers who won't be convinced, even when the team's performance or their own performance improves. When there is a choice, it is best to avoid having a hopeless skeptic on a team. The behavior of such a person can be disruptive and can consume management and coaching resources. Remember, the purpose of the pilot projects is to see what works for the majority of the developers. Disruptive or uncooperative team members will usually damage overall team performance and result in unsuccessful pilot projects. When such members are identified, they should be removed from their teams as quickly as possible.

TRAINING

Effective training is an investment, not a cost, and it produces near-term, measurable benefits that connect to business objectives. The TSP training includes knowledge transfer, but it is primarily oriented toward skill building and behavioral change. The courses include hands-on individual and group work that connects directly to the participants' roles and responsibilities in the TSP process. The training is put to use immediately during the TSP launch so that students don't have to wait to use what they have learned. Team performance then improves quickly, recovering the cost of training within a few weeks or months. The cost of not training, or using training shortcuts, is typically a failure to achieve the potential benefits of the TSP, often resulting in outright project failure.

As shown in Figure B.5 and described in Table B.4, TSP training addresses four different audiences: executives and senior managers, project managers and team leaders, software developers who are members of the development team, and other team members who don't have software development skills or responsibilities. Training proceeds top-down; executives and senior managers are trained first, then project managers and team leaders, and then the software developers and other team members. This approach builds top-down support. The senior managers understand what is being asked of their direct reports and the development teams, and the project managers and team leaders understand their roles and how TSP will affect the development teams. Building support and understanding from the top down reduces risk and resistance to change.

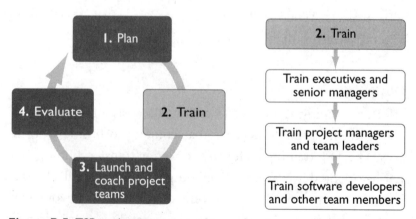

Figure B.5 TSP implementation: training

Table B.4 TSP and PSP Courses

Course or Seminar	Description
TSP Executive Strategy Seminar	A one-day seminar for executives and senior managers that introduces high-level concepts, benefits, business value, and the strategy for implementing the TSP
Leading Development Teams	A three-day training course for project managers and middle managers that introduces the concepts needed to lead self-directed teams
PSP Fundamentals	A five-day training course for software developers that introduces PSP and TSP using lectures and hands-on exercises where developers use the PSP to develop small software programs
PSP Advanced	An optional five-day training course for software developers that introduces advanced PSP and TSP concepts
TSP Team Member Training	A three-day training course for the team members who do not have software development skills and will not be writing software; examples are hardware engineers, business analysts, testing staff, and technical writers

The PSP training for developers is a critically important element of the overall training. The PSP training introduces fundamental concepts and behaviors that are required for a self-directed software team to succeed. These are concepts and behaviors that are not introduced in computer science and software engineering education. Without these behaviors it is nearly impossible to create a disciplined, measured, and self-managed team. The PSP training experience transforms the developers, and with proper instruction they learn vitally important lessons from the class programming assignments. Using progressively more advanced processes, they learn the value of following a personal process, having and using data, making personal plans, estimating, and managing product quality. Having seen the

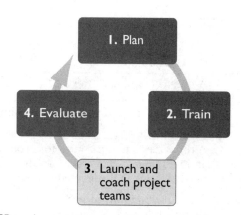

Figure B.6 TSP implementation: launching and coaching project teams

value of personal discipline during training, they are more willing to apply these concepts in practice. This PSP course and the TSP coaching model establish the conditions required for effective TSP teamwork.

As shown in Figure B.6, after training is completed, the project teams are ready to begin using the TSP. The TSP launch process is the first part of the TSP that you, your management team, and the development teams will experience. This is where these teams first begin to use TSP and to work with a TSP coach.

THE TSP LAUNCH PROCESS

The TSP launch process is shown in Figure B.7, and it combines on-the-job training with planning, estimating, and team building. It is the team's initial exposure to TSP coaching and the team members' first chance to begin acting like a self-directed team. The team will learn and use the TSP planning processes, methods, measures, and tools. During the launch the TSP coach will prepare them to use the TSP management and development processes and to integrate the TSP with their existing organizational processes and methods.

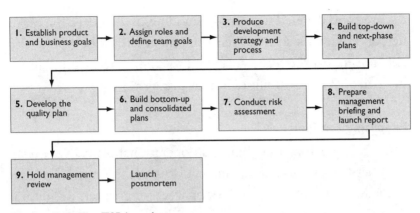

Figure B.7 The TSP launch process

The TSP launch process is a series of nine meetings followed by a launch postmortem. The project manager or team leader, the team, and the TSP coach participate in all nine meetings and the postmortem. The TSP coach plans, leads, and facilitates the launch. The other participants are assigned specific roles and responsibilities during the launch. Managers and observers are allowed only in launch meetings 1 and 9.

A business manager or product manager and a customer or customer representative must participate in meeting 1 and in meeting 9. In meeting 1 they present the business and product goals and objectives to the team. In meeting 9 the roles are reversed and the team presents its plans back to management. Then they negotiate. The business manager and product manager roles can be combined. Neither role is assigned to the project manager or team leader. These roles are typically the responsibility of the next level of management or above.

Peter Drucker said, "Unless commitment is made, there are only promises and hopes; but no plans" [Drucker 1974]. You need not know all the details of the launch, but you must understand how team commitment is achieved during the launch. The order and content of the launch meetings are designed to build a shared and detailed team understanding of the goals, the product, and the work so that each team member will be willing and able to support the team's plan and to commit to meeting his or her personal responsibilities in that plan.

Executing the Plan

The TSP launch process builds an operational plan: Every team member knows what he or she will be working on the day after the launch and for several days or weeks thereafter. As long as the team continues to maintain and follow its plan, the members will know what to do every day, and they will do their work with efficiency and without hesitation or delay.

Each team member has a TSP tool that contains his or her personal plan, including all the task and work product assignments, the risks and goals to track, the support mechanisms for gathering data while he or she works, and the means to track personal and team status. The tools make it easy to follow the plan, to gather data, and to track progress. Every week the team members review their tasks, order them by priority, and determine what they must do to complete their commitments for each week. Each day, they select a task from those planned for the week and click a button to start and stop time tracking. When they complete a task, they mark it as done. If they found and fixed defects while performing a task, they record these defects in a defect log. When they finish a work product, they measure and record its size.

Tracking the Plan

During the week, each team member reviews the status of his or her plan and assesses progress (earned value), resources used, estimation accuracy, and quality. The continuous feedback on progress against personal plans helps to keep each team member focused on the highest-priority current tasks. At any time, team members can review progress indicators for the week and for the cycle, including earned value, planned versus actual effort, plan growth, work in progress, process and product quality indicators, and many other indicators of progress or pending problems.

Each week the team members' plans are consolidated to produce a team-wide view of progress for the team's weekly meeting. Before the meeting, the role managers review the consolidated team plan from the perspective of their individual roles and prepare to report what they found at the weekly meeting. Among the topics reviewed are the items shown in Table B.5.

Table B.5 TSP Weekly Meeting Topics

Role Manager	Review Topic
Planning manager	Data quality
	Milestones and work completed last week
	Milestones and work planned for this week
	Schedule status and risk
	Resource status and risk
Process manager	Process fidelity
	Process improvement suggestions
	Defect prevention actions
Quality manager and test manager	Data quality
	Results of reviews, inspections, or tests completed last week
	Reviews, inspections, and tests planned for this week
	Product quality indicators and risks
Design manager, implementation manager, and support manager	Process fidelity
	Status of outstanding design, implementation, or support issues or risks
	Component postmortems (a postmortem on completed subsystems, components, modules, etc.)

The team leader, team members, and the team's TSP coach attend the weekly meeting. During the meeting each role manager reports on his or her findings, and each team member reports progress against the plan. These meetings also provide an opportunity for the team to coordinate work, make minor plan adjustments, and communicate dependencies or request assistance.

When projects start to slip their schedules, the problems first show up as small one- or two-day schedule slips. By precisely tracking status and promptly identifying such problems, teams can quickly address them while they are easy to fix.

The Cycle Postmortem

At the end of each project cycle, the team holds a cycle postmortem where each role manager reviews team performance from his or her perspective, and the members assess their personal and team performance. During the cycle postmortem the coach and team leader also compare team performance with the team's goals and plans and identify improvement goals for the next cycle or project. The team also assembles the cycle and project-to-date data for retention in the project file.

MANAGEMENT'S ROLE IN THE TSP PROCESS

Management is key to a successful TSP implementation. Management sets the organization's goals, monitors the work, motivates and rewards the people, and maintains the sense of urgency that keeps the organization energized. The TSP provides several ways to accomplish these ends. Among the most important of these ends is the point emphasized in Chapter 5: the need to align the workers' and managers' goals. For TSP teams, this process starts with the TSP project launch, and it is important that the managers understand how to fulfill their roles in this launch process.

Launch Meeting 1

In the first meeting of the TSP launch, management communicates its expectations for the project to the team. They tell the team what they want, including the business and product objectives; the definition of a fully and minimally successful result; schedule, budget, and resource constraints; and customer and competitive issues. This meeting sets the tone for both the launch and the project, so it is important that each manager be adequately prepared to fulfill his or her role. When teams understand management's objectives, they are more likely to devise plans that lead to successful business and technical outcomes. In making the plan, the team and all its members make a commitment. For them, this is a serious undertaking, and they will be spending many months of their time and energy striving to accomplish this plan. Without proper management preparation, these teams will not fully understand management's needs, and they will then be unlikely to do a superior job. That is why adequate management preparation for launch meeting 1 is so important.

The initial TSP pilot projects are also intended to guide the implementation and evaluation of the TSP. When preparing for meeting 1, managers should also consider this purpose and stress the importance of team ownership of the plan and the process, of gathering data, of self-management, and above all of doing quality work. The managers should work with the TSP coach to define quality objectives that can be measured and tracked throughout the project and then incorporate these objectives into the meeting 1 presentation.

Meeting 1 will probably take longer than expected. The team may ask more questions than anticipated or the product briefing could take longer than planned. Managers should keep their schedules flexible so that they can complete the meeting and answer all of the team's questions. The team cannot conduct a fully successful project or produce a superior product unless launch meeting 1 fully addresses all of the team's and management's relevant issues and concerns.

Launch Meetings 2 through 8

Meetings 2 through 8 will normally proceed without any management involvement, but management may be asked to clarify some issues. If the project goals do not appear to be achievable, the TSP coach and the team leader will seek management guidance on what to do. It is also normal for team members to have disagreements during the launch. This is because the launch process makes the team's goals and plans explicit, exposes assumptions, and builds a shared understanding among the team members. This cannot be achieved without surfacing differences of opinion. Management should not get involved in these discussions. If their help is needed, the TSP coach and the team leader will ask for it.

Launch Meeting 9—The Plan Presentation

Meeting 9 is the inverse of meeting 1. Here, the team makes the presentation and management asks the questions. This meeting will likely be quite different from plan reviews that managers have previously attended. To prepare for this meeting, managers should remember that they chose to pilot the TSP because, as in most software organizations, most of their software projects have been late or over budget or failed to deliver the promised functionality. According to the Standish Group's *Chaos Reports* for the past decade, only about one-third of all projects were able to meet all of their cost, schedule, and functional commitments. The other two-thirds were probably late the day they started. When did you find out that they were going to be late?

Was it at the beginning or near the end of the project when it was too late to recover? When would you like to know?

During the TSP launch, most teams discover that they can't build the product with the resources provided and in the time requested. When this is the case, the TSP launch process has teams build alternative plans based on the guidelines and objectives that management provided in meeting 1. Even if the project initially appeared to be feasible, expect to see alternative plans and be prepared to accept a plan that produces a realistic if not fully successful outcome.

The team's plan briefing should include a comparison of management's goals with the planned commitments. This comparison should clarify where the planned cost, schedule, resources, or functionality differ from your definition of a fully successful result. The briefing should also include the principal products produced, key milestones, key risks, the resources required, estimates of the gross size of the product, the overall schedule, and a quality plan. The briefing should provide all the information you need to select and approve from among the main and alternate plans. It should also include a schedule of milestones and deliverables to be used for project tracking.

Evaluating the Team's Plan

The team's briefing should be based on the team's plan. Managers do not need to review this plan in detail, but they must determine that it is a sound plan and that the team is fully committed to meeting it. In conducting this review, the questions to consider are given in Table B.6. Most of the questions will probably be answered by the team leader or by one or more of the TSP role managers. By asking both the team leader and some of the team members to answer their questions, managers can get insight into the team's level of ownership of and commitment to the plan.

Table B.6 Guidelines for the Launch Management Review Meeting

Question	Whom to Ask	Evaluating the Response
Does the plan include all of the work necessary to produce the planned deliverables?	Team leader Design manager Implementation manager	It should include all of the work promised in the plan briefing, although some items could be deferred to subsequent releases.
Is the near-term plan sufficiently detailed?	Team leader Planning manager	The near-term plan should have two to three tasks per team member per week.
Were size estimates made? What is the basis for these estimates?	Team leader Design manager Implementation manager	Typically size estimates are made, and they are based on an analysis of the size of similar products or components. Size estimates are needed for product work. Meetings, support, or services tasks may require direct effort estimates.
Are the tasks in the plan based on the team's defined processes?	Team leader Process manager	A defined process should be used as a template for all of the products and most of the work in the plan. Some work of a one-time or random nature can be planned directly as tasks.
What is the basis for the effort estimates for the tasks in the plan?	Team leader Planning manager	Effort estimates should be based on available data and/or made by the individuals who are assigned to the work. What specific data did the team use for making its estimates?

Table B.6 Guidelines for the Launch Management Review Meeting (*Continued*)

What is the average weekly resource availability estimate for the near-term plan? How were these estimates made? Are these estimates realistic?	Team leader Planning manager All team members	The average weekly hours for the team should be near 17 to 18 hours per full-time team member. New teams typically start with lower rates but gradually improve. Resource availability for the near term should be based on the estimates made by each individual team member. Each team member should agree that the estimates are realistic.
Is the team planning for a high-quality product? Does the quality plan include inspections and reviews for all products? What is the minimum size for an inspection team? What is the planned average review rate for software components? What is the planned pre-system-test yield?	Team leader Quality manager	Ask both the team leader and the quality manager for their views. All products should be reviewed by the producer and inspected by the team. The minimum size should be the producer plus two inspectors. The average review rate for software components should be between 100 and 200 new and changed LOC per hour. Faster reviews mean poorer-quality products. The planned pre-system-test yield should be 98% or higher.
Is this a plan that you can commit to meeting?	All team members Team leader	The team leader and all team members must agree.

Assessing Plan Feasibility

Projects are more likely to meet their objectives when the plans and the work are divided into manageable parts. The TSP uses the iterative or cyclic development strategy shown in Figures B.8 and B.9 to divide the overall plan into a series of cycles. Each of the cycles starts with a team launch or relaunch and ends with a postmortem. Between the launch/relaunch and the postmortem the team manages its work task by task, day by day, and week by week using structured weekly meetings.

The product development timeline is divided into separate releases, and each release is further divided into cycles or iterations. The cycles are not required to have fixed lengths, but they are typically a few weeks to a few months in duration. A cycle may represent all or part of a development phase, for example, design and develop one or more product features or compo-

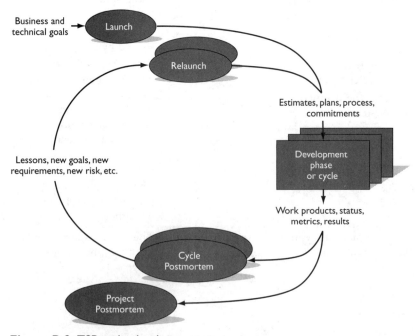

Figure B.8 TSP cyclic development strategy

nents. Each cycle has a clear outcome and a manageable duration. If the project plan includes multiple customer releases,
each release often includes one or more TSP cycles.

The product development timeline is bounded by a TSP
launch and a TSP project postmortem. Each cycle is also started
with a TSP launch or relaunch. If more than one project team is
using the TSP on the same product development timeline, the
initial TSP launch will include all teams. Subsequent cycle
relaunches do not have to be held at the same time but must be
coordinated to manage any inter-team dependencies.

This approach provides maximum flexibility for matching the
development strategy with the technical work. Together, management and the team(s) determine how to divide the work into
manageable segments based on business and technical needs.

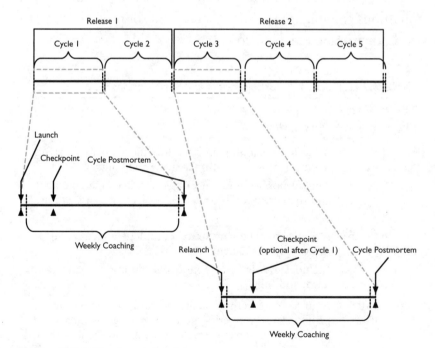

Figure B.9 TSP release planning

Management Reporting

Once a project is under way, management will want the TSP coach and the project manager or team leader to conduct periodic project status report meetings. These status meetings should review the actions planned during the prior status review, clearly describe project status, identify risks and key issues, outline the accomplishments planned prior to the next status review, and review and agree on action commitments. The reviews also provide an opportunity for management to motivate the team, to reinforce the desired team behaviors, and to compliment the team members for what they have accomplished.

The TSP provides four report formats for project status reporting: a period status report, a customer status report, a cycle postmortem, and a project postmortem. These TSP materials are described in Table B.7; the TSP coach can answer any questions you might have about these items or provide examples and other desired information.

Table B.7 TSP Status Reporting Scripts and Specifications

TSP Process Element	Description
Script STATUS	A guide to planning and conducting the periodic TSP management and customer status meetings
	The purpose of these meetings is to keep management and the customer informed of project progress, status, and risks.
Specification STATUS	A guide to making accurate, complete, concise, and informative management status reports
	Includes four levels of reporting: minimum, basic, standard, and full
Script TSP Postmortem	A guide to gathering, recording, and analyzing cycle and project data, comparing performance against goals and plans, and identifying areas where improvement is needed
Specification TSP Project Notebook	A high-level reference to the information and data prepared and gathered by the project team

Status Review Issues

Project managers typically do not look forward to project status review meetings with their management. The principal reason is that they are uneasy because they do not know their project status or they know that the project is in trouble. Preparing for a status review can also take a lot of the manager's and the team's time. However, with its detailed plans, metrics, and daily and weekly tracking, the TSP's self-directed team management style substantially addresses these concerns. Nearly all of the information required for the status reports is routinely prepared for each of the team's weekly meetings, and it need only be summarized for presentation to management. If the team's status is a surprise to the team, the team leader, or the TSP coach, you should consider getting external support, especially if the TSP coach or team leader has not already brought these issues to your attention.

There are six rules to follow during TSP status meetings:

1. Management must respect the privacy of individual team members' data. While it may occasionally be obvious who is responsible for a schedule delay or a product quality problem, managers must never single out such individuals.

2. Managers should recognize that a project that doesn't have accurate and detailed data can't be compared to one that does. The project without data is like a sports team that does not know the score. It will likely report that it is on schedule until it gets near a major milestone or delivery date.

3. Managers should treat the team like a team. They should not criticize or praise the team leader or any team member for problems or successes. They should hold the entire team accountable for addressing its problems and for coming back with answers and problem solutions.

4. Managers should reward teams for having and using data. They may not always like the picture the data paint, but if the team isn't recording and using data, the TSP will not work.

5. Managers must not overreact. TSP teams generally have a good understanding of their status, but they are not always on schedule, especially at the beginning of a pilot project. Think of the project like a sporting match; the team may fall behind, but in the early phases there is time for it to catch up. The data and lessons learned from each week and cycle will help the team find solutions to its own problems. The manager's job is to work with the TSP coach and the team leader to ensure that they solve their own problems.

6. Managers should recognize quality work. Superior work looks easy, so managers must focus on the team's performance and the quality of its work and not just on how hard the team worked. Hard work should be rewarded when it is productive but not when it is done to recover from the excessive test time needed to fix problems the team itself created.

During any TSP review meeting, managers should be alert to a few critical success factors. If they see issues in these areas, they should wait until after the meeting and discuss them with the TSP coach or the team leader as appropriate.

- Data quality: If the quality of the data gathered by the team is poor, TSP's self-directed team management concepts will not work. Discuss this with the TSP coach.

- Acting like a team: Teamwork is a critical success factor for the TSP. The members of the team, including the team leader, must support each other and act like a team. If managers see teamwork issues, they should discuss them with the TSP coach. A particularly sensitive issue here concerns the presence of an uncooperative or disruptive team member.

- Leadership issues: Leadership is most important. If the team leader is not motivating the team, maintaining appropriate standards, and building team cohesion, performance will suffer. Managers should be sensitive to potential leadership problems and check with the coach on the team leader's performance.

- Coaching quality: Coaching is a critical success factor for TSP. If the coach is not properly supporting the team, especially the pilot project teams, the TSP implementation could fail. Managers should discuss this with the team leader and then the coach. The organization may need external support for this issue.

- Management issues: If the existing policy, culture, or bureaucracy appears to be in the way, managers should discuss the issue with the TSP coach or team leader and support the team by removing such barriers.

SUMMARY

The strategy for implementing the TSP is based on the experiences, both good and bad, of many organizations. Success with this first step is important because a poorly implemented pilot program will make it difficult to convince later groups to try the TSP. A successful first effort will build internal support for moving past the early adopters to the early majority. Focusing on a few pilot projects will also help to ensure that the initial efforts have sufficient resources and support. The measured results and performance benefits that are typical with TSP will then help to build the momentum needed to accelerate the overall effort and to broaden it to cover the entire organization.

There are many things to consider in TSP implementation, but the basic steps are reasonably straightforward. First, staff an implementation team, train them, and if possible include an experienced external consultant. Develop a plan around the key steps: planning, goal setting, and team selection. Then train, launch, and coach the teams. Finally, evaluate the pilot results and then execute the overall implementation plan. If there are problems, find outside help from the growing community of TSP practitioners or from the Software Engineering Institute.

REFERENCES

[Conner 1992] Daryl Conner, *Managing at the Speed of Change* (New York: Random House, 1992).

[Drucker 1974] Peter F. Drucker, *Management: Tasks, Responsibilities, Practices* (New York: Harper & Row, 1974).

[Galbraith 1971] John Kenneth Galbraith, *A Contemporary Guide to Economics, Peace, and Laughter* (Boston, MA: Houghton Mifflin Company, 1971).

[Rogers 2003] Everett M. Rogers, *Diffusion of Innovation* (New York: Free Press, 2003).

[Sartain 2007] J. Sartain, "Critical Success Factors for TSP/PSP Adoption in a Consumer Software Company," European Software Engineering Process Group Conference, Amsterdam, sponsored by the Software Engineering Institute, the Netherlands, June 12–15, 2007.

Appendix C

Expanding TSP Use

This appendix describes how to broaden the use of the TSP across your organization. As shown in Figure C.1, it follows Appendix B, which describes how to get started with the TSP, and it precedes Appendices D and E, which address how to use the TSP in project, program, and organizational management.

At this point in your implementation process, you presumably recognize the benefits of using the TSP and are ready to proceed with a broad implementation effort. Because there is substantial available material on the TSP, however, this appendix will concentrate on the unique issues of implementing the TSP in an organization and refer you to other published sources for more general information about the TSP. The following topics are covered in this appendix:

- The overall implementation strategy
- The overall rollout plan

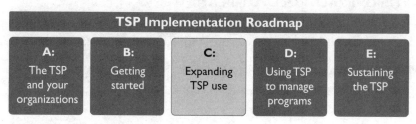

Figure C.1 Roadmap to the appendices

- Building local sponsorship
- Developing the local implementation plan
- Building coaching capability
- Other capability requirements
- When and where to use the TSP

THE OVERALL IMPLEMENTATION STRATEGY

The TSP is implemented with a combined top-down and bottom-up strategy. That is, the first step is to get top-level executive support and to produce an overall organizational plan. Then you start actual implementation at the bottom level with individual TSP teams. The first step in this process is to develop the organization's overall implementation plan and to get that plan approved by the senior executive sponsor. This first step was covered in Appendix B.

The next step is to produce a rollout plan and to select the part or parts of the organization with which to implement it. It is best to work with the senior managers in the part of the organization selected for initial TSP implementation and to get their sponsorship. Then, with their support, develop a local implementation plan. The local implementation plan should also follow the bottom-up team-based implementation strategy already described in Appendix B for the pilot teams.

THE OVERALL ROLLOUT PLAN

The first step in the rollout effort is for the overall corporate implementation team to develop the rollout plan for broad TSP introduction. This plan should be designed to produce the following four conditions in the organization:

1. Every part of the organization is using the TSP process and producing superior work. To do this, the TSP must be properly introduced and supported in all parts of the organization.

2. The initial implementation groups are successful and they are vocal supporters of the overall TSP rollout program. This is required to build and sustain the energy and momentum needed for successful TSP implementation.

3. The organization has the internal capability to ensure that the TSP is used properly and effectively.

4. The top executives continue to support the TSP implementation program and it is self-sustaining. This topic is discussed in Appendix E.

In developing the rollout plan to meet these objectives, you must address three issues:

1. Overcoming resistance to change

2. Building internal capability

3. Maintaining priority

Overcoming Resistance

As described in Appendix A, resistance to change is normal and natural, and you must not view it as obstructionism. The key to overcoming resistance is to address it rationally. Acknowledge people's concerns, and logically and factually address every one. Some people, particularly the early adopters, will accept logical arguments and references to other people's successes. Most, however, will adopt a show-me attitude, and many will be unwilling to change until they have either tried the change for themselves or are forced to change. There are two kinds of resistance to consider: internal and external.

Overcoming Internal Resistance

To address resistance within the organization, start by discussing the rollout strategy with the involved executives and senior managers. While doing so, identify the early adopters and, wherever possible, select the initial implementation groups from this set. Then, when these initial groups have positive results, use them as references in selling the early majority. As successes accumulate, the change program will gain momentum and internal resistance to change will gradually dissipate.

Overcoming External Resistance

External resistance generally comes from three sources: from suppliers, from partners, and from customers. If the suppliers are providing professionals to fill temporary team needs, you will likely face problems like those Microsoft encountered in India. The company found that temporary personnel who were not trained were not fully effective on TSP teams and that it was too expensive to pay for them while they were being trained. Microsoft's managers addressed this problem in two ways. First, they initially agreed to have the contractors attend PSP training with the Microsoft team members, but they would not pay for their time while doing so. Second, they announced that henceforth they would give preference to contractors who had PSP-trained staff.

For suppliers who develop products for you, the question of TSP use is best addressed during the acquisition phase. Then, when the supplier agrees to use the TSP, insist that this agreement be included in the contractual provisions and that their proper use of the TSP be independently verified. One way to do this would be with the SEI's TSP Organization Evaluation and Certification (TSP-OEC) process, described in Appendix E.

For organizations with which you are partnering on a larger program, you will generally have limited leverage. The most effective strategy in these cases is to treat these groups in much the same way as the groups within your organization and start by convincing their senior management. Also, if the work is likely to involve considerable interaction among teams from several internal and external organizations, a larger TSP multi-team process would likely be most effective. It is usually a good idea to tell the overall program customer about these discussions.

Overcoming Customer Resistance

This is the most challenging kind of resistance, and it is best addressed at the earliest possible time. If you are planning to introduce the TSP on a contract that is just beginning, start at the customer's most-senior management level and treat the customer resistance problem much like resistance from an internal group. Have the senior managers participate with your senior managers in a TSP executive seminar, and have the managers attend TSP management training along with your managers. This will provide these managers with the knowledge needed to monitor the TSP work, and it will start building the trusting relationships needed to cooperatively manage a multi-organization team of knowledge workers. Then, with a basic level of trust established, have the customer participate in meetings 1 and 9 of the TSP team's launch.

Building Internal Capability

When introducing any new method or practice into an organization, you must necessarily start with a limited foundation of knowledgeable and skilled people. In fact, most organizations that have introduced the TSP started with no internal PSP or TSP skills and had to retain external support to get under way. The skilled people who are most critical to TSP success are team leaders and coaches.

Because a skilled team leader is required for every TSP team, you might view developing team leader skills as the higher priority. This would be a mistake, however, because team leaders, after being trained, focus their efforts on building products. Conversely, coaches typically support multiple teams, and once they have been trained and qualified, they focus their efforts on developing people. This means that the coaches are force multipliers; one coach can train and develop many skilled and capable developers, managers, and team leaders. Therefore, the first priority in building internal skills should be training and qualifying internal TSP coaches.

Initially, because most TSP coaches are also qualified as TSP instructors, the internal coaches can act as instructors for the various PSP and TSP courses. However, as the demand for coaching and training increases, you will need to either qualify some internal PSP and TSP instructors or retain external ones. The coach and instructor development strategies are discussed further in later sections of this appendix.

Maintaining Priority

The priority issue is critical, particularly at the beginning of the TSP introduction effort. Unless a high priority is sustained, the energy and enthusiasm behind the effort will gradually wane, and momentum will be lost. While the TSP users themselves will be enthusiastic supporters, they will be busy with their projects and not have the time to sell the program to others. Therefore, without some central push, the local managers will often delay training their people or argue that this is the wrong time to introduce the TSP into their projects. This is nonsense, however, because the TSP can be introduced at almost any time during a project, and the earlier the better.

The TSP can be effective during the requirements phase, in design, and during implementation. However, we do not recommend introducing the TSP during final test. Another common delaying tactic is for management to say that they must wait for the end of a project phase to introduce the TSP. However, on real projects, no phase is ever really completed until final testing, and often not even then. Requirements typically change all the way through development and often after final delivery, design is generally in flux even through final testing, and implementation is necessarily involved in changes and fixes until the project ends.

An argument to wait until some phase is completed is, therefore, just a delaying tactic. An effective counter to these issues is an aggressive implementation plan coupled with regular progress reviews. Hold these reviews every week or two at the beginning, and if a senior manager would like to attend one of them, that would be even better. In any event, document the results of the review with a clear statement of any resulting action items, who is responsible for the action, and the due date.

Copy the executive sponsors on these reports and work with their offices to have them send the implementing managers short congratulatory notes for any major accomplishments or brief questions about problems and forthcoming actions. Just a modest show of continuing executive interest is usually sufficient to sustain the priority for the TSP introduction program.

BUILDING LOCAL SPONSORSHIP

Sponsorship is critical, and the principal objective of the first nine chapters and of Appendix A of this book was to enlist senior management as sponsors of the TSP introduction effort. As part of building sponsorship, a TSP Executive Seminar will have been given for the senior corporate executives. The next step is to broaden TSP use to other possibly remote parts of the organization. One or two of the senior executives of the first of these local groups to implement the TSP should have been invited to the initial executive seminar. If so, you should already have their support and be ready to obtain the support of the rest of the local management team.

If the local organization is large and several key executives and senior managers did not attend the senior-level seminar, another TSP Executive Seminar should be conducted for them. Then start the implementation effort by training the involved local managers and the members of their initial TSP teams. Following this, launch the first local TSP teams and proceed with the rest of the implementation plan. The key is to have the support of all of the organization's departmental and program managers and to make sure that the entire organization is aware of senior management's support.

It is important that everyone know what is being done before rumors start and people grow concerned about what is being planned for them. They should be informed generally about the overall effort and told that a detailed plan is being developed and that they will be informed about their role as soon as the plan is available. Also, and particularly for large organizations, once the plan is completed, discuss its details in an all-hands meeting.

In this meeting, it would be helpful to have one or two of the team leaders and some team members from the initial pilot projects attend and describe their experiences with the TSP and why they recommend that this group use it. If this communication is properly handled, several local project teams should volunteer to use the TSP for their projects. At that point, resistance to change should largely disappear, and as long as management priority is sustained, the overall implementation program should proceed relatively smoothly.

DEVELOPING THE LOCAL IMPLEMENTATION PLAN

When developing the local implementation plan, make sure that all of the involved groups are kept informed. However, the planning group itself should be kept relatively small and should consist entirely of people who either have attended a TSP Executive Seminar or otherwise have been TSP-trained and support the effort. You do not want doubters or skeptics on the planning team. It would also be helpful to include one or more members who were involved in the initial TSP pilot effort, are familiar with the time and resources required for the various actions, and understand the principal issues encountered and how they were addressed.

The planning work should follow the TSP team launch process and be coached by a qualified TSP coach. Representatives of all the involved groups should also be invited to attend launch meetings 1 and 9. When developing this plan, the planning group should consider the most common TSP adoption strategies and their pros and cons:

- Implement the TSP one department at a time.
  - Pro: It minimizes the need for management support and training.
  - Con: It delays broader exposure to and understanding of the TSP.
- Implement by one major program at a time.
  - Pro: It accelerates adoption by the program and will likely result in early and substantial benefits for that program.
  - Con: It maximizes the impact on the program and will likely require training all of the managers in the entire organization who are involved in the program.

- Implement the TSP by volunteer groups.

  - Pro: It maximizes the likelihood of early and substantial successes, and it will broaden exposure to the TSP.

  - Con: Assuming that the volunteers come from many parts of the organization, it requires that most of the organization's middle and senior managers be TSP-trained.

The key in selecting the implementation strategy is to ensure that all of the managers in the management chain above every TSP team are TSP-trained before their teams are launched.

Once the plan is approved and implementation starts, the tracking and reporting strategy should follow the approach outlined in earlier paragraphs on maintaining priority.

BUILDING COACHING CAPABILITY

The principal capability required for a successful TSP implementation program is a strong team of internal coaches. While you will almost certainly use external coaches to get started, and you will likely continue to use them to complement the internal staff, local coaches are necessary to provide the level of support that teams need to perform at their best and to continue improving their capabilities.

The importance of coaching and the roles and responsibilities of TSP coaches are covered in the book *TSP: Coaching Development Teams*, so these topics are not discussed here [Humphrey 2006a]. The focus here is on the recommended strategy for building and maintaining a coaching capability and the issues and challenges involved in doing so.

The strategy for building an internal coaching capability has five key elements, and they are all important:

1. Make coaching capability a high priority.

2. Define the coaching career path.

3. Establish a coach candidate identification program.

4. Qualify master coaches.

5. Monitor coaching performance.

Coaching Priority

To demonstrate the importance of coaching capability, start by naming at least two respected technical managers as coach candidates and get them trained and qualified as quickly as possible. This should have been done during the initial TSP pilot phase, but if it has not been done, do so right away.

The second part of making coaching a high priority is to have the coaching group report to a senior level on the corporate staff. The coaching team initially should be centrally staffed, funded, and managed. While the coaches will work with the local laboratories and groups to support their teams, they must be centrally staffed and funded or they will not be managed properly. The product work would always be given a higher priority and the coaching staff would be treated as a low-priority support group. The first senior manager who did not recognize the importance of coaching would then disband the group as soon as he or she could.

Even after the TSP program is fully staffed and after the local engineering groups have their own coaching teams, a central coaching staff must continue to manage the coaching career path, identify and develop new coach candidates, manage the master coaches, and monitor coaching performance.

The Coaching Career Path

Development professionals are often reluctant to take a coaching position because they don't appreciate how rewarding such a job would be and because they don't understand the career possibilities that coaching experience would provide. The coaching job concerns motivating people to do their best work as well as guiding and mentoring groups to help them become cohesive and highly productive teams.

It is imperative that senior executives recognize the importance of coaching and enable a career path for coaches. The principal reason that few technical people are promoted to executive positions is that few of them have developed coaching skills. While engineering groups have usually been managed with traditional methods, marketing and sales groups are composed of strong-minded individuals, and the most effective managers have typically developed coaching skills to lead them. This is because sales teams have all the characteristics of knowledge-working teams, and most sales managers know intuitively that a coaching management style will produce the best sales results.

Because high-performing marketing groups are easy to identify, their managers are typically promoted rapidly. That is why so many executives have sales and marketing backgrounds. To encourage developers to consider a coaching position, make it clear to them that becoming a coach would prepare them for a wider range of future careers than they could otherwise aspire to reach. For example, they could return to technical work, become project or program mangers, advance to a mentor coach position, or ultimately even be considered for more senior management jobs.

To reinforce the benefits of a coaching career, make sure that when people move on from a coaching position, their next jobs are obvious promotions. Also, as the benefits of coaching experience become more widely understood, list coaching experience as a desirable background for project and program managers, laboratory managers, and director- and executive-level positions.

Coach Candidate Identification

If your organization has an established program for identifying high-potential employees and planning for their long-term development, consider adding the coaching position as a useful broadening assignment [Humphrey 1997]. If you do not have such a high-potential program, establish something similar for identifying potential team leaders, program managers, and engineering directors, and include prior coaching experience as a desirable prerequisite.

Finally, post the coach openings where members of the development community will see them, and circulate descriptions of the job openings and their requirements. Once the coaching job openings are known and the potential career advantages of having coaching experience are widely understood, there should be no problem in recruiting coach candidates.

Training and Certifying TSP Coaches and Mentor Coaches

The SEI has a program for training and certifying TSP coaches and mentor coaches. To become certified, a candidate coach must have been certified by the SEI as a PSP developer and have been mentored and recommended by a mentor coach. To provide a reasonable number of coaching candidates, encourage your developers to become PSP-certified and initiate the actions required to develop and certify your own mentor coaches.

Coaching Performance

Some people make outstanding coaches and others do not. The SEI coach certification program will ensure that all certified TSP coaches are qualified and capable of performing the coaching job. Beyond this, however, some coaches will be much more effective than others in motivating superior team performance. By identifying these superior performers and getting them certified as mentor coaches, you can rapidly improve the performance of your entire coaching community.

As described in Appendix E, the SEI has established a program for evaluating the performance of TSP-using organizations and for certifying those that demonstrate proficiency with the TSP process. This certification process is typically used to assess and improve a TSP organization's internal performance, to demonstrate capability to potential customers, or to evaluate the capability of potential suppliers. The TSP organization certification data could also be used to identify the coaches whose teams do consistently superior work and to urge them to become mentor coaches.

OTHER CAPABILITY REQUIREMENTS

When launching a TSP program, you will need some qualified PSP/TSP instructors. Initially, you can use external instructors, but thereafter you could qualify some instructors of your own. Unless your organization is large, however, the ongoing teaching workload would probably not be sufficient to warrant a full-time instructor staff. Therefore, after the initial developer and manager training workload, your existing TSP coaches could handle any sporadic needs because many are also qualified as PSP/TSP instructors. If you decide to retain external instructors, make sure that they are properly qualified by the SEI.

Beyond the coaching and instructor positions, the other capability requirements are for qualified and capable team leaders and developers. The team leader job is critically important. When team leaders do not support the TSP, their teams will not use the process properly and they will not perform measurably better than they did before TSP introduction. Thus, it is essential that all TSP team leaders attend TSP team leader training before their first team launch.

A common problem, particularly for team leaders who are under heavy cost, schedule, or customer pressure, is their ability to maintain their teams' fidelity to the TSP process. When team leaders do not insist on process fidelity, the team members will likely stop gathering some data, holding regular status meetings, providing accurate status reports to management, or maintaining quality standards. One answer to this problem is to make process fidelity a key job requirement for team leaders and to give it equal weight with project performance.

Softtek addresses this process fidelity problem by maintaining an independent fidelity audit system for evaluating TSP teams. The audits focus on the teams as units and do not reveal any information about individual team members. The team leader is then held accountable for the results of these audits, and he or she can also hold the team coach accountable for providing adequate assistance to the team in maintaining its process fidelity.

The team leader job is described in the book *TSP: Leading a Development Team* and will not be covered further here [Humphrey 2006b]. Similarly, the required skills for developers are described in the book *PSP: A Self-Improvement Process for Software Engineers* and are not covered in this book [Humphrey 2005].

Beyond these skills, the final need is for a modest staff to guide and monitor the TSP transition and implementation program itself. Here, the most consistently successful strategy has been to use the central coaching group as a team and to have them monitor and guide the overall TSP effort. This team should use the TSP process to plan and manage its work, and in its initial launch it should produce a complete plan, including its needs for management, clerical, and other support.

WHEN AND WHERE TO USE THE TSP

The TSP can be used with project teams of any kind, and it has also been used for various kinds of non-project activities. Examples are testing groups, maintenance departments, support activities, and running a corporate executive office (see, for example, the Quarksoft story in Chapter 2). We suggest, however, that organizations initially focus on using the TSP for managing their development projects and that they not attempt to use it for non-project or support activities until they have considerable project experience and a number of experienced TSP coaches.

Another time when a TSP introduction might not make sense is when an organization is in the middle of another massive change program. Organizations can withstand just so much change at any one time, so you should not attempt too many disruptive changes at once. Organizations are constantly changing, however, so change is a fact of modern organizational life, and as long as the scope of the TSP does not overlap with the other changes in such a way as to cause confusion or conflict, the TSP can be implemented while the other changes are being made.

When you get arguments about conflicting change programs, examine the changes involved to determine whether they would conflict with the TSP effort. Because the TSP process will not conflict with whatever environments, languages, or development methods your groups select, making changes in these areas at the same time as TSP introduction should not cause problems. Assuming this is the case, treat this argument as another excuse for inaction.

The TSP has also been used for various categories of teams and activities, and the SEI has developed custom versions of the process to fit the specific characteristics of such work. The categories involved are

- Multidisciplined teams
- Distributed teams
- Functional teams
- Large-scale programs

Multidisciplined Teams

Organizations are increasingly finding that multidisciplined teams are more productive and creative than single-skill teams. Vicarious Visions, a division of Activision, has used the TSP to develop a great many video games, including the recent hit game Guitar Hero. For this work, the company includes programmers, game designers, artists, and hardware engineers on its game-development teams.

The typical experience with such multidisciplined teams is that they do better work far more rapidly and efficiently than they could have when they worked as separate specialists on common projects. The bond of common goals and plans and the close and cohesive team relationships of TSP teams foster highly creative interactions that produce results that are not typically achieved by more traditional development groups.

One of the most effective ways to improve organizational efficiency and reduce project cycle time is to use multidisciplined teams. When software programs include their related requirements and testing groups, for example, they can often cut months from their schedules. Similarly, when an integrated hardware and software project forms a combined team for requirements specification, systems design, software and hardware development, testing, and manufacturing, they can generally make substantial cost, schedule, and quality improvements. For large programs, cycle times can often be cut by a year or more.

If a multidisciplined team has fewer than about 15 to 18 members, the standard TSP process is perfectly appropriate. For larger multidisciplined projects, the SEI has developed a custom multi-team process, or TSPm. Because this TSPm process is thoroughly described in the book *TSP: Coaching Development Teams*, it is not discussed here [Humphrey 2006a].

Distributed Teams

In the modern workplace, it is now normal to have project members distributed across several locations. As shown by the project described in Chapter 3, however, such teams can still be cohesive and productive as long as they have common goals, processes, and plans. We have found with the TSP that the common bond of the team commitment is far more powerful than either a single working location or membership in a common organization. Even when team members work for competing organizations, if they follow the TSP launch process, agree on common goals, and produce and commit to a common plan, they can still form a highly cohesive and effective development team. Depending on team size, either the standard TSP process or the multi-team TSPm process will work for such teams.

Functional Teams

Functional teams are groups that provide some kind of ongoing support. Examples of such work are software maintenance, IT support, and testing. While these groups typically do challenging and highly technical work, they usually do not have the kind of clear and compelling mission that is common for development teams. The goal of developing and delivering a product provides an obvious focus that all team members can understand easily.

If functional teams can identify a common goal, they can still be formed into cohesive and highly productive groups. The challenge is to define a real and compelling goal that they can all understand and commit to meeting. One example of how to do this is Jason Ziemer's Enterprise Engineering Department at the Naval Oceanographic Office of the Stennis Space Center (NAVO). His group provides technical support to U.S. naval ships on station throughout the world. One of their key jobs is responding to engineering change requests (ECRs) from the fleet. Because these requests are often from ships that are in a war zone, rapid response is important.

In its TSP team launch, Jason's ECR team established a goal of reducing ECR response time, and the entire team worked as an integrated unit to do so. The team ended up cutting response time for small ECRs from an average of 17.5 days to 4.8 days and for medium ECRs from 122.6 days to 26.5 days. Improvement goals of this type can be highly effective in motivating functional teams. Appendix E describes how management can use a continuing improvement program to maintain the striving for excellence organizations need to remain competitive.

The TSP functional process, TSPf, is designed to support such teams. It is described in the book *TSP: Coaching Development Teams* [Humphrey 2006a].

Large-Scale Programs

With the rapid advances in technology, modern-day systems are becoming ever larger and more complex. Consequently, their development must involve ever-larger and more complex engineering programs. The TSPm process can support multiple-team projects of up to about 150 to 200 or so members, but beyond that, a larger and typically unique process is required for each program. In customizing such a process, the principal factors to consider are the following:

- The system architecture
- The development organizations involved
- Program management
- Team coordination

The System Architecture

As was the case for the multi-team project described in Chapter 3, the key to effective teamwork is a clear and compelling team goal. For development work, that goal is usually a product or a major product component. It follows that, in defining the process required for a large-scale systems program, you must establish the overall system architecture before deciding how to structure the development process or the organization that will develop it. Once that architectural definition is established, you can define the system's principal components.

Assuming that each of these major components can be developed by a single multi-team of 200 or fewer members, the basic process and program organization structure can be defined. The objective is to have one TSPm multi-team responsible for developing each of the system's major subsystems or components. If any components are larger than any single multi-team could handle, the system architecture should be further refined. Once the architecture is defined, the structure of the development organization can be established. It is essential to define the architectural structure before the organizational structure because otherwise, systems tend to become structured much like the organizations that developed them. Such politically based designs generally have multiple problems.

The Development Organizations

With the overall development organization structure defined, the next step is to define and staff the development multi-teams. Start by identifying the needed skills for each component team, and then staff these skill needs from the available resources in the various involved organizations. This process is typically complicated by the fact that several organizations will have cooperated in the bid to obtain the development program, and the development responsibilities for each of the system's presumed subsystems and components will already have been specified in development contracts.

Because of the ability of the TSPm multi-team process to integrate the work of widely distributed teams, however, these contractual and responsibility problems should not be insurmountable. This is because, with the TSP, engineers from any one of the organizations could be assigned to work on any of the teams, even if they were managed by other than their home organizations. The only issue is to ensure that the members of all the teams participate in the launches for their teams and that their assignments be clearly defined and approved by all of their respective managers.

Because there may be many management and contractual issues to settle before the proper skills can be assigned to the development teams, these arrangements should be given a high priority. Otherwise, the quality of the resulting system will likely be compromised. With the team structure and staffing defined, the remaining steps concern program management and team coordination.

Program Management

In managing TSPm multi-teams, overall team leadership is provided by a leadership team that is led by the project manager [Humphrey 2006a]. The other members of this leadership team are the team leaders for each of the unit TSP teams that make up the multi-team. Each of the unit teams follows the standard TSP process in doing their work, and the team leader represents the team on the leadership team.

The leadership team monitors the progress of the unit teams, resolves inter-team issues, and, where necessary, balances team workload and resources among the unit teams. Similarly, for a large program, an overall program management leadership team should be established and led by the overall program manager. The leaders of each of the component multi-teams would then be members of this leadership team. Just as with the TSPm leadership team, the program management leadership team monitors the progress of the component multi-teams, resolves inter-team issues, and, when necessary, balances workload and resources among the multi-teams.

While such a multi-team structure will handle most situations, it still leaves open the question of how the many multi-teams and unit teams will coordinate their work and how the many team members can be kept informed and involved. This is critical because the team members must be actively involved in managing their own projects. Only then will they be personally responsible for managing their own work and feel empowered to identify and resolve the many issues that are common to large programs. Providing this level of involvement is a team coordination issue.

Team Coordination

One of the qualities that makes TSP teams effective is the strong feeling of ownership the members have for their work. They understand the overall job, they manage their own work, and they are aware of the issues that involve them and their teams. As a result, they feel empowered to identify issues and problems and either to resolve these problems themselves or to refer them to another team member who will get them resolved.

To ensure that this is done and that there is an owner for every issue that is likely to arise, each TSP team member takes responsibility for one or more team member roles. TSP teams typically have eight standard team member roles:

- Customer interface manager: handles customer and requirements issues
- Design manager: handles design issues
- Implementation manager: handles implementation issues
- Test manager: handles testing issues
- Planning manager: handles planning issues and produces the periodic management status reports
- Process manager: handles process issues and monitors process compliance
- Quality manager: handles quality issues and monitors product quality
- Support manager: handles team support issues

These role managers do not do all of the work in their areas, but they do monitor the work and identify and resolve issues. For example, the design manager will likely be the lead designer and establish the team's design standards, but he or she will not necessarily do all of the design work.

Role-Manager Teams

On a TSPm multi-team, each of the unit teams defines a standard set of team member roles, and coordination across the entire multi-team is maintained through a set of role-manager teams. That is, there is a role-manager team for each of the standard TSP role-manager jobs, and the role-manager team members are the role managers from each of the unit teams. There is a role-manager team for the customer interface managers, for the design managers, and for each of the other team roles.

Role-manager teams are responsible for handling cross-program issues within their areas of responsibility and for performing any special tasks that the leadership team assigns to them. For example, the planning managers from all of the unit teams form a planning manager team, and this team coordinates and resolves planning issues among all of the unit teams. When these role-manager teams cannot resolve issues, they take them to the leadership team. This role-manager team structure provides the development team members with ready access to all members of the multi-team, and it enables the members quickly to resolve issues, clarify questions, and identify and escalate impending problems to senior management.

The reason it is so important to identify these issues is that major program problems almost always start as minor issues that, if identified early enough, could have been quickly resolved. Minor issues are invariably first recognized by working-level team members who generally raise them with their immediate management. Usually, nobody but the working-level engineer who first sees a problem appreciates its significance, and because nobody typically feels responsible for issues that do not affect his or her immediate work, the issue is usually ignored and not addressed until it is too late to prevent a major program problem. Without some way to identify and resolve rapidly the many issues that are common to large programs, problems are common and delays and overruns are almost universal. The TSPm role-manager teams are a proven way to handle this early-warning problem.

To ensure that the role-manager team capability is available to the members of all of the multi-teams in a large program, the overall program leadership team requires a small staff to support the role-manager teams and to ensure that they maintain the kind of open and cooperative relationship needed to quickly identify and resolve major issues. The structure of this program management staff must depend on the specific program situation and the preferences of the program management team. However, its role is critical and it should be established when the overall program is initially structured.

SUMMARY

Expanding TSP use across a large organization involves five principal steps: establishing an overall implementation strategy, defining the rollout plan, building sponsorship, developing local implementation plans, and building internal capability. This appendix addresses each of these topics and describes how to handle the issues that most commonly arise.

REFERENCES

[Humphrey 1997] Watts S. Humphrey, *Managing Technical People: Innovation, Teamwork, and the Software Process* (Reading, MA: Addison-Wesley, 1997).

[Humphrey 2005] Watts S. Humphrey, *PSP: A Self-Improvement Process for Software Engineers* (Boston, MA: Addison-Wesley, 2005).

[Humphrey 2006a] Watts S. Humphrey, *TSP: Coaching Development Teams* (Boston, MA: Addison-Wesley, 2006).

[Humphrey 2006b] Watts S. Humphrey, *TSP: Leading a Development Team* (Boston, MA: Addison-Wesley, 2006).

D

Using the TSP to Manage Programs

This appendix describes how managers and executives can use the TSP data and methods to help them manage their programs and organizations. As shown in Figure D.1, it follows Appendix B, which describes how to start introducing the TSP process, and Appendix C, which discusses the issues of broadening TSP use across an organization or a large engineering program.

Once your people are using the TSP, you will have several new tools to help manage your operations. This appendix describes how to use these tools to address many of the issues that long have plagued managers of large-scale development work. The appendix covers the following topics:

- The program management problem
- Establishing aggressive but realistic plans

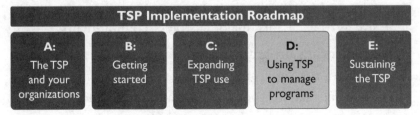

Figure D.1 Roadmap to the appendices

- Monitoring program status
- Identifying and resolving issues
- Managing quality
- Dealing with the customer
- Management's continuing responsibilities

THE PROGRAM MANAGEMENT PROBLEM

In this appendix, we assume that you are managing a large multi-facility program consisting of several subsystems. The work is performed in multiple locations by several hundred to a thousand or more hardware and software developers and support personnel. Managers of companies, divisions, laboratories, or large departments also face many of these same program management problems. We do not, however, address the non-development issues on which senior managers typically spend considerable time such as legal, financial management, marketing, personnel, facilities, services, and advanced technology. While TSP methods could be used in these areas just as effectively as for development, we do not recommend applying it to them until you have considerable TSP experience and a number of qualified coaches. The topics we discuss in this appendix relate to the development work itself, and they are the following:

- **Establishing aggressive but realistic plans.** The issue here is establishing program plans that are aggressive enough to maintain a sense of urgency but not so aggressive as to likely miss major customer commitments.

- **Monitoring program status.** Program status is a serious problem for large programs because development groups often appear to be on schedule until they suddenly announce a major schedule slip. This problem is particularly common for programs that involve a substantial amount of software work.

- **Identifying and resolving issues.** This topic relates to the trust topic we discussed in Chapter 5. The challenge here is to identify issues early enough to do more than merely react to the resulting crises.

- **Managing quality.** Quality management is impossible in a crisis-driven environment. The reason is that quality problems only become crises long after there is any way to mitigate or prevent them. If you do not manage quality until it becomes a crisis, you are not managing quality; you are reacting to quality problems.

- **Dealing with the customer.** This subject also concerns the trust issue, but here you are on the other side. As long as things are progressing according to plan, customer relations will be good, but when programs start missing commitments or having unpleasant surprises, customer relationships will quickly sour. Then again, instead of managing the customer relationship, you will be reacting to a new set of crises: those caused by an irate and suspicious customer.

This appendix describes how to use the TSP methods and data to address these issues.

ESTABLISHING AGGRESSIVE BUT REALISTIC PLANS

The task of establishing an aggressive but realistic plan involves a trade-off: balancing the risk of missing commitments with the need for a challenged and motivated workforce. To be successful, your teams must work smarter and better than the competitors, but they must also meet their commitments. Your job is to ensure that their plans are as tight and aggressive as possible but also that the technical work is feasible and the resources available are likely to complete the job in the required time.

Building Team Motivation

To get a plan, you obviously must tell the team what you want. That is the first part of the management job in TSP launch meeting 1. The second and even more important part is to motivate the team members to produce as aggressive a plan as they can.

Motivating people is a leadership problem. The need is to convince your potential followers to accept your goals as theirs and to then do their utmost to meet them. For development groups, this motivation problem is pretty simple when the job is building an exciting new product. Then all you need to do is to explain why the product is exciting and why your business goals are important.

The more difficult challenge is when the product isn't that exciting. Examples would be reworking an older existing product or providing maintenance support for installed systems. Because the product is not inherently exciting, the challenge is to make the work itself exciting. The description in Appendix C of how Jason Ziemer did this with his maintenance team at NAVO is an excellent example of this. He challenged them to cut their response time for engineering change requests (ECRs) from the U.S. Navy's fleet. The team members were highly motivated by this challenge because they knew that their customers were in warships on station in battle zones. They actually cut the response time for many ECRs from weeks to days. They did this for a job that everybody had previously viewed as routine and boring.

Making work exciting is an important part of building team motivation, but there is another and even more important part:

making the team members feel like partners with management. Here again we have the trust issue. The only way to make knowledge-working teams feel like partners with management is to be honest with them; explain exactly what you need and why. An excellent example of how to do this is the way Peter Bartko, the former CEO of EBS, handled the schedule problem with a large team the company had charged with developing an important new system for online currency trading [Humphrey 2002].

In TSP launch meeting 1, Peter described the company's business situation, the competitive challenges, and why it was important to have this new system available in one year. The team spent an entire week developing the plan, but they could see no way to deliver the product in less than two years. While Peter was clearly disappointed, he ended up accepting the team's plan. However, the team members now understood the business need and were also concerned about the two-year schedule. As they proceeded with the design, they soon figured out how to produce a reduced-function system version within one year. They then revised their plan and met their new one-year commitment. The power of motivated and committed teams is extraordinary. If you trust them with the facts, they will be creative partners and will keep thinking about better ways to meet your goals.

Assessing the Plan

After TSP teams produce their plans, they present them to management in launch meeting 9. Now management must switch its role. Instead of pushing for the most aggressive plan you can get, you must assure yourself that the plan is realistic and achievable. Because development work typically involves building new products or adding new enhancements to existing products, developers often argue that they cannot estimate and plan the work. They reason that because the work is new, there is no way to judge the time it will take to do it. Experience shows, however, that this is not true. Even though the overall product may be new, a large percentage of the work will be similar to prior work. Therefore, if data on the product sizes and development times for this prior work are available, they can be used to help estimate the size and development time for the new product.

In the launch meeting 9 plan presentation, your challenge is the reverse of that in meeting 1. With a highly motivated team, the principal risk now is that the team members will have produced a more aggressive plan than they can possibly meet. So, in meeting 9, probe the team's plan and make the members prove that it is realistic and achievable. In examining plans, the principal risks concern the plan's completeness and the realism of the size and resource estimates.

When development groups make plans, unless they previously have made and worked to similar plans, they often omit key tasks, such as final product build, integration testing, and product documentation. The biggest risk, however, is that motivated development teams often overcommit themselves. While it is appropriate to give the teams aggressive goals, after they have produced a plan and done their best to meet your goals, you must force them to defend their plans.

The best strategy is to recognize that all plans assume that the work will proceed pretty much as planned. However, particularly with high-technology programs, surprises are common and surprises almost always involve more work. To allow for these surprises, ensure that the program plans are conservative and that if nothing goes wrong, the work can be accomplished during normal working hours. Then, when the surprises come, the teams will have the reserve capacity to handle them. If you start with a team that is stretched to the limit, every change or surprise will be a disaster.

Even if the plan does not meet your original needs, the key is to understand first what it really takes to do the job and then to address any cost and schedule problems. The TSP process provides three complementary ways to assess the likelihood that a development plan's commitments are achievable: assessing the size, resource, and quality plans; balancing resources and schedules; and reviewing the plan's risks.

The Product Size Estimate

With the TSP's estimating methods, the team gathers historical data on the sizes of similar previously completed products and uses these data to estimate the likely sizes of the new products. While size estimation is typically error-prone, experienced TSP teams rapidly accumulate a substantial volume of historical size data, and these data help them to make progressively more accurate size estimates.

In reviewing size estimates, the key concern is with the source and reliability of the size data and the likely confidence intervals for the resulting estimates. Statistically sound confidence intervals are typically available only for the smallest components that TSP teams develop, but TSP teams can provide informed judgments on the likely high and low size ranges for even large systems. From these ranges, you can explore the likely best-case and worst-case resource and schedule ranges for the program.

The Resource Estimate

TSP teams are taught how to estimate product size and development time, and they are shown how to gather and use data on prior work to improve the accuracy of their estimates. They also learn the value of gathering data on the sizes of the products they develop and how long it took to develop them. Most developers are surprised by how predictable their development work becomes once they have even a modest amount of personal and team productivity data.

With historical productivity data, TSP teams can produce estimates that are more accurate than they have produced in the past. Therefore, to assure yourself that a development plan is accurate, ask about the data used to support the size and resource estimates. Have the teams explain what data they used, the projects from which the data came, and how similar those projects were to this new job. Then ask the developers about their confidence in the accuracy of the productivity figures they used in the estimate.

The Quality Plan

It is also important to probe the quality plan and assure yourself that it has been competently prepared, is realistic, and presents suitable milestones and benchmarks for tracking. These topics are covered in the later section of this appendix on quality management.

Balancing Resources and Schedules

With the plan, and still in launch meeting 9, the next issue is to balance the available resources to achieve the desired schedule. The key issue in making a program plan is the total effort required to do the work. Then, to achieve the desired schedule, you merely assign enough developers to the job. This of course assumes that all the developers can be used productively throughout the job. Deciding how many developers can be assigned is a management job, and determining how best to use them is the team's job.

If, in meeting 9, the team presents a schedule that is longer than you want, it will probably also have presented some alternate plans that do meet your schedule but take more resources or produce a reduced-function product. The management question, then, is one of establishing priorities: Are there lower-priority jobs from which the needed resources can be obtained? In all of these discussions, it is important to recognize that the cost of the job will not be changed significantly by adding or reducing staff.

For most development work, the cost of the job is determined by the required number of engineering months of work. For example, if the original request was for a 12-member team to produce a product in 12 months and the team estimates 15 months, the costs are obviously more than hoped: 180 versus 144 engineering months. Now, however, once you have reviewed the plan and concluded that the work really will require 180 months of work, the actual cost will be essentially the same whether you assign 12 engineers to do it in 15 months or 15 engineers to do it in 12. This, of course, assumes that the team agrees that it can productively use all 15 engineers for the entire 12-month period. Experience shows that arbitrarily imposing an early date is not an effective way to compress schedules.

Reviewing Plan Risks

In the TSP launch, teams assess and evaluate the risks they see in doing this job. They also assign likelihood and impact ratings and assign the highest-priority risks to team members to monitor. In launch meeting 9, the teams present this risk assessment and describe their mitigation plans for the highest-priority risks. The management job is then to ensure that the team has addressed all of the right risks, that the mitigation plans are sound, and that the team knows when to call on management for help in addressing the risks.

MONITORING PROGRAM STATUS

Large programs, just like large organizations, typically have many interrelated parts, and problems in any one part often mean that there are or soon will be problems with the other parts.

If these problems are not recognized and promptly corrected, the overall program will then have problems. On most programs, senior management rarely sees such problems until it is too late to do anything about them.

If every team and every project in a large program maintains its schedule and meets its cross-program commitments, the program as a whole will almost certainly meet its commitments. To ensure that this happens, every manager at every level of a large program must ensure that every project or group of projects within his or her purview either stays on schedule or is following a realistic recovery plan. When this is not the case, that manager should escalate that issue to higher management and get help in addressing it.

When managers behave in this way and when they have precise and timely data on all of their project teams, large programs are most likely to perform in accordance with their plans and to meet their commitments. The TSP team weekly status report provides the data required to manage programs in this way.

The Earned-Value Measure

TSP teams use a precise and objective form of earned value (EV) to determine project status. As with traditional EV measures, the TSP assigns each task a planned value (PV) that is that task's planned effort as a percentage of the total project's planned effort. Once that task is completed, its PV is converted to EV and accumulated to give the total project EV to date. The PV is used regardless of how much effort the work actually took, and there is no credit for partially completed tasks. The total EV compared to plan shows whether the project is ahead of schedule or behind.

For example, if a project had an EV of 25.0 compared to a planned PV of 33.3 at a given point in time, that would indicate that it was (33.3% • 25.0%) = 8.3% behind schedule. For a 24-month project, the 33.3% PV at this point would mean that about one-third of the work should have been done, and that about 8 months would have elapsed. However, for this team, only about one-quarter of the work has been done, or about 6 months of work in 8 months. If nothing changed, this project could be expected to take 32 months to finish instead of the planned 24 months, meaning it will be 8 months late.

Not only does the EV metric provide a precise measure of project status, it allows management to determine which parts of a large program are in trouble and by how much. To do this, however, every team on a large program must use a precise EV measure that is calculated from objective and auditable data. Because TSP teams use such measures and calculate their EV status every week, the EV for the entire program can be calculated from all of these parts, and managers can determine quickly which parts of the program are in trouble and why.

An Example Status Report

Figure D.2 shows a typical program-level status summary report. Charts like this are called long-pole reports because they identify that part of the overall program that, if not corrected, will be the gating item on the overall program schedule. On the left is the average EV status for the entire program compared to the planned status at this point. The numbers above the bar give the month when that group of teams is projected to finish. Because the overall program is scheduled to complete in 24 months, it is now about a month behind schedule.

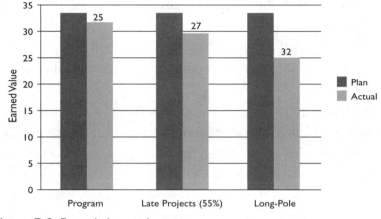

Figure D.2 Example long-pole status report

The key to keeping large programs on schedule is to recognize that the program's status is determined by the one part of the program that is furthest behind schedule: the long-pole project. To help determine the magnitude of the schedule problem, the right-hand bar in Figure D.2 shows the EV status of this long-pole team. It has completed only 25.0% of its planned tasks compared to 33.3% of the value planned so far, so it is 8.3% behind schedule at this point or about 2 months late. The number above the actual bar for the long-pole project shows that if the team continues working at its historical rate, it will finish in 32 months instead of the committed 24 months.

To indicate how widespread this lateness problem is, the middle bar in Figure D.2 shows the percentage of the program's teams that are behind schedule and by how far. In this case, 55% of the teams are behind schedule with an average projected delivery of 27 instead of 24 months for those teams. However, because there could be several very late teams in this group, the recovery plans for all of the late projects should be reviewed, and senior program management should review the recovery plans for those that are in the most serious trouble.

The reason that 55% of the teams being late is not necessarily a concern is that when large programs are working to accurate plans, on average, half of the teams will be a bit behind schedule and half will be a little ahead. The time to get concerned is when the percentage of the teams that are late becomes much larger than 50%, when the average delay becomes large, or when, as could be the case here, a few of the teams fall seriously behind schedule.

The Limitations of Earned-Value Measures

While the EV measure can be very helpful, it can also be misleading. The reason is that the accuracy of the measure requires two things: that the original plan be realistic and that the work be of high quality. For the first item, the program plan must be based on a realistic distribution of time among the program's tasks and phases. This is typically possible only when teams use historical data in making their plans. Suppose, for example, that a team planned to spend six months developing a product and only one month testing it. This could be realistic if the team had data to support such a short test time, but if not, the team would likely think it was on schedule right up until the beginning of the final test and then face a four- to six-month schedule delay. That is why it is important for management to examine a team's plan in launch meeting 9 and to verify that it is based on realistic and relevant historical data.

The second thing that EV measures require is that the work being tracked be of high quality. Here again, consider the example of the team that planned for six months of development and one month of testing. Suppose instead that they made a more realistic plan and scheduled four months for testing. While this would almost certainly be a more accurate plan, it still would not provide a very good basis for estimating when the job would be done.

The reason is that for poor-quality products, testing times are inherently unpredictable. In this case, while testing could be completed in three or four months, it could also take six to eight months or more depending on the kinds of problems encountered.

In net, when plans are based on realistic historical data and the work is of high quality, the EV measure can provide very useful insights into program status.

IDENTIFYING AND RESOLVING ISSUES

While the traditional way to identify issues is through management status reviews and reports, the most important way is for the development team members to identify the issues they see and to either resolve them personally or to escalate them to someone who can handle them. The reason this is so important is that the development team members normally can see the early symptoms of major problems long before they become visible to anyone else. This is one of the great advantages of maintaining a trusting workplace environment and empowering self-directed teams.

In a trusting environment, the teams take responsibility for their jobs and assign roles to their members. When they identify important issues that could impact their work or even other issues that could affect the overall program, they refer these issues to the responsible role managers on their teams. These role managers can either resolve the issues themselves or escalate them to the appropriate management. As long as management addresses the issues when they are raised, and as long as they don't shoot the messengers, they can expect to get early warning of most key issues. This will enable them to resolve most problems before they become crises.

For the more traditional way of identifying issues through management reviews and reports, TSP data can provide useful

Table D.1 Weekly Team Status Report—Week 35

	Plan	Actual	Plan/ Actual
EV for the week	0.962	1.060	0.907
EV program to date	33.7	26.1	1.291
Task hours for week	225	255	0.882
Task hours for program to date	7,875	6,825	1.154
Task hours for completed tasks	6,120	6,610	0.926
EV per task hour to date	0.00428	0.00382	

insights. Again, using the example of the team that had earned only 25% EV in eight months instead of the 33.3% planned and was two months late, the key questions are why the team is late and what can be done to recover. Here, the data in Table D.1 provide some useful facts.

Estimating Accuracy

The first point to consider is the accuracy of the team's plan. If the original plan was inaccurate, it is best to recognize it as quickly as possible and to take immediate corrective actions. Remember, however, that all plans are subject to error, and that even when a large program has an accurate overall plan, about half of the teams' plans will be underestimates.

The accuracy of a TSP team's plan can be determined from the line for task hours for completed tasks. This shows that the team estimated that it would take 6,120 task hours to complete the tasks it has finished so far but that it has actually taken 6,610 hours. This means that so far the work has actually taken 7.4% more time than originally planned. The best assumption at this point is that this 7.4% increase in work will apply to the rest of the job. The next question then concerns how to reallocate program resources or to otherwise recover the lost time and get back on schedule. The EV data shown in Table D.1 are helpful for identifying schedule problems, but they do not identify problem causes or suggest possible recovery actions. For that, the task-time measure is more useful.

The Task-Time Measure

Several of the items in Table D.1 refer to task hours. These relate to the TSP's task-time measure. On most projects there are two categories of work: those tasks that have clear and defined completion criteria and those that do not. The first category consists of the standard development tasks such as defining requirements, producing designs, inspecting or reviewing products, and testing. As well as being clearly defined, all of these activities have specific completion criteria.

The second task category consists of all those ill-defined things the developers must do to get their jobs done. These include meetings with management, helping coworkers, setting up or rearranging computing facilities, answering e-mail, getting supplies, or providing help to another project. While these tasks are generally necessary and can take a lot of time, it is usually easier to treat them as overhead rather than trying to estimate, measure, and track every one.

There are three reasons for this. First, including such tasks in the plan reduces the quality of the estimates. This is because most projects have many tasks that cannot be estimated accurately from historical data, have no defined completion criteria, and must be estimated arbitrarily. The second reason not to include these items is that it takes time to make such estimates. The third reason is that having such estimates does not help in managing programs.

This means that the task-time data shown in Table D.1 concern only that time the team spent in accomplishing the development tasks that are in the team's plan and that are measured by EV. A final point on task time is that it varies widely by organization. When developers have well-defined processes and plans, they tend to be more efficient. They don't wait for their boss to tell them what to do next; their plan tells them. When they want to find out how to perform some task, they just check with the defined processes and procedures.

Task-Time Experience

Experience shows that in most organizations, the weekly task hours per developer vary from about 12 to 20 hours for a standard 40-hour week and that new TSP teams tend to start at the low end of this range. With increased TSP experience and with management's help in reducing distractions and diversions, weekly task time typically grows to between 15 and 18 hours a week fairly quickly. Beyond that, specific steps such as rearranging office space, providing clerical support, or limiting meeting and other management-initiated activities to specific days or times of the day are usually required.

Task time is a variable that TSP teams can influence. As these teams gain experience, they learn how to use their time more efficiently so that task-hour performance typically increases over time. For example, the 15-developer team shown in Table D.1 had planned for 15 weekly task hours each over the 35 weeks of the project to date, or for 225 hours a week and 7,875 hours to date. However, the team has been able to work only 6,825 task hours so far. This could be because of other assignments, sickness, or any of a number of reasons, but the team is clearly quite late, so some changes are required.

From the data in Table D.1, however, it is also clear that the team has already taken steps to recover its schedule. The members increased their weekly task time from the average of 6,825/ 35 = 195 hours a week to 255 hours for the latest week. This is actually more than the team originally planned, and it required an average of 17 weekly task hours per developer instead of the 15 hours originally planned. The next question is: If the team can continue working at this rate, when will it finish? Here, the bottom figure in the table is useful. With 0.00382 EV per task hour, the 255 weekly task-hour rate will generate 0.974 EV per week. Because there are $(100 - 26.1) = 73.9$ EV to go, the team will take $(73.9/0.974) = 76$ weeks or about 17.6 months to finish the job. Counting the 8 months already taken, this comes to 111 weeks or nearly 26 months instead of the planned 104 weeks or 24 months.

To finish the job, the team must spend a total of $(255 \times 76) = 19,380$ task hours. To do this in the 69 weeks remaining would require 281 task hours per week. With the present staff of 15 developers, this would take an 18.7 weekly task-hour average, which is more than the team has been able to achieve so far. With one more developer, the task-hour rate would have to be 17.5 hours a week, and with two more, it would be 16.5. Any new developers would probably not be fully efficient from the start, so it would be prudent to add two developers to this team as quickly as possible.

Managing Task Time

Because increasing a team's weekly task hours provides such important benefits at no apparent cost, managers are often tempted to direct their teams to increase their weekly task hours. In one case, for example, a manager directed the team to increase its weekly task hours from 17 to 20 hours a week. This was a serious mistake, however, for the task-hour rate actually dropped. Making such edicts is a very bad idea for three reasons.

First, to meet a 20-hour weekly task-hour edict, the more experienced TSP team members would just modify their plans to more precisely define some of their ill-defined tasks. For example, they could then include a project coordination task and record the time they spent on miscellaneous activities against it. While this would not increase the time they spent on development tasks, it would immediately satisfy any management edict to increase task hours.

The second reason that such an edict would be a mistake is that it would relieve the developers of responsibility for managing their own task hours. With the edict, management has declared its intention to manage task hours, so the team members are now merely working to management's edicts. Because management now owns the task-hour problem, the teams are not motivated to continue improving. In every one of the few cases where management has issued such edicts, the teams' actual weekly task hours dropped, generally quite substantially.

The third reason that such edicts are unwise is that they demonstrate that management does not trust the developers to manage themselves. By issuing an order to increase weekly task hours, management also is abdicating its responsibility to support the engineers and to help them to resolve the problems that limit their ability to increase task hours by themselves.

MANAGING QUALITY

Effective quality management must start at the very beginning of a program. This is not generally possible, however, because few software or systems development teams have any quality data until system testing starts. That means that the typical quality-management technique is to urge the developers to produce quality work. However, because most developers have always tried to do quality work, and because software people spend almost half of their time in test trying to get their products to work, they believe they already are trying to produce quality work.

To manage quality at the beginning of a job, you must have data, and the TSP provides the needed data. With the TSP, engineering teams produce a quality plan, and in that plan they define how they intend to manage quality: the time they will spend in each development phase and the defects they expect to inject or remove in that phase. Furthermore, because TSP teams have been trained in quality-management methods, they know how to make quality plans that, if followed, will produce high-quality products. This means that the most effective quality-management strategy is to monitor team performance and to ensure that the members are following the quality plan that they produced.

In conducting such reviews, the measure of goodness is the reverse of that used when reviewing development plans. For development work, the objective is to finish tasks as quickly as possible. In quality management, however, all of the steps except testing involve the developers appraising their products to find and fix defects. In these steps, the developers work alone or in teams to examine all aspects of their products and to ensure that all required functions are included and properly implemented. This is an exacting and time-consuming process, and when developers are under intense schedule pressure, they tend to rush through these appraisal activities. Unfortunately, when they rush, they miss a lot of defects.

The TSP has four basic quality measures: review yield, process yield, review rates, and the ratio of the time spent appraising products to the time spent in developing them. These measures are defined in Table D.2. As is clear from these definitions, the yield measures are available only late in a program because they cannot be calculated until most of the product's defects have been found.

Table D.2 TSP Quality Measures

Quality Measure	Measure Definition
Review yield	The yield of a project phase is the percentage of the defects in the product during the phase that were removed by the end of that phase. This measure is used for every defect-removal phase.
Yield before test	Yield before test is the percentage of all the defects in the product that were removed before the start of final system testing.
Review rate	This measures the rate at which the developers review or inspect a product. For example, if a developer took 10 hours to review a product of 988 lines of code, the rate would be 98.8 LOC/hour.
Appraisal-to-development ratio (A/DR)	A/DR measures the ratio of the time spent reviewing or inspecting (appraising) a product to the time spent developing that product. A/DR can be calculated for a project phase, for any group of phases, for an entire project, and even for an entire program.

The yield-before-test measure provides an excellent overall measure of the quality of a development job. That is because testing removes only a fraction of the defects in a product, and a truly high-quality development process should remove all or most of the defects before the start of testing. TSP teams consistently achieve yield values of 95% or more, and many reach yields of 99% and even 100%. In fact, in one study, one-third of the TSP teams had no defects found by their end users [Davis 2003]. The review-rate measure is useful in determining how effectively the developers performed a specific review or inspection step, but it is not as helpful in examining the overall quality performance of a team, a project, or an entire program. For that, the appraisal-to-development ratio (A/DR) is most useful.

The A/DR measure compares the time spent appraising the quality of a product with the time spent in developing it. This measure is highly predictive, and it is available at almost every stage of the development process. Figure D.3 shows a plot of the defects found in testing compared to A/DR for 8,100 programs written by experienced software developers during PSP training. From this chart, it is clear that higher values of A/DR are associated with fewer test defects.

Because it takes time to review programs, it would be expensive to increase A/DR above the point where improvement becomes marginal. Figure D.4 shows average data for these same developers for test defect levels and review hours per thousand line of code. While this chart suggests that developers should spend about 10% to 15% of their development time appraising their work, these data are for small stand-alone code modules. For more complex or larger products, we have found that teams do most effective reviews when they spend at least half as much time reviewing and inspecting their products as they spent in developing them.

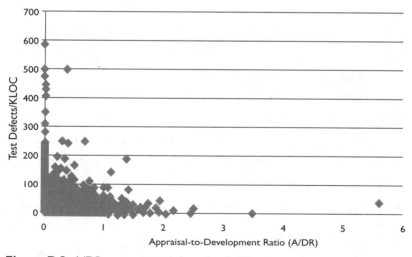

Figure D.3 A/DR versus test defects for 8,100 programs

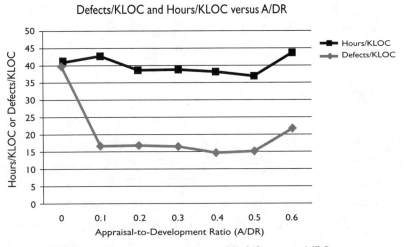

Figure D.4 Test defects and review hours/KLOC versus A/DR

Figure D.5 shows data for 11 components of one larger project that suggest that the A/DR value be at least 0.45 or higher. This means that the development teams must spend at least half as much time appraising their products as they did developing them. While larger values would probably improve product quality, A/DR values above about 0.5 would likely be only marginally

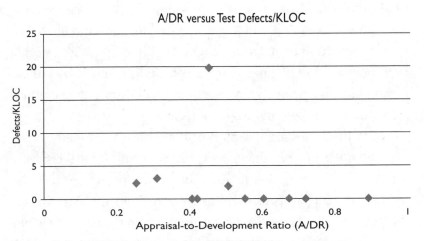

Figure D.5 A/DR versus test defects/KLOC of 11 program components

effective. Because the optimum A/DR operating point will differ by type of work, each organization should analyze its own TSP data to establish its own guidelines.

Program Reviews

If you do not regularly conduct program reviews, you should consider doing so on at least a quarterly basis. Appendix E describes how to address quality and financial issues in such reviews, but you also should examine schedule and cost status. However, to ensure that the development groups continue to view quality as THE top priority, consider reviewing quality performance first followed by schedule and cost performance. Here, for the projects that have not yet completed final testing, examine the teams' A/DR data and compare them with the teams' quality plans.

For those projects that have completed final testing, examine the yield-before-test results as well as the A/DR data. A typical A/DR report should look like Figure D.6. This figure shows the planned and actual A/DR by phase and to date for the program. If you wish, you could also ask for detailed A/DR reports on all of the individual teams in the program. In this example, the actual A/DR values for all project phases are substantially below those planned. On a large program, this could suggest that everyone has A/DR rates that are a little low, but it could also mean that some projects have adequate A/DR rates while others aren't doing reviews and inspections at all.

When programs are clearly not following their quality plans, ask why not and what they plan to do about it. Typical recovery actions would be to identify the most defect-prone product elements and to re-inspect them and clean them up. Actions like this could be performed at any program phase from requirements through implementation. In the example shown in Figure D.6,

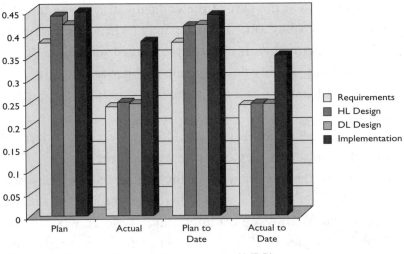

Figure D.6 Appraisal-to-development ratio (A/DR)

if management had been reviewing the A/DR data, the problem should have been caught and corrected at the requirements phase.

In the schedule review, examine the long-pole reports like that shown in Figure D.2. These will show which parts of a program are furthest behind and will likely determine the overall program schedule unless addressed immediately. The key questions from any such reviews should concern the recovery plans and the checkpoints for reviewing performance against these recovery plans. The financial review could address profit per EV status versus plans in much the way that Quarksoft management does for its teams (see Chapters 2 and 7).

DEALING WITH THE CUSTOMER

Before Allied Signal merged with Honeywell, it had a contract with the U.S. Army to develop a large and complex weapons system. The development team was using the TSP and was making good progress until the Honeywell–Allied Signal merger was announced. The U.S. Department of Justice had approved the merger but only if the part of the company developing military products was spun off. Unfortunately, when the company announced the merger, it had not yet worked out all the details of the spin-off, so this development group was told that they were affected and that some of them would either be laid off or have to move.

Over the next month, the developers were so concerned about their jobs that they did little work on the project. When the details of the merger were finally announced and the engineers could get back to work, there had been a substantial schedule slip. What was most interesting, however, was how the availability of precise data on project status affected the customer negotiations.

In the project's implementation phase, the team had planned a series of builds, and the army had assigned some of its engineers to work with the team on build testing. This provided them early experience with the product, but it also exposed them to the TSP process and the weekly team status meetings. As a result, in the recovery negotiations with the customer, everybody knew exactly how far the project was behind schedule and why. Even though the customer was unhappy with the delay, everybody knew that there was no point in rehashing history, so they just concentrated on working together to solve the problem. Even though the final delivery date could not be recovered, the developers were able to make some adjustments to help the army minimize the impact on its overall acceptance-testing and deployment plans.

One major reason that customer relations become strained is lack of trust, and this lack of trust generally stems from incomplete or misleading information. When development teams don't have precise data on their work, they cannot know their schedule status, so they are forced to guess. Because these guesses are usually wrong, when managers use the information the developers give them, the customers soon learn that they cannot trust what the managers say.

Open, clear, and honest communication with the customer is the key to establishing trust, and trust is essential for resolving problems and for maintaining a cooperative and productive customer relationship.

MANAGEMENT'S CONTINUING RESPONSIBILITIES

Program managers have a lot to do, and to keep their programs under control, they must prioritize their time. Unfortunately, with the high frequency of crises on most large programs, the crises must take first priority, leaving little time for anything else. With self-directed teams and a data-driven management system, the number of crises is sharply reduced, and program managers typically have more control over how they spend their time. To most productively use this extra time, they should give priority to three things: maintaining the focus on quality, ensuring effective program-wide communications, and sustaining continuous improvement.

Maintaining the Focus on Quality

The reason that quality must be the top priority is that poor-quality work is the principal cause of most program problems, and the cost and time needed to rework defective products are usually the gating items on most program schedules. As noted in Chapter 8, the fastest and cheapest way to do any job is to do it right the first time. That is one of the principles of the TSP, and to ensure that all parts of a large program follow this principle, program managers must continually emphasize quality when giving talks, while conducting program reviews, and when speaking at meetings. Instead of just talking about quality, however, talk about specific numerical goals and status against them. Without numbers, all you can do is talk about quality, and, unfortunately, generalized quality talk can quickly become repetitious and boring. Rather than motivating effective action, you will then be discouraging it. So talk about quality frequently, but use numbers when you do.

Ensuring Effective Program-Wide Communication

The issue here concerns communication at every program and management level. The principal concern is that on most technical topics, the working-level developers have the most accurate and timely information, and the quality of this information typically declines with every step on the way up the management chain. The TSP multi-team process and role-manager teams provide a powerful vehicle for establishing and managing communication that is timely and accurate.

The role-manager teams are the key to maintaining program-wide communication, but they require management support. This support is not hard to provide, however, and typically requires only that the leadership team periodically ask the role-manager teams to address key programmatic problems and issues. For example, the design managers could be asked to recommend design standards for the overall program, or the planning managers could be tasked with resolving schedule interdependencies among several program teams. Also, provide a management mentor for each role-manager team and have that mentor ensure that the role-manager communication network is functioning, that key issues are communicated up the management chain, and that these issues are tracked to resolution and the originating developer is informed of the outcome and thanked for his or her efforts.

Also, for large programs, the program manager must maintain a small program-manager staff. Because big programs typically have several large subsystems, and because each subsystem will have its own multi-team process and set of role-manager teams, a staff is needed to establish and facilitate communication among these multiple role-manager teams. While this level of communication is helpful in maintaining team morale and motivation, it also enables the early warning and resolution of critical program problems.

Sustaining Continuous Improvement

Continuous improvement is the subject of Appendix E.

SUMMARY

Managing large programs involves establishing aggressive but realistic plans, continually monitoring program status, identifying and resolving issues, managing quality, and dealing with the customer.

- In establishing plans, the key activities are to build team motivation, assess team plans, balance resources and schedules, and review plan risks.

- Monitoring program status involves, among other things, using the earned-value (EV) measure to identify the most troublesome parts of the program.

- In identifying and resolving issues, the job is to identify and resolve problem causes.

- Quality management is critically important, and it must begin at the start of every program. The A/DR measure provides the data needed to monitor quality performance at every stage of the program.

- The availability of objective and complete TSP data provides the foundation for establishing and maintaining a trusting and cooperative customer relationship.

The program manager must also attend to three continuing senior management responsibilities:

- Maintaining a focus on quality
- Ensuring effective program-wide communication
- Sustaining continuous improvement

REFERENCES

[Davis 2003] N. Davis and J. Mullaney, "Team Software Process (TSP) in Practice," *SEI Technical Report* CMU/SEI-2003-TR-014, September 2003.

[Humphrey 2002] Watts S. Humphrey, *Winning with Software: An Executive Strategy* (Boston, MA: Addison-Wesley, 2002).

E

Sustaining the TSP

This appendix describes how to sustain the TSP effort once it has initially been established, and it outlines several ways to use the TSP methods and data to monitor and support a continuous improvement effort. As shown in Figure E.1, this appendix is the final of the five appendices in this book, and it assumes that the TSP is already in place and being used by many of the development teams in the organization. The challenge addressed in this appendix is maintaining and improving the effectiveness of the organization's development teams.

WHY CONTINUOUS IMPROVEMENT IS IMPORTANT

Every study of the subject has concluded that the rate of change in advanced economies is higher than ever before and that this rate continues to accelerate. This means that the best and most capable competitors in just about every industry are continuously adopting newer and better methods. It also means that

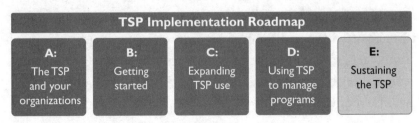

Figure E.1 Roadmap to the appendices

those businesses that do not improve will be exposed. As Thomas Friedman has said, the world is flat, and with the Internet and disappearing national boundaries, competitors can spring up anywhere at any time [Friedman 2005].

So far, this book has focused on initiating a major improvement program that involves adopting the TSP. However, initiating an improvement and sustaining that improvement are two different matters. This appendix describes how to sustain the TSP improvement program and how to use the TSP in that sustainment effort. It covers the following topics:

- Improvement examples
- Improvement risks
- The principles of lasting improvement
- Executive financial reviews
- The executive quality review
- The executive role in continuous improvement

IMPROVEMENT EXAMPLES

Many improvement programs are, in a sense, self-defeating. The problem is that most improvements are initiated to address specific problems. Then, once the improvement is in place and the problem is no longer a concern, the need to improve disappears. If the improvement had been thoroughly and completely made, however, it would have included the means to sustain itself, but few improvement programs do that. Therefore, once management's attention is distracted by more pressing issues, organizations generally revert to their prior habits. Over time, the original problem then reappears, and a new improvement effort will be required.

This is a common problem when improvements are made to solve specific problems. Because there is an almost infinite number of ways to fail, fixing problems one at a time is a never-ending chore. That means that an improvement strategy based on learning from failure will be ineffective and counterproductive. Improvements should be introduced as part of a comprehensive improvement effort, and they should include the means to sustain themselves over time. The following two examples illustrate this improvement problem.

Example of a Failed Improvement Program

Some years ago, Michael Fagan found that if teams of software developers inspected their programs before testing them, they could both improve product quality and sharply cut testing times [Fagan 1976]. After demonstrating his method in one of his company's laboratories, he convinced senior management to install it throughout the development group. This was done, and the improvement was very effective: It cut testing times almost in half.

Several years later, after many of the original managers and executives had moved on, project managers began to complain about the time these Fagan inspections were taking. Senior management agreed that the inspections could be optional and that each development laboratory could decide whether or not to use them. When the programming quality people objected that testing times would increase, management pointed out that testing time was not a serious problem, so requiring everybody to do inspections was not justified. While it took a few years, testing time did increase significantly and a new program was needed to reintroduce software inspections into all of the development laboratories.

When the original purpose of an improvement is to address an immediate business pain, once the improvement is in place and the pain is gone, the executives will no longer be concerned, and they will give it a lower priority. When priority drops at the executive level, it will also drop at every lower management level. Organizational priorities are very sensitive to executive priorities, and unless senior management continues to be regularly involved in some way, improvement programs will generally die out.

A Successful Improvement: The IBM CI105 Program

Jack Kuehler, when he was IBM president, initiated a very successful improvement program. The company had already issued a corporate instruction called CI105 that required every new IBM product to be measurably better than its IBM predecessor product as well as better than its best competitor. This policy had already been implemented by the hardware groups with enormous success, but the software groups had said it could not apply to software. However, Jack Kuehler insisted, and he had the software quality staff establish a program for measuring and reporting software quality against the CI105 criteria [Humphrey 2009].

The IBM software quality staff established the required measurement standard, and they also posted the results for all the key products on an online executive quality-reporting system. Just as with the hardware, the results of the software CI105 program were extraordinary. The number of customer-reported defects for each of the covered products dropped by 50% in each of the succeeding years.

The key to sustaining this improvement was that the senior executives regularly reviewed the marketplace performance of the key products in their laboratories, and they included the CI105 quality data in these reviews. When a product didn't meet its planned quality levels, they called for recovery plans, but they didn't beat up or criticize the program manager. Jack Kuehler had insisted on aggressive quality goals, and he knew that if they beat up people for missing their goals, they would set conservative goals. He also contended that if everybody always met the quality goals, they were not trying hard enough.

IMPROVEMENT RISKS

In making any major improvement, there are two key risks to avoid: simplistic measures and dead-end improvements.

Simplistic Measures

An excellent example of the simplistic measurement problem is the SEI's work with Capability Maturity Model Integration (CMMI) and its predecessor, the Capability Maturity Model (CMM). When the CMM was first developed, the U.S. Department of Defense (DoD) saw that it could be very effective in improving the cost and schedule performance of its software suppliers. DoD issued a ruling that all of its software suppliers must achieve at least maturity level 3 before they could be awarded contracts.

This was a challenge because the CMM (and later CMMI) had established a five-level set of improvement criteria. These were called maturity levels, with maturity level 1 being the lowest. This lowest level was where most software organizations then worked, and they typically missed their cost and schedule commitments by large margins. Levels 2, 3, 4, and 5 then defined various grades of improvement beyond maturity level 1. Because moving from level 1 to level 2 and then on to level 3 took considerable time and effort, this DoD edict got a lot of attention, and an entire software-process-improvement industry was established to support these organizations with their improvement efforts. Today, many of the leading organizations that contract to supply software products and services are rated at CMMI level 5.

The CMMI example also indicates one of the risks of mandating an improvement program. When the DoD issued its edict, many software organizations were at CMMI level 1 and would have to get to level 3 to stay in business, so they started crash improvement efforts. While this might seem like a positive development, it had one unfortunate result: It changed the improvement focus from achieving measured performance improvement to achieving a maturity level. The problem then was that, as in any improvement effort, people started to focus on the measurement system rather than the intended end result. So the goal became to achieve a maturity level to qualify for the DoD's business even if that didn't improve the development process.

While one might argue that this would be cheating, and it would certainly seem like a waste of a potentially helpful improvement program, it is perfectly normal for people to look for easy ways to solve their problems. The only counter to this problem is to keep the measurement system focused on performance-related items and to use a variety of measures. Single-dimension measurement systems always present the risk of such misuse.

Dead-End Improvements

A second problem that is also illustrated by the CMMI concerns dead-end improvements. The problem here is that soon after maturity levels were adopted by the DoD to evaluate software suppliers, commercial industry started to use them as well. This has been very helpful in motivating improvement, but once many major software suppliers reach maturity level 5, CMMI is no longer an effective marketplace differentiator. At that point, the motivation to continue with CMMI improvement is greatly reduced and can even disappear. Even though the organizations that reach maturity level 5 would presumably still be performing far better than they did before, once the focus on CMMI improvement is lost, organizations can be expected to revert to their prior practices. Then, just as with the earlier example of Fagan inspections, the original performance problems will ultimately reappear and the improvement cycle will have to be started all over again.

So, while coupling an improvement effort to marketplace performance can temporarily help to sustain its priority, once the specific improvement becomes more common in the marketplace, the motivation to sustain that improvement will gradually disappear. While this could take many years, the only ultimate answer is to follow the credo once expounded by Art Anderson when he was IBM's Senior Vice President for Manufacturing and Development [Humphrey 1997]: "There is always room for improvement." To sustain this credo, establish a continuous improvement program.

THE PRINCIPLES OF LASTING IMPROVEMENT

The persistence of an improvement depends on three things: worker benefits, adequate support, and management priorities. Because all of these are related, the problem of sustaining an improvement requires attention to all three.

Worker Benefits

If the people who must implement the improvement find that it helps them do their jobs, they will want to continue working in that way. Then, assuming that they can do so by themselves, they probably will. Furthermore, the people doing the work often cannot really tell if the improvement helps them or not, but if they think that the improvement helps and it is convenient, it will also likely stick. For software development, only simplistic and stand-alone improvements like development tools and environments are of this type. The more difficult improvements like Fagan inspections typically require some training and support.

One of the things that makes many of these improvement programs difficult is that they have deferred benefits. Often, in fact, these deferred benefits are for groups other than those making the changes. That means that the people who must change their personal practices will see little or no immediate benefit. More personal examples of such deferred-benefit changes are stopping smoking, losing weight, and taking up regular exercise. While the benefits of such changes are unquestioned and even life-saving, the changes do not generally stick without some kind of continuing support.

Adequate Support

The typical kinds of support required for complex changes involve such items as training, consultants, coaching support, and tools. New design methods typically require training and consultant support, and Fagan inspections also require training and the availability of qualified inspection moderators. The TSP also requires training, the availability of qualified coaches, and the use of suitable support tools. Providing such support usually requires building a competent support staff and providing adequate funding. Because getting adequate funding for staff activities is always a problem, improvements that require staff support always require management support. The problem of getting management support, however, always concerns management priorities.

Management Priorities

Management's ability to sustain any kind of orderly priority depends almost entirely on whether the organization is crisis-driven or plan-driven. Because crisis-driven organizations typically cannot sustain complex improvement programs, the first improvement step must be to fix the crisis-driven management system. That is why, for example, the CMMI improvement program calls for improving to level 2 before doing anything else. The level 2 items are designed to prevent crises before they happen. However, moving from a crisis-driven to a plan-driven environment can take a long time.

Any organization that is concerned about sustaining a TSP improvement program has presumably already instituted an initial TSP improvement effort, so it probably is not operating in a crisis environment. In this case, the issue of management priority principally concerns executive priorities. While the executives who initiated the TSP improvement would likely agree that it should be sustained, if they don't devote any time to the subject, the lower-level managers will also focus on other topics, and the improvement effort will soon lose its priority. To sustain continuous executive attention, the improvement must be connected to something that executives regularly monitor. This will then sustain its priority throughout the organization. For the TSP, the best candidate is to connect the improvement program to the financial performance of the business.

EXECUTIVE FINANCIAL REVIEWS

Once a clear connection is made between an improvement program and the organization's financial performance, the executives should regularly review that improvement program's performance as part of their regularly scheduled financial reviews. As mentioned in Chapter 7, Cesar, the CEO of Quarksoft, did just this, and it served to show continued executive interest in the effectiveness with which the TSP teams performed. In organizations where the costs of developing, testing, and supporting the organization's products are significant financial concerns, such a strategy can be very effective.

To couple the TSP improvement program to financial performance, the first step is to consider the controllable costs in an engineering organization. At least for software, the principal cost is the engineering staff, so the cost-control question concerns the factors that influence the number of engineering months of work required to do any given job. This effort is determined by three things:

- The knowledge and skill of the engineers
- The size of the job to be done
- The efficiency with which the job is done

Engineering Knowledge and Skill

The knowledge and skill of the engineering staff in an organization are not controllable items. The organization has presumably already obtained the best staff it could find and has done whatever it could to ensure that this staff has the required knowledge and skill for the jobs that need to be performed. Beyond that, getting additional skills is always desirable. However, changing the skill mix in an organization is not a controllable item, at least not in the short term. So, while important, skill mix is not a controllable cost item.

The Size of the Job

The size of a job and its cost can be changed only by changing the functions and properties of the product to be produced. Once the functions are defined, however, size is no longer a variable. Then the cost of doing the job is determined by the efficiency with which the engineers do the work. So, while job size is a variable at the very outset of a job, once the job is under way, the functions of the desired product are largely set, so job size is no longer a controllable cost. While that issue could always be reopened, that is not something that can be done easily or without considerable additional engineering cost and customer debate.

Job Efficiency

The most efficient way to do a job is to do it right the first time. This means that there are two elements to job efficiency: the cost of doing the job the first time and the costs of fixing all the errors and mistakes the engineers made when they didn't do their work perfectly. Here, the costs of doing an engineering job the first time are largely determined by how big the product will be, the development strategy, and the tools and methods to be used.

As noted above, the product functions are typically established before the job is started, and the product development strategy is established when the work is started. Thereafter, these items are set and can be changed only at great cost in time, money, and confusion. As a result, they are not controllable costs. Similarly, the design methods and development environments and tools must be set at the beginning of the job and not changed. Making changes in design methods or development tools in the middle of a job generally causes considerable disruption and adds costs rather than cutting them. Consequently, even the development strategy, tools, methods, and environments cannot be considered as variable costs.

In summary, the only item that can be considered a variable cost in development work is the cost of fixing all the mistakes and errors the developers made when first developing the product. This means that the cost of quality (COQ) is the only major controllable cost in engineering development work. While smaller items like the level of clerical support, training, and facilities are always adjustable, they are not major items and certainly are not things that can or should be monitored by executives as they manage the organization. This means that any financial review of the TSP improvement effort must focus on quality costs and the activities that increase and decrease those costs.

THE EXECUTIVE QUALITY REVIEW

With the scale of modern software products, even the few defects each developer leaves in his or her product can, when combined with all the other developers' defects, cost a great deal of time and money to fix in test or when the product reaches the customers. What few developers realize, however, is that the costs of fixing their defects extend far beyond the development phases. In integration and system testing, traditional development groups spend as much or more time and effort fixing defects as they did in development. Then, even after extensive testing, the customer typically finds even more defects in acceptance testing. Even after that, there is usually an extensive maintenance period that may extend for several years, and, depending on how widely the products are used and how defective they are, this later maintenance phase can cost far more than all of the development and testing work combined. So coupling an improvement effort to financial performance can be very effective, but all of the quality-related costs must be clearly and regularly presented to senior executives.

The Cost-of-Quality Measure

The financial measure that covers the costs of correcting defective work is the COQ measure described in Chapter 8. These costs can be displayed in several ways. Figure E.2 shows quality

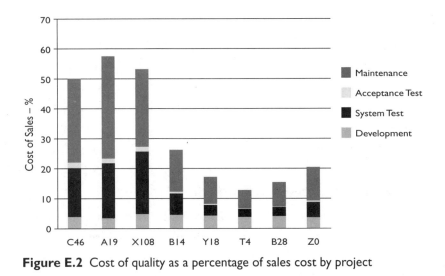

Figure E.2 Cost of quality as a percentage of sales cost by project

costs as a percentage of the cost of sales for eight different projects. As shown in the figure, there are four principal quality-cost elements: maintenance, acceptance test, system test, and development. For maintenance, acceptance testing, and system testing, the entire activity is typically considered a quality cost, but for development, the quality costs are only those activities concerned with preventing, finding, and fixing defects. These elements could also be shown by organizational unit or over time.

In Figure E.2, for example, the data for project X108 are typical of a large-scale, high-volume systems program that would take about 100 engineers 26 months to develop using traditional methods. Here, the total cost of development is about 20.4% of the cost of sales, and the cost-of-quality portion of these development costs is 4.8%. However, the non-development quality costs significantly exceed the development costs with system testing at 21% and maintenance at 26%. Thus, while direct development costs are only 20.4% of the cost of sales, after including all the associated quality costs, the true contribution of this product to cost of sales is 69%. That is why a focus on managing the cost of quality is so important.

The COQ measure is very useful for portraying historical costs, and it provides an effective way to show the financial consequences of a quality-management program. However, by the time the COQ is reported, the work has already been done and the costs have been incurred, so it is too late to control those costs. To control quality costs, the appraisal-to-development ratio (A/DR) measure described in Appendix D is more effective.

The Appraisal-to-Development Ratio

The A/DR measure described in Appendix D provides a way to anticipate quality problems in time to fix them before too much development time and effort have been wasted building a defective product. A/DR charts can provide early warning of problems in any part of the development organization. This is accomplished by showing the A/DR levels for products in each development phase. Then requirements or design problems can be detected as early as at the end of the requirements or design phases instead of waiting to find and fix them in system testing or in the customer's office. Because the late discovery of requirements defects can cause a major product redesign or even an entire project failure, early discovery is highly desirable.

A chart showing A/DR by phase for 11 components of a system is shown in Figure E.3. As is clear from this chart, the defective components had low A/DR values in the design phase, so, with the early warning available from such charts, these quality problems could have been recognized and corrected before implementation work was even begun. While component 1 also had design problems, the extensive appraisal effort spent during coding apparently caught its problems. Skipping design appraisals and trying to find design problems during implementation is not a good idea, however, as demonstrated by component 6.

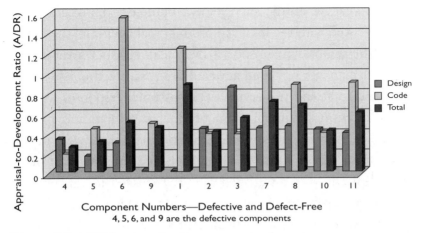

Figure E.3 A/DR by phase for 11 components of a system

THE EXECUTIVE ROLE IN CONTINUOUS IMPROVEMENT

Without some level of sustained executive interest, no improvement program will survive for long. In addition to the financial review process just described, other key topics executives should consider for sustaining the TSP are the following:

- Maintaining priorities
- Mandating action
- TSP certification
- Rewarding success

Maintaining Priorities

An excellent example of how to maintain priorities is the IBM customer satisfaction program. IBM reviewed the customer satisfaction for all of its major products, and the surveys were conducted annually. They were completed by key customer managers who worked directly with the products being covered. Because the survey responses were known to generate action, a high percentage of customers completed them.

Each year, when the survey was completed, the results were first reviewed with the involved product managers and then with the IBM senior vice president over that product area. Every product manager who had any significant satisfaction issues was expected to attend this review. The customer responses were in seven categories ranging from product capability and performance to usability and installability, and the ratings were in five levels from very dissatisfied to very satisfied. Any product manager with any very-dissatisfied rating was asked to explain that customer's problem and what was being done about it. Consequently, when any product manager received any such rating on any product, he or she immediately visited that customer to understand the problem and to agree on a way to resolve it. Product managers who didn't have good answers to these questions were usually in trouble.

In addition to keeping the customer satisfaction topic at the top of every product manager's priority list, this executive level of interest also had a very positive effect on customer satisfaction: The very dissatisfied customers quickly became satisfied. Reviews of this type could be conducted in any business area.

Mandating Action

Once the executives in an organization have seen enough data from an improvement program to be convinced of its effectiveness, they are often tempted to issue a mandate requiring everyone to adopt it. Such mandates can make a lot of sense but only under certain conditions. First, there must have been enough experience with the new method that its effectiveness is generally recognized. At that point, the principal resistance will generally be from the few people who typically resist any change. Second, there must be sufficient available skills and resources to install the change generally. Mandating that everyone do something that the organization cannot support could cause considerable confusion. Third, it must be clear that the change really should be adopted by everyone. If there are cases where the change would not make sense or where implementation should be delayed, these cases should be identified and given an exception. Finally, there must be some way to objectively verify that the mandate was actually carried out.

With these caveats, a mandate can make a lot of business sense. Once newer methods are known to be substantially more effective than those currently in use, there comes a point where people must adopt them. As technology advances, there is normally some small percentage of people who just will not adopt. Once the executives decide to mandate adoption, those who won't adopt must be reassigned or told to find other work.

TSP Certification

As systems grow larger and more complex and as the risks of damage or personal injury from defective software increase, customers and the general public will increasingly demand contractual protection. Just as with management edicts, these contractual provisions require some objective way to verify that they were implemented properly. For the TSP, the SEI has established a TSP certification program to meet this need.

The various elements of TSP certification address development professionals, development teams, and entire development organizations. In addition, the certification program also covers TSP instructors and TSP coaches. The developer certification is currently available internationally through the PSP developer certification program. Because PSP skills are needed to effectively participate on TSP teams, PSP developer certification is highly desirable. This certification only attests to knowledge and understanding, so the only requirement is that the candidates pass a PSP certification examination.

The SEI also currently certifies TSP coaches. A TSP coach must know and understand the PSP and TSP methods and be capable of coaching development teams, so a TSP coach certification requires that the candidate be PSP-certified, pass a TSP certification examination, and satisfactorily complete a coach-mentoring program under the supervision of an SEI-authorized mentor coach. TSP coach certification is also available from the SEI. Certification for TSP instructors also requires successful completion of an examination and a trial instructional program.

Certification for TSP teams and organizations (with the TSP-OEC process) requires that all team members be properly qualified, that the teams be properly formed and coached, and that the teams' results be of high quality. This last point is objectively verified through analyzing the data the teams gather while doing their work. In addition to the criteria for TSP teams, the TSP organizational certification program includes ratings for customer satisfaction and TSP coverage as well as all the criteria required for TSP teams.

Once an organization has reached a reasonable level of TSP usage, executives or customers could have various parts of that organization TSP-certified and then regularly hold reviews of the results. Because these certification results give considerable detail on the organization's performance, they provide an objective basis for measuring that organization's performance as well as the degree to which it has met any edicts or contractual requirements to use the TSP.

Rewarding Success

In any business like software where people have traditionally been recognized and rewarded for working hard, it is difficult to switch to a different reward system. Because it is obvious when people are working late at night and coming in on weekends to fix those last few test defects, it seems only natural to reward them for all of their efforts. While that would be entirely reasonable if there were no alternatives, once newer and better methods are known and some teams are regularly producing products that have few if any test defects, the criteria for success must shift from rewarding hard work to rewarding quality work.

Quality work is often done quietly and efficiently, and quality products typically are delivered on time and work when put into test, so it is often hard to recognize the great personal skill and discipline required to do such work. Highly skilled and competent work looks easy, but that is only because the professionals have honed their skills and built the personal discipline needed to consistently apply these skills to their work. Here, the measures described earlier for COQ and A/DR can help to identify and reward the high-performing teams. The team members, team leaders, and coaches should also be asked to identify any members who should receive individual recognition.

REFERENCES

[Fagan 1976] Michael Fagan, "Design and Code Inspections to Reduce Errors in Program Development," *IBM Systems Journal* 15, no. 3 (1976): 182–211.

[Friedman 2005] Thomas Friedman, *The World Is Flat: A Brief History of the Twenty-first Century* (New York: Farrar, Straus and Giroux, 2005).

[Humphrey 1997] Watts S. Humphrey, *Managing Technical People: Innovation, Teamwork, and the Software Process* (Boston, MA: Addison-Wesley, 1997).

[Humphrey 2009] Watts S. Humphrey and Grady Booch, *Oral History of Watts*

Humphrey, CMH Reference number X5584.2010, Computer History Museum, 2009, www.computerhistory.org/collections/accession/102702107.

About the Authors

WATTS S. HUMPHREY

Watts S. Humphrey (1927–2010) joined Carnegie Mellon University's Software Engineering Institute (SEI) in 1986 after a long career as a manager and executive at IBM. A Senior Fellow at the SEI, Humphrey was the founder of the SEI's Software Process Program and primary author of the SEI's software process maturity model. In 2005, he was awarded the National Medal of Technology—the highest honor given by the president of the United States to America's leading innovators. His principal focus in recent years was on knowledge work and its impact on software and systems development.

During his 27 years with IBM, Humphrey was Director of Programming and Vice President of Technical Development. He also managed all of IBM's software product development work, including the first 19 releases of IBM's principal computer operating system, OS/360. Before his retirement, he served as Director of Programming Quality and Process. While at the SEI, he introduced the concepts of Software Process Assessment and Software Capability Evaluation, which evolved into Capability Maturity Model Integration (CMMI). He also led development of the Personal Software Process (PSP) and the Team Software Process (TSP).

Humphrey earned graduate degrees in physics from the Illinois Institute of Technology and in business administration from the University of Chicago. He was a Fellow of the Association for

Computing Machinery (ACM), an IEEE Life Fellow, and a member of the Malcolm Baldrige National Quality Award Board of Examiners. Humphrey was awarded the 1993 Aerospace Software Engineering Award presented by the American Institute of Aeronautics and Astronautics and an honorary Ph.D. in software engineering by Embry-Riddle Aeronautical University in 1998. In 2000, the Boeing Corporation presented him with an award for innovation and leadership in software process improvement, and in 2010, the Illinois Institute of Technology recognized him with its professional achievement award.

Humphrey's publications include many technical papers and 13 books, including *Winning with Software: An Executive Strategy* (2001), *PSP: A Self-Improvement Process for Software Engineers* (2005), *TSP: Leading a Development Team* (2006), *TSP: Coaching Development Teams* (2006), and *Reflections on Management: How to Manage Your Software Projects, Your Teams, Your Boss, and Yourself* (2010). His most recent book, *Leadership, Teamwork, and Trust: Building a Competitive Software Capability*, is his eleventh published by Addison-Wesley. He held five U.S. patents.

JAMES W. OVER

James W. Over, who has been with the SEI since 1987, is manager of the TSP Initiative and is a senior member of the technical staff for the Software Engineering Process Management Program. Over has led SEI's TSP Initiative since its inception, transitioning the TSP into organizations in the United States and abroad. He has received the SEI Director's Award for Excellence, the SEPM Director's Award for Quality Innovation, and an award from

Boeing Corporation for innovation and leadership in software process improvement. He has more than 35 years of technical and management experience in the software engineering industry. Over is the coauthor of several SEI publications on software process definition and improvement. He attended Northern Illinois University.

Index

A

accelerating projects, 149–152

acceptance phase, Conner's change model, 192–193

acceptance tests
  benefit of implementing TSP, 170
  evaluating pilot projects, 204
  productivity gain with TSP, 177–178
  as quality-cost element, 299
  Softtek product offering and, 10

accuracy
  communications, 120
  estimating, 216–217, 263–264, 271–272
  limitations of EV measures, 269–270
  as performance indicator for TSP team, 40–41, 107, 111, 122

ACM (Association for Computing Machinery), 307–308

acquisition phase, overcoming resistance of suppliers in, 234

Acquisition Support Program (ASP), SEI, 165

Activision, using TSP, 166

Adobe, using TSP, 164–165

A/DR (appraisal-to-development ratio) measure, quality
  executive review of, 300–301
  overview of, 276–279
  program reviews, 280–281

Aerospace Software Engineering Award, 308

aircraft
  managing quality of safety on, 127–128
  operational procedures example, pilot preflight checks, 78

Allied Signal, 113–114, 281–282

American Express, 19

Anderson, Art, 293

appendices, roadmap to, 162–164

application software, developed with TSP, 167–168

appraisals
  cost-of-quality measure for, 126–127
  management conducting performance, 180
  managing quality of, 276

appraisal-to-development ratio. *See* A/DR (appraisal-to-development ratio) measure, quality

ASP (Acquisition Support Program), SEI, 165

assessment
  management not using personal data for, 108–109
  of program plan, 261–263
  reviewing program plan for risk, 265–266
  risk, during TSP launch, 215

auditable data
  accuracy of TSP, 120
  handling poor performers, 109–111

More from Watts S. Humphrey

Reflections on Management: How to Manage Your Software Projects, Your Teams, Your Boss, and Yourself

ISBN-13: 978-0-321-71153-3

This book collects Humphrey's best and most influential essays and articles sharing insights that will be indispensable for anyone who must achieve superior results in software or any other endeavor.

PSP^{SM}: A Self-Improvement Process for Software Engineers

ISBN-13: 978-0-321-30549-7

This is the essential guide to learning how to apply the disciplines of the Personal Software Process (PSP) in a contemporary software development environment.

TSP^{SM}: Leading a Development Team

ISBN-13: 978-0-321-34962-0

The Team Software Process (TSP) provides software engineers with a framework for building and maintaining effective teams. This book is a guide for the people who will lead those teams.

TSP^{SM}: Coaching Development Teams

ISBN-13: 978-0-201-73113-2

In this practical guide to TSP, Humphrey shares the methods that have proven most effective for coaching high-octane TSP teams and their leaders.